# THROUGH ORPHANED EYES

*A story of two people, two nations*

The verses on page 45-46 have been quoted from the song 'Ae mare Waton Ke logo' sung by Lata Mangeshkar, written by Kavi Pradeep and composed by C Ramchandra. With grateful acknowledgements for the same.

# THROUGH ORPHANED EYES

*A story of two people, two nations*

AJAY SINGH

PENTAGON PRESS

**Through Orphaned Eyes**

*by Ajay Singh*

ISBN 978-81-8274-859-0

First Published in 2015
Revised Edition: 2016



*Published by*
PENTAGON PRESS
206, Peacock Lane, Shahpur Jat
New Delhi-110049
Phones: 011-64706243, 26491568
Telefax: 011-26490600
email: rajan@pentagonpress.in
website: www.pentagonpress.in

*Branch*
Flat No.213, Athena-2,
Clover Acropolis,
Viman Nagar,
Pune-411014
Email: pentagonpresspune@gmail.com

Printed at Aegean Offset Printers, Greater Noida

**For my Parents**

*Who believed in the words,*

*Even before they were fully formed.*

# ACKNOWLEDGEMENTS

For two years, this book has played on my mind, seeking to find release. Yet, it would never have taken form had it not been for all those who did so much to help it find expression. I am eternally grateful to:

My wife Monisha and daughter Ragini – who put up with two years of moody, cantankerous behavior as I struggled with the words. And whose inputs helped the book find its final form.

My parents – who believed in me and gave me the support to write.

My in-laws, Col and Mrs Naik – who stood by me in their usual silent, steadfast way, giving me self-belief and strength.

My brothers, Abhay and Akshay – with whom I shared my thoughts and ramblings, and who helped give form to the concept.

Chetan – for that one drunken evening of narration when he looked at me and said, 'Just write it.'

Kiran – One of my dearest friends, who gave me so much insight on the happenings of 1984 and in whose beautiful home I wrote the entire chapter on that momentous year.

To the Indian Army – which shaped my thoughts and beliefs, and gave me the experiences that are reflected in the book.

And finally to all of you who read it – with the heartfelt hope that you will enjoy it.

# CAST OF MAJOR CHARACTERS

## INDIA

**The Hero**. The unnamed Indian. Comes to India on 15 Aug 1947, in the trauma of Partition. Through his eyes we see the nation through its formative years, its wars, its fears, its hopes for the future. An orphan himself, his final act expresses the anguish most Indians feel at being orphaned by its own leaders.

**Masterji**. His uncle, who becomes his father and raises him up as his own. A principled, devout Indian who teaches his sons the values of 'Indian-ness.'

**Nivedita**. His wife. A steady, supportive figure, who stands by him though his years in the army and beyond.

**Gaurav.** His eldest son, an army officer who is killed in one of the decisive battles at Kargil

**Supriya**. His daughter. An Odissi dancer, who attains repute as one of India's leading classical dancers.

**Vikram.** His younger son. A rising executive, who like the new generation of Indians is brash, confident and self-assured and asks only for a level playing field to showcase his skills. He is trapped in the Taj Mahal hotel during the Mumbai attacks of 2008.

**Kunal and Vishal.** Masterji's children and the hero's foster brothers. They rise in their careers, one to become a leading nuclear scientist, the other a management guru.

**Baba Randhawa**. Their Sikh neighbor, whose home is targeted during the anti-Sikh riots of 1984.

**Bharat Haladi**. A corrupt politician who is involved in a slew of scams and criminal cases. Yet, he rises in his political career and becomes a leading Prime Ministerial candidate.

## PAKISTAN

**Shahnawaz Khan**. The hero's brother. Born in a sugarcane field on 14 August 1947, he is brought up by a childless Pakistani couple. He joins the Pakistani army and rises to become the head of Pakistan's Inter Services Intelligence.

**Shahryar Khan.** His father, who finds Shahnawaz after a communal carnage during Partition and takes him home. He rises to become a General in the Pakistan Army and participates in the thrust into Kashmir in 1947-48 and the offensive into India in the 1965 Indo-Pak War.

**Shazia.** Shahnawaz's wife. A beautiful, talented singer, who attains national fame as the 'Nightingale of Pakistan.'

**Salim, Mehtab and Aftab.** Their sons, part of a Pakistani generation frustrated with the lack of opportunities in their own nation.

**Suleiman**. Shahnawaz's comrade and buddy in Afghanistan and Kashmir. He saves Shahnawaz's life in the Kargil operation and becomes part of the family.

**Nazneen**. Shahnawaz's mother, who accepts him after initial reservations and then brings him up as her own.

**Baitullah Wazir.** An Afghan warlord who participates in the battles against the Soviet occupation of Afghanistan aided by Shahnawaz. He moves to Pakistan in the wake of the US invasion of Pakistan in 2001 and establishes the militant organization, 'Tehrik-e-Taliban' there. Initially a friend, he becomes an avowed enemy of Shahnawaz and the Pakistani state.

# Timeline of Events

| India | Pakistan |
|---|---|
| | **1947** |
| **India gains Independence** (15 Aug) Hero comes to India with his father in the chaos of Partition. | **Creation of Pakistan** (14 Aug) Birth of Shahnawaz. (14 Aug) Found in sugarcane field by Shahryar Khan and adopted by the family. |
| | **Kashmir War** (1947-48) |
| Indian troops land at Srinagar Halt of Pakistani advance. | Pakistani Invasion of Kashmir (Oct). Shahryar leads the invasion with tribal warriors. |
| Destiny of Kashmir and the two nations change | Raiders halt to rape and loot and Delayed short of Srinagar. |
| | **1948** |
| Assassination of Mahatma Gandhi (30 Jan). Hero father dies. Orphaned, Adopted by Masterji | Death of Jinnah (11 Sep) |
| | **1958** |
| India in the Nehru Era. | General Ayub Khan takes over in a military coup |
| Democracy, Secularism take root. | Shahryar participates in the coup and helps overthrow the President. Rises in his career. |

| | |
|---|---|
| **1962** | |
| **Indo-China War (Oct)** | |
| Crushing defeat of India<br>Hero joins army. Becomes a Sapper. | |
| **1965** | |
| **Indo-Pak War (Sep)** | |
| Hero helps halt offensive by flooding the fields ahead of the approaching Pakistani tanks. | Pakistani launches offensive into India. The offensive flounders and Shahryar, the GOC, is killed. |
| **1966** | |
| **Death of Shashtri – Indira Gandhi takes over** | |
| Marriage to Nivedita | |
| **1968-70** | |
| | Shahnawaz commissioned in Pak Army at a time of brewing rebellion in East Pakistan. |
| **1971** | |
| Hero moves to Calcutta with his unit. | Pakistani troops flown in to East Pakistan to quell rebellion. Shahnawaz amongst them. Participates in operations against Mukti Bahini and sees atrocities on both sides. |
| **Indo-Pak War (Dec 71)** | |
| Indian Army advances into East Pakistan.<br>Hero moves in with his unit. | Shahnawaz occupies defences. Repulses Indian attacks. |
| **16 Dec – Pak army surrenders at Dacca** | |
| Hero participates in the surrender ceremony. | Shahnawaz surrenders with his unit. |

| | |
|---|---|
| **1972** | |
| In charge of Prisoner of War Camp at Barrackpore.<br>Meets Shahnawaz, develop closeness.<br>Birth of his son Gaurav. | Shahnawaz taken prisoner. Meets the hero at POW Camp.<br>Repatriated to Pakistan after a year in captivity. |
| **1974** | |
| Conduct of Nuclear Test. | Bhutto takes over as President |
| **1975** | |
| Imposition of Emergency.<br>Hero witnesses excesses of the Emergency.<br>His father arrested and forcibly sterilized. | |
| **1977** | |
| Emergency revoked, elections held. | General Zia-ul-Haq deposes Bhutto, military rule in Pakistan again. Islamisation sets in. |
| **1979** | |
| | **Soviet invasion of Afghanistan. Pak helps Afghan Mujahidin**<br>Shahnawaz joins the ISI and sent to Afghanistan to befriend Mujahidin. Meets Baitullah Wazir. Inducts Stinger Missiles into the War.<br>Shahnawaz marries Shazia, a talented singer. |
| **1984** | |
| **Unrest in Punjab, Attack on Golden Temple, Assassination of Mrs Gandhi, Anti-Sikh riots.**<br>Participates in Operation Blue Star.<br>Witnesses Anti-Sikh riots, gives refuge to a Sikh family. | Pak involvement in Punjab and Kashmir begins. |

**1989**

| | |
|---|---|
| | Soviet withdrawal from Afghanistan, Pak shifts focus towards Kashmir |

**1992**

| | |
|---|---|
| Growing insurgency in Kashmir<br><br>Hero leaves the Army. Masterji dies. | Shahnawaz commands unit on Line of Control. Helps foment insurgency in Kashmir with help of Baitullah Wazir. |

**1993**

Economic reforms announced
Era of economic growth begins
Hero gets a job in an IT firm and prospers.

**1998**

| | |
|---|---|
| **Nuclear Tests by India.** | **Pakistan's nuclear tests.** |
| | 1999- **Kargil operation** |
| | Shahnawaz takes over Brigade, is responsible for Kargil operations Operation meets initial success. |
| Son Gaurav in Kargil operations | Kargil operation fails. |
| | Shahnawaz appointed as Commander of the Brigade at Islamabad. |
| | Oct 99 – General Musharaff's coup, takes over as President. |
| | Shahnawaz helps in coup. Becomes Musharaff's trusted man and becomes Deputy Director ISI. |

| 2000-2001 | |
|---|---|
| **The New Millennia. India's economic success story gathers momentum.** | **11 Sep 2001; attacks on World Trade Center in USA.** Pakistan forced to join USA in its war against Islamic terrorists. Mujahidin groups from Afghanistan move inside Pakistan. Establish themselves inside Pakistan. Turn against Pakistan. |
| **2002-2005** | |
| Congress led UPA government comes to power with Manmohan Singh as PM in 2004. | Terrorist groups intensify activities against Pakistan. Form Tehrik-e-Taliban under Baitullah Wazir. Demand Islamic law in Pakistan. |
| **2007** | |
| **India wins T-20 World Cup Final against Pakistan** Viewed by Hero's family in India and Shahnawaz's family in Pakistan | |
| **2008** | |
| | Shahnawaz becomes Director of ISI. Plans Mumbai attacks. |
| (Festival of Peace held in Mumbai. Hero's daughter Supriya, who is a rising Classical dancer, and Shahnawaz's wife, Shazia, a nationally acclaimed singer, participate together) | |
| | Terrorist attack on Mumbai sponsored by Pakistan. |
| Attack on Mumbai. Taj Mahal hotel under siege. Son Vikram trapped inside hotel. | |

| | |
|---|---|
| **2009-12** | |
| India's success story slips | Increased terrorism in Pakistan. Army intensifies operations against them. Shahnawaz initiates it. |
| **2012 -13 and onwards** | |
| Growing frustration at corruption, Growth rate plummets, jobs dry-up Corruption increases. New scams emerge every day. Economy flounders, Hero loses job.<br>Hero expresses his anger at the growing corruption in the nation, by his culminating act. | Shahnawaz leads the battle against the Taliban. Will he be able to save his nation from its cancer or does he himself succumb to it? |
| **Will India regain its success story?** | **Will Pakistan win its war within?** |

# CONTENTS

# THE BIRTH OF TWO NATIONS – THE DEATH OF HUMANITY

## Sheikhupura, Pakistani Punjab, August 1947

I do not know the exact year of my birth. But then, I don't think anyone does. It was in the year of the great flood, they say. That would make it 1941 or 1943 or 1947 or so. It could also make it sometime in the mid-thirties, or at any point in the unrecorded history of my time and that of my country. It could be as far back as 2500 years ago when the floods ravaged the Indus valley and carried away an entire civilization. But then, the year of my birth is immaterial. On paper, they recorded it as 15 August 1947, the day I was carried in my father's arms, shocked and numb with terror, into the land of my new born nation.

1947 was the year of the floods. The rains began late that year, around early August or so. But when they did its waters swept away two countries in its wake. I recall little of the torrents of water, but I remember the flood of tears that never seemed to stop. I remember the fear and the aching tightness in my throat, I can still feel the pounding of my father's heart as he carried me from our home in *Nehar ki Haveli,* Mohalla Ganesh Kund, Village Sheikhupura, Post Office Shahdara, District Lahore toward the East where they said our new country was. I did not understand then the concept of a new land or a new country then. As far as I knew, Sheikhupura, our happy, sunlit village was our land and country. Our brick lined house with its wide courtyard and mud walls was our home. But that home and land were not to be ours any longer. It had been repossessed by another God.

The memory of that house is still so strong. I can see those three rooms with startling clarity; its charpoys, the pictures on the walls, the *chullah,* the cow-shed in the courtyard. I recall the exact texture of the door on the main gate – the door that splintered. At times I can taste the cool, sweet water of our well- the well in to which the women jumped. But, these images come in spurts. My mind has blocked out most else. I do not remember the face of my mother at all. I don't recall the name of a single friend or cousin or neighbour. But I remember the smells of the dung-plastered floor and of food cooking over a wood-fire in the kitchen. And I remember the earthy aroma of the first rains, in the last monsoon we experienced there. It was a light drizzle sometime in June or July 1947, but it preceded a storm over our divided land.

For years thereafter, the smells of a first rain never brought on the comforting coolness that it usually does. Instead it filled me with a dark feeling of impending doom. It brings back locked memories of shouting mobs, screams and attacks. I don't wish to recall any of it again, but deep in my subconscious the images remain alive, throbbing like a freshly cut wound. I rip apart the scab that has formed over them every now and then and re-open the wound. Then the images come back and the blood flows anew. Then the image of my mother comes back. My mother in her blue sari, waddling with the clumsy, heavy gait she had developed in the last month of her pregnancy. I remember her laugh, and at times, I can hear her scream.

With the rains, our house had also started filling up with people, Friends, relatives, neighbours, total strangers who shuffled in; small bundles on their shoulders, uncertainty in their eyes. My father's house, being the largest Hindu house in the predominantly Muslim village of Sheikhupura, drew them like a magnet. They came with their wives and children, their goats, cows and chickens; they came with hope and despair, seeking safety in a fortress of flimsy bricks and sun-dried mud.

The violence around us had been gathering steadily. There were stories of brutal communal riots in Lahore, Sialkot and Gujranwala; in Amritsar, Ferozepur and Gurdaspur – in the entire Punjab which was going mad. There were the stories of silent trains steaming into silent stations. And the stories were coming closer to our own village with each passing day.

For days the Hindu families of our village of Sheikhupura huddled within our home. In togetherness there was strength. There were visits by our Muslim neighbours, who smuggled in buckets of *chaas* and bundles of *rotis*, at least in the initial days. They were our friends since childhood. Friends who had celebrated *Diwali* and *Id* together, who had helped in the birth of children and calves, who had condoled deaths, who had helped plough the fields and harvest the crops. We had been friends for generations – Hindus, Sikhs and Muslims. Why then this hardening of eyes now. Why then these calls to leave.

In spite of the communal madness closing in, I don't think any truly believed that we would be leaving for good. Many had buried their valuables in a hidden corner of their fields, where they would be safe. Many had handed over their cattle and livestock to their Muslim neighbours for safe-keeping till they returned. Because, of course they would return. It was their land. Their village. One land, one village wasn't it?

No it wasn't. The land had already been divided. The towns, the villages, the lanes, the fields, even individual houses had been cut by the cold strokes of Sir Cyril Radcliffe's pen. His pen ran from the mountains and vales of Kashmir in the North; it cut through the greens fields of Punjab, clipped through the deserts of Rajasthan and Gujarat till it reached the neutral waters of the Arabian Sea. Punjab was cleaved in the worst way possible; not with a surgeon's scalpel but with a butcher's axe, the East falling to India, the West to Pakistan. In the South, the division was slightly more precise. Rajasthan and Gujarat fell on this side; Sindh and Baluchistan on the other. 2500 kilometres to the East the same ruthless pen cut its way through the vast province of Bengal, creating East Pakistan. It was not merely a travesty. It was a mockery, which would have been comical in its ludicrousness had it not been for the scale of the human tragedy that unfolded on both sides of the line.

We were amongst the statistics of that tragedy. One of the six million who moved from one side of the line to the other. For us then, there was no India there was no Pakistan. There was only that land, that village where we had lived all our lives. Now we were told that this land, this village was no longer ours. Because of our religion, our land lay on the other side. That line drawn on the map told us, "You have never lived here. You don't belong. Now go".

## II

The violence in Sheikhupura began with the attack on Bhanwar Lal, the local grocer, who had been selling salt, tea, grain, sugar to the village for decades now. He too had been torn between leaving the village and staying behind hoping to tide out the storm. That day, when he opened his shop late and occupied his usual place on the counter perhaps he was just hoping to clear some unsold stocks before finally bolting the shutters. Customers were few. Most were familiar faces to whom he had supplied provisions for years. It was one of these familiar figures that walked in that morning, spoke briefly and then slasheda matchet repeatedly across Bhanwar's face and chest.

A week later, Mange Ram the peddler was found dead by the pond on the outskirts of the village, his throat slit. His cycle with its colourful festooned wares was nowhere to be found. It emerged a week later, ridden triumphantly by one of the local goons, flaunted brazenly as a symbol of victory, or one of the spoils of war.

It were these instances and the chants of *Allah-o-Akbar* reverberating with increasing intensity that drove the Hindu families into the huddled sanctuary of my father's house with its ten foot high walls and large courtyards. The Sikhs of the village converged towards the safety of the *Gurudwara*. And from its cool, comforting confines, the *kirtan*- their prayer hymns continued to play. We had heard the *kirtan*, wafting over the village every dawn and dusk, for as far back as one could remember. But, now, in its calm, sonorous tones there seemed to be a hint of despair.

For over two weeks, the Sikhs sought sanctuary inside the *Gurudwara,* waiting for one of the infrequent military columns to help take them out to safety. And in that time, the intensity of the mob built up like a wave around them. And then one evening in the first week of August, they stormed the *Gurudwara*.

The mob, crazed with misplaced religious fervour, hurled itself against the barred *Gurudwara* doors. The doors held on longer than anyone would have imagined, till they finally burst open under the fury of the seething mob. Then came the carnage, a brutal, senseless carnage which ended with each one of the sixty odd defenders clubbed, knifed, hammered and torn to death in an orgy of bloodletting. Those who died early were the lucky ones. They were quite ingenious those days in the inflicting of the most painful and gruesome deaths. And, as always, the women suffered most – those who had not the time or the courage to hurl themselves in the solitary *Gurudwara* well. Their suffering would last throughout the night, in the days and nights that followed till the long night finally consumed them.

And when the mob finished its orgy of killing, looting, raping and desecration, it turned its attention to the other bastion of Hindu-Sikh refuge. My father's home with its twenty odd Hindu families behind its flimsy walls.

More than sixty years after it all happened, images of that night come back to me like a bad photo montage. I hear the calls of *"Allah-o-Akbar"* rising like a war-cry; I hear the cries approaching. I hear the frenzied pounding on the door, the wailing of women, the isolated shots, the sound of a Jeep revving up, whining with pent- up energy and then slamming against the door. Then the sounds of the wood splintering, the torrent pouring in and the screams becoming louder and louder still.

And I remember the images of my father, his face contorted in terror, fleeing the crumbling gate, scooping me in his arms, rushing screaming for his wife in the terrified frenzy of the courtyard. Even in the red haze that seemed to surround me, I noticed my aunt and two nieces contorting in the death throes, their throats and wrists slashed. The mob had not yet made their way to the inner part of the house, but many of the women were already dead. Some had hurled themselves in the well in the courtyard. Those in the inner sanctum had stabbed themselves with blades, kitchen knives, anything that was available – even a *dupatta* to strangle their young. Anything that would deliver them from the fate that lay in store if they were caught alive by the frenzied mob that had hammered down the door.

It is strange how strong the instinct for self-preservation is. My father loved my mother dearly. In her advancing pregnancy he had lavished an affection on her that in that day and age would seem almost unmanly. She was due any day now, and at her most vulnerable. Yet he could not have spent more than two or three minutes searching for her in that charnel house of crying, terrified women. Perhaps he presumed that she too had taken her own life. Perhaps he realized that it was too late anyway. He fled from the room, rushed out through the back wall from the waist-high opening that was kept for the animals and plunged into the sugar cane fields beyond. His frenzied flight carried us away from our village, and the flickers of flame that had begun consuming the place we once called home.

The mob had come armed with jerricans of kerosene and petrol – standard tools of their trade. In those days, it was not enough to just kill and maim, the last vestiges of existence had to be obliterated as well. And as they splashed petrol on the shops and houses of the Hindu community and threw their burning torches within, the flames rose indiscriminately. The wooden huts with dry thatched huts ignited like matchsticks themselves, petrol fuelling the flames. Fanned by the winds, the flames spread. Tongues of fire leapt from one house to the next, and then the one beyond, not caring if the tinder belonged to Hindu or Muslim. The level, indiscriminate wind carried the flames without favour or partiality, consuming all in its wake.

By the time the mob re-filled their jerry cans with water instead of petrol and splashed it ineffectually on the spreading flames, it was already too late. The fire was out of control, tearing away at houses and cow-sheds, chicken coops and vegetable gardens, destroying walls and doors and roofs. By the next morning, the new morning of 14 August 1947, only two monuments, the symbols of both its love and hatred, remained standing. The blackening turrets of the mosque and the *gurudwara* were all that remained in the burnt out village of Sheikhupura. But they did not seem majestic or proud any longer. Rather they seemed tarnished and steeped in sorrow and shame.

**III**

We walked and ran all night. Or rather my father walked and ran with me in his arms. I was too scared to let go of my vice like grip around his neck, too scared to be abandoned as my mother had been. We hid in the sugarcane fields all day, moved all night, bypassing the villages. We avoided the roads and moved along a railway embankment where we linked up with a column of refugees – a long, pitiful line of humanity moving slowly eastwards.

In that line there were thousands like us. Some had their lives earnings wrapped up in a piece of cloth or balanced in a small tin trunk on their heads. Others had their lives possessions- or at least what remained of it- strapped onto the back of a donkey or inside a bullock cart. But most of the millions who trudged eastward or westward, depending on the nation their religion ordained them, carried nothing but a deep reservoir of sorrow and hate. They would carry that weight for much of their lives and for many it would be simply too much to carry.

We crossed Lahore early next morning. Lahore was in flames. This beautiful jewel of Punjab was the worst affected in the country. It's almost equal population of Hindus and Sikhs and Muslims let loose a spate of strikes and retaliation that raged beyond reason, beyond control. We bypassed the city but even from the distance could hear the sounds of a populace gone mad. And that evening on the 15th of August 1947 we reached the check post at Wagah on the Grand Trunk Roadand walked into our new land. We crossed the check posts, first on the Pakistani side, then the Indian one and entered our new nation. Across the road a banner in saffron, white and green proclaimed "*Jai Hind*"; another in green, facing the opposite direction shouted out "*Pakistan Zindabad*". These banners were the only things that welcomed us, the millions of us, into our new land. Most of the country- two countries now- were simply too enraptured in the celebration of their birth to really care.

# PAKISTAN – OUR DREAM, OUR NATION

Lieutenant Colonel Shahryar Khan was a methodical, punctual man. And this morning, as always at 8.30 on the dot, his car glided in through the gates of Probyn's Horse, the old, proud cavalry Regiment that he commanded.

He had been commanding his regiment for two years now. He had been with the Regiment and his men for over twenty years, had lived with them, trained with them, fought wars with them. It was his home, his family, but now the family would split. Today he would supervise the breaking up of his beloved Regiment. Today was the day his Rajput and Sikh soldiers would be leaving his Regiment to go to their new land – India.

With the Partition of India, the Army was being divided like everything else in the dominion. Regiments and battalions were allotted to either nation depending on its religious composition. The purely Muslim or completely Hindu Regiments would be allotted to Pakistan or India as the case would be. And in Regiments which had a mixed composition of Hindu and Muslim troops, such as Probyn's Horse, the Hindu soldiers would leave for India. In their place would come in Muslims from other Regiments which had been allotted to India. The breaking up of units which had held together for decades – in some cases, for centuries- was a painful, often bitter process, and Shahryar Khan was determined that in his Regiment the transition would be as smooth and painless as possible.

The Quarter guard bell chimed the half hour just as he entered the office and as always, the sense of heritage struck him. A flag of the regiment, ornately embroidered in gold thread, adorned one wall. On the other wall were the mementoes of past victories and glories – a painting of an attack on Kandahar in 1890, a flag of a Baluchi warlord captured in 1913, deliberately placed upside down, the muzzle brake of a German Panzer destroyed in 1942, a glass encased pistol of a captured Italian officer from Abyssinia. Directly above the Commandant's chair were the portraits of the previous Commandants of the regiment. His photo would be next in line. What would be his own legacy to his unit?

"May I come in, Sir?" Major Mahavir was there at the door, saluted and entered. He was Shahryar's Second in Command but more than that, they had been friends for years. They were commissioned in the same Regiment, had patrolled together, hunted together and had riotous whiskey-fuelled evenings in their younger days. They had faced bullets and tank fire together and in all the years, he had never known Mahavir to flinch once. He had never seen him lose that calm, dignified composure. But now his eyes revealed a hidden tension.

The coffee came. It was a daily ritual, that morning cup of coffee which the Commanding Officer and his Second in Command had together when they discussed the events of the day. Today would be the last day of that ritual.

"Mahavir, I am sure you have things under control. Are they all ready".

The 'They' were the Sikh and Rajput troops of his unit about to depart for India, under Mahavir. And yes, they were ready. They had packed their uniforms, collected their pay, paid off their debts, and were all set to leave for their own homeland.

"They are ready, Sir. But with your permission we would like to leave a little early. We want to reach India by last light. There is much violence in Lahore and we are being badly targeted".

The 'we' jarred. It had never been 'we' and 'you'. It had always been 'us'.

"Okay Mahavir, you can leave by ten. You should make it across the border by nightfall that way. And yes, there is one more thing. Each one of your men will carry their personal weapon and twenty rounds of ammunition. You are going to need it on the way."

Mahavir's eyes widened. He knew the implications of this command. Strict orders had been received from the Headquarters of the newly raised Pakistan army that departing troops were to be issued with no arms or ammunition whatsoever – to conserve the precious weaponry for their own army. The soldiers who left for their new nation were unarmed and defenseless, and easy prey for the rampaging mobs. Shahryar was deliberately disobeying orders to ensure that his men would reach their new nation safely.

Almost involuntarily, Mahavir reached across the table and clasped his CO's hand "Thank You, Sir".

They said no more. They did not have to. They finished their coffee in silence. Then the two old friends shook hands for one last time, embraced and saluted. It was a long salute. In that gesture they saluted each other, their common regiment and each other's new nation. They would meet just once more again, and when they met, they would not be friends or comrades. They would be enemies firing at each other.

The office seemed very silent once Mahavir had left. From outside came the sounds of a squad marching past, a truck revving up, a shout from an NCO to a dawdling recruit; the daily sounds of a regiment. Then from a mosque in the vicinity came the call to prayer. Involuntarily, Shahryar turned towards the direction of Mecca, knelt and bent his head in response to the muezzin's call to prayer. And the first words of his prayer spilled out. It was "Pakistan Zindabad". His regiment may have been divided, but his new nation had just been born.

# THE IDEA OF PAKISTAN

*For many Pakistanis, their nation is 2000 years old. It began not on the blood soaked day of 14th August 1947, but way back in the sixth century when the teachings of Islam came to Indian shores. It took root with the great Muslim empires of the Khiljis, the Tughlaks and the Mughals. Why, Pakistan, the land of the Muslims, had been in the sub-continent all throughout. It just needed to be established as a distinct political identity.*

*The idea of a separate land for India's Muslims was articulated for the first time by Mohammed Iqbal in 1930. Iqbal, the Muslim poet, who also gave India its hauntingly beautiful national song, "Saare Jahan se Accha, Hindustan Hamara" – a song sung all over India even today.*

*The vague concept got form in 28 January 1933 in London when Rahmat Ali, a 41 year old law student at Cambridge first defined the contours of a new state carved from the Muslim majority provinces of Punjab, Afghanistan, Kashmir, Sindh and Baluchistan. From their letters came the name PAKSTAN – which then became Pakistan, the land of the pure. Rahmat Ali's concept remained dormant for over a decade. It was only when Mohammed Ali Jinnah, the thin-lipped leader of the Muslim League, adopted it in the Lahore Declaration of 1940 that it gathered momentum.*

*Jinnah's inflexibility and iron will won. The Congress leaders reluctantly agreed to his demand for the partition of the country and the creation of a new state - Pakistan- in the Muslim dominated provinces. Pakistan was born, on 14 August 1947, one day before India attained independence. It was the creation of a new nation that led Shahryar Khan and millions of other devout Pakistanis rushing to their prayer mats, to thank fervently "Pakistan, our Land, our Dream, is born".*

## THE BURNING VILLAGE

Shahryar did not have time to savour the birth of his new nation; or even feel a touch of sorrow at the departure of half his Regiment. Just hours after Mahavir and his men had marched out for India, he received his first official call as an officer of the newly created Pakistani Army. Yet he would wish that the call had carried happier tidings and was not so representative of the madness that had gripped his new nation.

It was his Brigade Commander on the line. There were no preliminaries, "Shahryar, mobilize every man you have got. You are moving for Internal Security duties. Virtually every town, every village in Punjab is aflame with communal rioting."

"You will move your unit to Sheikhupura. It is one of the worst affected areas. Be ready to move within two hours." This move to Sheikhupura, the first operational action that Shahryar would perform for his new nation, would change his life forever. In some way it would also impact the future course of his nation.

Shahryar and his men had witnessed destruction and death in the Punjab over the past few months but Sheikhupura surpassed all the horrors that they had seen before. The entire village, except for its *Masjid* and *Gurudwara*, was razed to the ground. It lay smoking and smouldering, and everywhere were the dead. The dead with knife wounds, the dead with heads and limbs torn apart, the dead pounded to a pulp with hockey sticks and clubs, the burnt dead, the unmarked dead, the mutilated dead. They lay in ditches, in the alleys, by the fields, in the burnt houses, in heaps around the *Gurudwara,* anywhere that they had gone to hide and had been pulled out by the mindless mob.

The fire was under control by now. Well, not really under control, it was just that there was nothing left to burn. The villagers sat glum and sullen by the road side, as they surveyed the shattered remnants of their homes. In their eyes, they seemed to blame God himself for the punishment that he had unfairly wrought upon them. They were merely doing his work, weren't they? They killed in his name, didn't they? Then why did he strike down their homes in this manner?

Shahryar organized the relief operations as best as he could. He cordoned off the smouldering area, directed teams to beat out the fires that were still burning, others to salvage anything that could be saved. There was nothing to be done for the dead, they were simply too numerous. But he moved the injured for rudimentary treatment, and sent teams to search for other dead or wounded. That was when they discovered the dead woman and her new-born child.

She lay in a heap in a blue sari inside a sugarcane field on the outskirts of the village. There were no external injures on her and she seemed to have died of shock. She must have died just after giving birth. The child was next to her, still linked to his mother by the umbical cord. God knows how he had survived so far. It was lucky the dogs had not got to him. In those days, dogs had taken a fancy to human meat. There was so much of it around and so easily available.

The Medical Orderly with them had never assisted in child birth before, but he cut the umbical cord, cleaned the child with warm water and the last of his antiseptic lotions, dried him with surprising tenderness then swabbed him in a rough military towel. But now what. Without his mother the child would not survive for more than a few hours. And here in the sullen, burnt-out village, there was none who would even acknowledge the baby, leave alone give a helping hand.

Shahryar often wondered why he made the next decision. The child was nobody's child. An unclaimed orphan, one of thousands of infants abandoned in the trauma of partition. He could have left the child with the village headman, with the knowledge that it would be abandoned in the same field as soon as they left. He could send it to the nearest Military Hospital where they would make a few perfunctorily efforts and then simply forget it till it wasted away. He need not have done what he did next, but his order just seemed to slip out. "Take this child to my home".

Perhaps that particular day – 14 August, had something to do with it. On the day of Pakistan's birth, Shahryar could not simply abandon the first new-born he had seen in his new-born nation. Damn it, that child had the dust of his new nation sticking to him. He needed a chance to live. To grow big and strong and find his own place in the world, just as his own nation did.

His wife, Nazneen would know what to do with it, she always did. She would tend it, feed him and ensure he survived. Then they could hand him over to the refugee camp or the orphanage, or wherever he belonged.

It did not work out that way. The child came home pink with crying-was washed and swaddled in a clean cloth. A lactating sweeper of the neighbourhood was got to nurse the child. He slept, awoke, cried, was fed, cleaned, fed again, cleaned again, cried, fed, slept and settled quite naturally in the maids' room. Nazneen went down to see him often; made sure he was clean and fed. A fortnight later she got him up to their room. A month later he slept there. Then he made the room his own.

He remained in the room for a month, then two, then six. Then the talk of finding a suitable orphanage for him stopped. Nazneen lavished an attention on him that released years of pent up emotion of their childless marriage. The child seemed to complete the vacant spaces of their lives. He had moved permanently into their room now, and around eight months later, she announced very matter of factly, "I have called the *Maulvi* home this Sunday for his Baptism. I have already thought of a good name for him. We will call him Shahnawaz Khan".

# OUR NEW LAND

## Delhi -1947

We reached the refugee camp at Atari around noon on 15 August. That would be our home for the next two months, if you could call a strip of blue plastic tented over our heads and a single grey blanket spread beneath a home. That was all we had then. That and the memories of what we left behind.

I opened my eyes only at Atari. Throughout our long flight I clung on to my father's neck, eyes shut tight, face buried in his neck, not letting go. He carried me with the same desperation with which I clung to him. Perhaps he too was clinging to me for support, for some measure of contact with our past lives from which we had been so cruelly uprooted.

I did not let go of him even in the refugee camp. Not when he went foraging for food, not when we lay on our thin sodden sheets at night, not even when he went out to relieve himself in the fields. I never cried though. I just kept my eyes tight shut, my brain refusing to register any image, refusing to remember any of the sights that it had seen, refusing to see even now.

We had travelled with nothing except the clothes on our backs and some small change in his pocket. He gave away the silver bracelet he always wore for a handful of rice. He gave away his thin gold chain for a few *rotis.* We ate what little the camp offered, we lived beneath the plastic sheets that passed off as tents in that open field at Atari. For two months we stayed in that camp of ghosts and wraiths. We watched people come and go, lie-down and die. We watched children being born, we watched others die. Death was a daily occurrence here, almost an hourly one. Many simply lay down, closed their eyes and never opened them again. Many left because they had just lost the will to live, and many like us, continued even though we nothing to live for.

We left the camp around mid-October. The light mists of the Punjab winters were just settling it and in its haze, the ordered fields of mustard and sugar cane stretched out as far as the eye could see. Neat irrigation channels crisscrossed the fields, tall eucalyptus trees reached heavenwards. It was a fertile land, this Punjab of ours. It was a generous, kind and forgiving land. You would not think that this land could have produced the men who did all that they did in those days of 1947. But itdid -on both sides of the fractured earth.

When we boarded the train that morning. The madness had subsided a little bit, but Atari station still had the silent, funereal air of a cremation ground. A palpable sense of death hovered like the light mist over its platforms. Trains began and terminated here now. They no longer went further west towards Lahore like they earlier did. We alighted our compartment, ticketless of course, took a vacant seat, heard the shrieking blast of its whistle, felt the rhythm of its wheels pick up tempo as it carried us past Amritsar, Jallandhar, Ludhiana, Panipat and into the congested, confused heart of Delhi. I clung on to my father throughout the journey, face buried in his neck, but somewhere along the way, I opened my eyes, and stared stonily through the window as my new land unfolded before my eyes.

## II

We spent the night at Delhi Railway Station. The Station was festooned with lights and banners. The tricolour was everywhere; greeting us at the platforms, outside the Station Master's office, over the lavatory doors, in the waiting room and the ticket counter – everywhere. The station still had the air of festivity of a nation rejoicing its new-found freedom. The incalculable human cost of that freedom had not been really comprehended as yet.

We spent the night at the station and then left next morning on foot, looking for an address scrawled on a yellow, badly dog-eared postcard. It was the address of the last link that we had left with any sort of family. The address of Girdharilal Sharma, my father's brother, my uncle, who would soon become my own father. We searched for the address all day – C-3 Janakpuri, Delhi Cantonment, an address that would soon become my home. We wandered through the lanes, asked directions and then finally arrived at the doorstep with the brass plate which read, Girdharilal Sharma, BA. Here my father put me down. I heard the doorbell ring, saw the door open, registered the look of shock in my uncle's eyes and saw my father collapsing in his arms, crying pitifully, sobbing painfully like a child who has been permitted to cry only now.

We stayed together for just around three months there and then my father left. He left on the morning of 30 January 1948. I remember the date well. There was mournful music playing all day on the radio, flags were at half-mast and in the streets people were mourning and weeping. Not for my father, of course, he was a mere statistic, but for another father. That same morning, Mahatma Gandhi, the father of our nation, had been shot by a Hindu nationalist during a prayer meet at Birla House, New Delhi. The bullets fired into the chest of the frail old man took away the Father of the Nation, a father whose values no longer seemed relevant, whose teachings seemed hopelessly outdated- but a father all the same. His legacy of non-violence had gone long ago, squandered by wasteful sons who no longer believed in it. And when he left, his pyre lit by his old friend and comrade, Jawaharlal Nehru, on the cold bank of the Yamuna River, the nation lost a little bit of its past. It also lost a little of its soul.

My own father left the same day. He slept early that night and did not awake -ever. No one knew the exact reason for his death. The doctor couldn't tell and no one bothered with the niceties of the post mortem or things like that. But I knew the reason for his death. He too died of wounds to the heart. He too died of grief. Of grief and guilt that tore him from within. The guilt of fleeing, leaving behind my mother and his unborn son when the doors came splintering down. The guilt of running, terrified, when the mob burst in. The guilt of having survived, when she could not.

There was no father to bury my neck into now. No father, whose rough smell of earth, sweat and unwashed clothing would permeate into my nostrils and give me the vague reassurance that he was there. No father, whose coarse stubble would cut into my check when I pressed my face against his neck, No father to remove his turban and wrap its thin fabric around my shaking shoulders when the night set in. I was orphaned now. Truly, in every sense of the term.

But I found a father. I never could bury my face tight against Girdhari, but I held his hand. And he held mine. He guided it to light my father's funeral pyre. He held it when he took me back home. He held it as he walked me to school – the school he taught at. He held it with the same ease and nonchalance with which he held the hands of his own two sons. With him, I learnt to open my eyes and see that there were not just mobs and flames outside, but comfort and love within. I learnt to speak. And then to write. And slowly still to laugh with them in my new home. Because home it was- they never let me feel any else. I never heard any argument with him and his wife about my presence. I never heard the dreaded words, "What do we do with this boy?" The room never hushed when I entered. My two younger siblings took to me with the natural ease of only the very young. I played marbles with them, fought over my winnings, wrestled with them, told them outrageous ghost stories at night, stole mangoes together, attended weddings and celebrations together. My aunt, no, my mother, never seemed to differentiate either. She fed me with the same gusto as she did her other sons, placing one more *paratha,* scalding hot, straight from the *tava* to my plate, even though I was too stuffed to take another morsel, with the command, "*Kha, Puttar*" She cuffed me on my head as frequently and as vigorous as she did her other sons. She called me a donkey and an idiot as often as she did them. She didn't embrace me so much though, but she ruffled my hair often and combed it, and taught me to tie my shoelaces. I grew up in that warm, boisterous; happy home and here I truly belonged. I was no longer from *Neher ki Haveli;* Mohalla Ganesh Kund; village Sheikhupura; Post office Shahdara; District Lahore. I was now the eldest son of Girdhari Lal Sharma, from C-3 Janakpuri, Delhi Cantonment, New Delhi 110058, India – growing and evolving with my new country.

## KASHMIR – BEAUTIFUL, VEXED KASHMIR

*The communal carnage that marked the birth of the two nations soon subsided. But another major dispute surfaced – one which would plaque relations between the two neighbours for decades thereafter. It involved Kashmir, beautiful, beautiful Kashmir which formed the crown on both their maps and which was coveted by both Nehru and Jinnah. This Muslim dominated state was ruled by a Hindu Maharaja, Maharaja Hari Singh, who first toyed with the idea of joining Pakistan, then joining India, then remaining independent. As he vacillated, courted by both sides, Pakistan launched an ambitious plan to capture Kashmir by military force.*

*This plan was simple. Since regular Pakistan army troops could not be sent into the independent state, tribal warriors from the North West Frontier Province would be sent into Kashmir on the pretext of waging jihad to help their Muslim brothers. The tribals, led by Pakistan officers in civilian clothing, would storm into Srinagar, capture Hari Singh and force him to accede to Pakistan. By the time, the Indian army responded, if they did, Srinagar would have been secured and Kashmir forcibly annexed into Pakistan.*

*The plan came within an ace of success. Yet the planners had not bargained on the lawless nature of the tribals. As they stormed through Kashmir, they halted at each town and village to loot and rape. In their frenzy, they were beyond the control of their Pakistani officers. Their frequent stoppages cost them time, in which Maharaja Hari Singh finally agreed to join the Indian Union.*

*Almost immediately, Indian troops were airlifted into the troubled state. Hopelessly outnumbered, the newly arrived Indian troops fought a series of delaying battles to gain time for reinforcements to arrive. Slowly, their strength built up. The Pakistani led tribals were kept at bay and then pushed back. Srinagar was saved, Kashmir became part of India and the geography of the both nations altered irrevocably thereafter.*

# The Open Road to Srinagar

## October 1947

Shahryar Khan was not court-martialed for his act of giving weapons and ammunition to his departing troops – though he came perilously close to it. Because of his impeccable track record (so far at least) he got away with just a censure. The new Pakistani army needed all its officers, especially brilliant ones like Shahryar. Yet, he was ordered to relinquish his command immediately and move on posting to Abbotabad, a small Frontier town near the newly formed India-Pakistan border.

But then Abbotabad was not too bad. The sunny little town at the foothills of the Himalayas was a much-favoured holiday resort, a stopover on the road to Kashmir. It was quiet and serene, and there would not be much work here. If nothing else, he would have time with his family.

He was wrong. Nazneen did never join him at Abbotabad, not even for a holiday. She continued at their home in Lahore, tending Shahnawaz who was slowly becoming the focus of her life. Nor would he spend much time in Abbotabad himself. Just two weeks after his move there, he got a 'Personal and Confidential' signal summoning him immediately to a meeting at Army Head Quarters, and then that he understood the true reason for his posting to Abbotabad.

### II

There were twenty of them in the Operations Room of Army Headquarters, all of them equally clueless as to why they had been called to this hallowed room at such short notice.

Major General Akbar Khan, the Director General Military Operations of the Pakistan Army strode in. He began without preamble, "We have gathered today for a mission of national importance. I have no need to tell you that what I say here will not be repeated. You will take no notes, you will discuss it with no one. You will act as we tell you, in complete secrecy and with absolute speed."

"Pakistan has been created at great cost and immense sacrifice. The great *Quaid-e-Azam's* vision has come true; but…," he slammed his hand on the table. "We have been cheated by the Hindus and the British, by Nehru and Mountbatten. The Pakistan we got is not the Pakistan we asked for. Look what they have given us".

His aide unfurled a map of the Indian Sub-continent. There, shaded in green was marked the map of Pakistan. It was the Pakistan they had dreamed, the Pakistan they had wanted. The green swath began from Kashmir moving southwards to cover almost all of Punjab and extended further downwards nibbling parts of Rajasthan and Gujarat. Two other blobs of green were marked – the Provinces of Hyderabad and Junagadh-stood out as islands in the orange that surrounded it. To the extreme East was another triangle of green, East Pakistan.

"What we have got instead," he unfurled another map violently. This time he did it himself, "Is this". It was the map of Pakistan as it existed in its present form. Athin strip of green covering Western Punjab, Sindh. Baluchistan and the North West Frontier Province. There was no Hyderabad, no Junagadh and most importantly, no Kashmir.

Akbar jabbed at the map – right at Srinagar, the heart of Kashmir, "This is ours. Kashmir is ours. It is ours morally, rightfully, legally, whatever way you look at it. Ninety percent of the population – Ninety percent," his voice screamed, "are Muslims, part of us," he continued, his voice rising, "But, what does that Maharaja Hari Singh say. He first says he wants to be independent. Then he says, he will join Pakistan and then he says he may go to India. And you knew something, the indicators are that he is going to join India."

Akbar paused. "But Gentlemen" Akbar Khan allowed himself the luxury of a smile. "We will not allow Kashmir to get away from us. *Hamne haqse le liya hai Pakistan. Ham lad kar le lenge Kashmir.*" (We have got Pakistan by right. We will claim Kashmir by force)

"Even as we talk today, twenty thousand warriors are gathering for *jihad.* They are our Afghan and Pathan brethren from the North West Frontier Province who will be the soldiers of Islam in this battle. They will lead the battle; they will take Kashmir for Pakistan".

Shahryar's years of military upbringing somehow could not digest the idea. He stood up. "Sir, why send these tribals. Just give the command and the Pakistani army will march into Srinagar. We will get Kashmir for you".

Akbar smiled, a little sarcastic smile with just a hint of a sneer, "Shahryar, idealistic and naïve as always. Pakistan cannot attack Kashmir. A direct Pakistani attack will give that bastard Hari Singh an excuse to join India. The Indian army will also enter Kashmir, if Pakistani troops are involved."

"But..." Shahryar stood up again, only to be silenced by a wave of Akbar's hand.

"The tribal fighters will go in. They will be in their tribal dresses, they will be in civilian trucks, and they will go in to fight a *jihad* as independent soldiers of Islam. Once they are in Srinagar, Hari Singh will be forced to join Pakistan and Kashmir will be ours."

"And that is where you all come in. Each of these battalions will be commanded by Pakistani officers. Each one hand-picked, each one amongst the best in the land. You all. You will each have only one officer and five Junior Commissioned Officers with you. God knows you will need some kind of help to control that rabble." He permitted himself a wry smile.

"And yes, one more thing. I suggest you all get some *firhans* and pajamas. For Operation GULMARG – that's what we'll call the operation – all of you will be in civilian clothes."

## III

Shahryar threw himself into his new task with his usual methodical efficiency. He wrote to Nazneen, asked her not to come to Abbotabad. She didn't sound too surprised, when she replied, nor particularly disappointed. She had become used to these cancellations of plans by now and in any case she was completely pre-occupied with Shahnawaz. His men and equipment started trickling in. Captain Javed Burki, a fine young officer from the Baluch Regiment reported to him a day after his return. Five Junior Commissioned Officers also came in, already in civilian attire. They would each command a column of his battle group -if you could call a horde of screaming tribal warriors that - on their road to Srinagar.

And Srinagar it was. Shahryar had been given command of the main thrust line and had been tasked to take his force straight into the capital. It was not far, just 180kilometres of open road, past Muzzafarabad, Baramula and then Srinagar. He could be there in twenty four hours. All he had to do was just drive with the foot on the accelerator along that open, undefended road straight to Srinagar.

"Speed is the essence," Akbar Khan had emphasised repeatedly. "Speed and secrecy. Just reach Srinagar and capture the airfield and all of Kashmir will fall into our lap."

Shahryar's new soldiers also came in. A horde of Pathan tribesmen, led by their warlord, Rahimtullah Wazir, their shaggy, bear-like leader. Forget the secrecy. They roared into Abbotabad cantonment perched in their jeeps and Ford trucks shouting, "*Allah-o-Akbar*," "Pakistan *Zindabad*," "Hindustan *Murdabad*," firing their weapons in the air in riotous celebration for the coming battle. Damn it. If there was even one Indian agent here it would have been a dead giveaway that something was afoot.

But for all their lack of discipline they were fighters all right. These wild tribesmen of the Afridis, Wazirs, Masoods and Hazaras clans had fought all their lives. It was their calling. Life and Death held no meaning for them. Human attachment and compassion was non-existent. And they were fearless. All Shahryar had to do was to drive their passion-filled energies towards only their target – Srinagar.

Now, as he crouched with them in the darkness along the border they were silent. Rahimtullah Wazir crouched next to him, tense and expectant. His men were dispersed in the shadows beyond. And then a single yellow flare arced through the night in a streaky parabola and exploded in a burst of light. A second followed, red. The third, yellow again. That was the signal. The invasion of Kashmir had begun. Operation Gulmarg was on its way.

## IV

Shahryar's columns crossed the border at 2200 hours dot on the night of 24 October 1947. The initial advance was easy. The border guards of the Kashmir State Force were simply brushed aside, their throats slit. Within just an hour Shahryar's column roared into Muzzafarabad, their first objective.

The small town of Muzzafarabad was asleep when Shahryar's raiders burst into it. Shahryar had planned it well. First, a silent road block behind the town so that no one could leave and carry warning of the raiders, then a force to the telephone exchange to snip the wires, another to the police station and barracks of the Kashmir State Force. Securing the town would not take more than six hours.

It didn't. It took just four. The unprepared police forces fled at the first sign of the raiders. Most simply dropped their few weapons and surrendered. In just a few hours, the electric sub-station, the telephone exchange and radio station were in their hands and the town was totally under their control. He detailed a small force to hold the town and ordered his force to move out again on the road to Srinagar. He moved ahead in the leading jeep, along with Captain Javed Burki, and it was only when he was fifteen odd kilometres from the town that he realized with a shock that he was all alone. There was no other vehicle behind him. His column had simply vanished.

He considered calling Rahimtullah Wazir on the radio, then decided against it. If the message was intercepted, it would give away surprise at the initial stage of the operation itself. He turned his jeep around and moved back towards Muzzafarabad, to locate his lost tribal warriors.

The first signs of what was really happening struck him only when he approached Muzzafarabad. His tribesmen were still there. They had not left Muzzafarabad at all. They roamed the streets, shooting randomly, smashing the shop doors, entering houses, grabbing, looting, pushing whatever they could get their hands on in to the backs of their trucks. His raiders had gone berserk in that hapless town.

Rahimtullah Wazir was there, leaning against his truck parked in the centre of the town, nonchalantly smoking a cigarette as he watched his men take their fill. His own truck was being loaded with sacks of grain, a bicycle, electrical fitments, dammit, even a street lamp.

Shahryar exploded. "Rahimtullah, what the hell is going on here? Get your men together. We have to move for Srinagar."

Rahimtullah continued looking in the distance appraising each item that his men were collecting,watching the women carried like sacks on the shoulders of his Pathan warriors. Watching what was being taken, what was left behind.

He didn't even stop smoking his cigarette. "*Janaab*" he answered coolly, "We were told that in Kashmir we would get the world's best women, defenceless men and easy plunder. We were promised all we could carry."

"What women? What loot? Our task is to take Srinagar. We can't waste time here."

"*Janaab, Gussa mat ho jayea*. We will get you your Srinagar. But we have to also get what we came here for, no." He smiled evilly, turned away and went to join his men.

It was a losing cause. Shahryar could do nothing to sway these wild men. The column finally restarted late the next night, when the tribesmen had taken everything that was not bolted down, every woman they could find and had their fill of loot and plunder. They were ready for Srinagar now. After all, they had been told that there was even more loot there, and the women even more beautiful.

In spite of the delay Shahryar was still optimistic. Even now they could still reach by the next afternoon if they moved fast enough. He led the column himself as always, and this time he kept Rahimtullah Wazir with him in his vehicle. In spite of his personal dislike for the man, he needed him and he was the only one the wild tribesmen really listened to.

They crossed Chakoti by first light on 27 October. It was still around a hundred and twenty kilometres to Srinagar now, around ten to twelve hours of driving in these winding roads. They crossed Uri, 80 kilometres now, and then they reached the last staging post at Baramula just 40 kilometres from Srinagar. This would be the last halt before his force moved on to Srinagar.

The radio cracked to life. So close to Srinagar all radio transmission were banned altogether for fear of being intercepted by the enemy. A call now would have to be something very urgent.

It was Akbar Khan. "That bastard Maharaja Hari Singh has agreed to join India last night. The first flight of Indian troops flew in this morning. Luckily it is too small a force to do anything much, but the main force will be landing tomorrow. Shahryar, it is touch and go now. Reach Srinagar before the Indians arrive tomorrow or we have lost Kashmir forever."

Shahryar put down the set, stunned. Nobody had expected the Indians to move so fast. But... he calculated, 40 kilometres from Srinagar. Four to five hours of travel time. Another three to four hours to secure the airfield. Who knows, he could just beat the damned Indians, yet. That little force that had already arrived in those seven aircraft could not be more than a company or two, no match for his force. He could brush them aside, and if he stopped the main force from landing, he could still secure Srinagar.

Shahryar could still reach there. But he was to be thwarted again. He was to be delayed again. His tribal warriors were gone again. This time their target was the defenceless hamlet of Baramula.

There was little in Baramula. Most of the town had fled as news of the approaching marauders reached the town. Only one small structure still retained signs of human activity. The small chapel and hospital of the Franciscan Missionaries of Mary, where fourteen European and Indian nuns still remained tending the sick and wounded, caring for those that were left behind and praying for their beautiful valley.

Wazir's animals descended on them with the manic intensity of the possessed. The hospital was first – its patients knifed, the bottles of saline and plasma shattered, the medicines and bandages besmirched. The quaint 19$^{th}$Century chapel of brick and stone with ivy clinging lovingly to its walls was next. The grotto was dynamited, the small donation box with its humble contents looted, the stained glass windows removed; even the brass door knobs unscrewed and carried away. Then it was the nuns. The aged sisters in their grey flowing robes who stood clutching their crucifixes helplessly as the tribesmen swooped upon them.

They violated them shamelessly, repeatedly. Those frail, elderly ladies, old enough to be their mothers and aunts. They violated them with triumphant whoops – flaunting their manhood, shrieking with glee.

Shahryar rushed to the chapel from where he could hear the screams. Nothing these animals did should have surprised him any longer, but this sight shook him to the core.

He ran to the nearest Afghan, lying atop an elderly nun. Her body was rigid with fear, her eyes glazed. He had ripped her robe off and was astride her, his pajamas pulled down; thrusting wildly, whooping with exultation.

"Leave her, you bastard." And then Shahryar slapped. A violent, open-handed slap across the contorted face. A slap that contained all the contempt and anger he felt inside.

Shahryar was a strong man and the blow would have knocked down most men. That man didn't ever notice it, even though a trickle of blood burst from his lip and his face turned red with shock. He continued humping, he continued whooping.

That was when Shahryar lost the last vestiges of control. His revolver was in his hand, the weapon cocked, as he always kept it during action. He flicked his thumb, released the safety catch and pressed the trigger.

If the slap had sounded like a pistol shot, the shot rang out like a cannon. Half the face of the sparsely bearded youth atop the nun blew off with the impact, his body hurled violently backwards.

For almost a minute, Shahryar stood over the body of the young Pathan, his pistol smoking. The nun still lay supine beneath. Maybe she was in shock. Who knows, perhaps she was already dead. Maybe she was dead even before this brutal assault, one of the many that she would have endured. From the corner of his eyes, he saw Rahimtullah Wazir approaching, other Pathan and Afghan warriors converging, unslinging their weapons. Shahryar knew that in this moment everything could just finish. The march to Srinagar, the plan to take over Kashmir, his own life, everything.

It took an effort of will to get control of his voice. Wazir was still looking at the dead Afghan. "Come; get your warriors of Islam together. Our *jihad* lies ahead and God has given us only a few hours to attain his purpose."

It was the right thing to say. For a long while, the two men looked at each other. Wazir spoke first, "We will do God's work then. After that, there are other duties to my own people that I must perform."

Shahryar knew what he meant. The Pathan code of vengeance was strong. Their tribal enmities lasted generations. The boy he had killed was Rahimtullah Wazir's nephew, his sister's son. The tribal laws demanded revenge, And revenge they would. May be not right now, may be not tomorrow, may be not even next year or the year after. But revenge they would. Shahryar himself would be spared the revenge. Rahimtullah would die that night, killed by a man Shahryar considered a friend, a brother – a man whom Shahryar himself would kill. The friendship and enmity between Shahryar's family and the Wazir clan would transcend generations – when their own sons would become friends and comrades, and then sworn enemies. Sixty years later, the Wazir clan would take the life of his grandchild, in another act of retaliation. Their hatreds were strong and transcended generations, and they always extracted an eye for an eye, blood for blood, a life for a life.

## V

Shahryar reassembled his column again. The wild tribesman moved with surprising alacrity and reacted with a respectful deference that was not there earlier. They responded well to strength, these men, and a hard, unrelenting leader always inspired respect in their eyes.

Shahryar moved out from Baramula again with him and Rahimtullah in the lead and Captain Burki in the last vehicle. It was around 2000 hours now. It would take four hours to get to Srinagar. Another two to occupy the heights and secure the airfield. The Indian aircraft could not land before six or so in the morning. I can make it dammit. I'll still make it.

Involuntarily he pressed his foot to the accelerator as the thought crossed his mind. And then, just twenty meters ahead of him, the ancient iron and wood bridge spanning the Baramula Nala – the last obstacle on the way to Srinagar – exploded in his face.

The impact flung Shahryar from his jeep. His jeep veered off the road and tilted dangerously on the side. Behind them, the thirty odd trucks, packed with tribesman closed in like a concertina towards the destroyed bridge. Then a burst of automatic fire rang out and the leading truck erupted in flames.

It did not take long for Shahryar to assess the situation. The Indian advance party had got there. They had moved out from Srinagar to fight them away from the town and keep them at bay. They intended to delay them here.

Yet the firing was not so intense. It was just a single automatic and some small caliber weapons. Obviously it was just a small squad on the other side. If he got across the *nala* he could clear them and move the rest of the way on foot. But how could he get across.

It was Rahimtullah who showed the way. In these thick wooded mountains, so akin to his own land, he was in his element. His practiced eye saw the ledge around half a kilometre to their right. Beyond that, there was another crossing place on the slightly higher reaches of the mountain. The men could get across, clear the enemy position and then rush for Srinagar on foot.

The Afghan tribesmen moved in absolute silence. They moved like mountain goats, reached the crossing place and began crossing in silence. Then the flare arced across the night sky, exploded over them with a hiss, and bathed the pitch-black October night with its light.

A well-trained soldier would have stiffened at the first indicator of the flare, remained statue-still till it died and spluttered into darkness once again. The tribesmen didn't. They rushed headlong to find refuge behind boulders, behind trees, anywhere to find cover from the light that made them naked and vulnerable.

The automatics opened up again its tracers probing like fingers into Rahimtullah's men. Four fell like puppets whose strings have been abruptly cut, in the first burst itself. Two more collapsed in the next. Then the second flare came, perfectly timed, just before the first had died down. Three more bursts of fire came in its twenty second flight;two more lay dead or dying. Then the firing stopped even though the Afghans were still firing blindly in uncoordinated, aimless bursts of return fire.

But Shahryar had got a rough idea of the location from where the fire had originated. Slowly, very slowly, he led the file on a wider, even more circuitous route from where he could roll down on the Indian defenders.

They moved slowly, silently. Each step they took, each meter they walked consumed precious time. Every now and then the fire opened up again, sending his men to the ground, not willing to move. Each burst of fire burnt time, precious time. As they closed in to the spot while the Indian fire was last seen, another burst opened up. This time it was less than 30 meters from where they were.

At that range the effect was lethal. Rahimtullah took the brunt of the first burst. The burst shattered his chest and abdomen, hurtling even that powerful brute of a man to the ground. But the Indian had given away his position. At that close range his gun flashes could be clearly seen. Every weapon opened up in that direction. There was a staccato of return fire; another burst from a carbine, another small volley, single shots from a rifle. Shahryar emptied his magazine in the direction of the fire, saw the flashes of its ricochets, saw a figure there jerk backward as his bullets found their mark. Then he lifted his hand, motioned it forward and led his tribesmen in an adrenal-fuelled charge towards the Indian position.

There were three of them inside the small foxhole, all dead. One was a burly Sikh NCO, his sten carbine still in hand, the other, a boy, just fuzz on the cheeks, his rifle lying next to him. The third was slouched over his Light Machine Gun. There were three empty magazines to the side; perhaps the one mounted on his weapon was his last. From the amount of blood that had seeped onto the ground he would have lain badly injured for quite a while before that last exchange of fire. He was dead too, killed by a burst to his chest.

Shahryar moved forward and yanked the Indian across his weapon. The Light Machine Gun swayed on its bipod, tilted and fell. Shahryar turned the dead Indian on his back – and recoiled with shock.

He could never forget that face. How could he. That calm, serene face had sat opposite his table every morning, sipping coffee. He had never known that face to lose its composure and it never did. Mahavir's face was as calm in death as it had been in life. Pale, lifeless and blood-stained but still composed and serene.

From the village in the distance below, he could hear the muezzin's cry, calling the faithful to prayer. It was getting light now. Even if he rushed to Srinagar with all that he had, he would never be able to reach the airfield before the Indians arrived. But then it was already too late. The sun was slowly coming up, bathing the hills with light. And with daylight came the sound he had been dreading. From the direction of the South came the steady drone of engines, increasing in intensity as they approached closer. It was the sound of Dakota aircraft, Indian troops in their bellies, coming in to land at Srinagar airfield. The Indian army had arrived.

# GROWING PAINS

## India, 1948-1962

Those were heady days, the years in which we grew from childhood to adolescence towards slow maturity, in the years of the 1950s and 60s. They were the days of wild excitement, of expectations, of achievements and disappointments, filled with all the pain and confusion of adolescence. But grow we did. Me, my brothers, our nation; we grew through those years together and watched ourselves evolve.

Those days of youth, I still recall as amongst the happiest of my life. But the scars of the past remained embedded in my mind. For years, I would awake crying; dreaming that I was looking for my mother in an endless refugee camp packed with dead and mutilated bodies, all in blue saris. The dream came to me for years, usually surfacing when I was ill or upset. It gradually receded but never really went away. It came to me after decades, on the night of 26 November 2008, the night my own son was trapped in the Taj Mahal Hotel during the terrorist attack on Mumbai. Some dreams, I guess, never really go to sleep.

As I grew, I watched my own country grow though Masterji's eyes. Yes, my father was always that – 'Masterji'. That small, slight man in his immaculate white *kurtas* and the Gandhi cap perched on his head was always Masterji. He was Masterji to the students of the school he was the headmaster of, Masterji to the shopkeepers, Masterji to the children of the neighbourhood through which he cycled, giving tuitions to augment his small salary; Masterji to the postman, to his friends, to his wife, and eventually even to the three boisterous children of his brood.

The title sat well on him. He lived that role, lived to teach. Like all others in those heady days, he had been swept by the mood of nationalism and the expectations of the great, new India. He was amongst the millions that had been mesmerized by Nehru's 'Tryst with Destiny' speech at the stroke of midnight on 15 August 1947. And once he had been lodged in Tihar jail with Nehru, during the 'Quit India' movement. He had met Nehru on his walks around the prison yard, exchanged '*Namastes*' and a wave of the hand. He recounted his days in prison with pride, the same pride with which he showed off his left hand, permanently bent at the forearm, fractured during a non-violent protest at the Ram Lila Grounds.

Through his eyes, I saw the story of India, heard of its two millennia old civilization; of the Indus Valley and Harappa, of Asoka and Akbar and Shivaji, of the perennial infighting, of the repeated rape, pillage and conquest of our nation by outsiders, its two centuries under British yoke, its struggle for independence and then freedom – freedom, glorious freedom.

I remembered the lessons well. How couldn't I? After all, every evening, me and my two brothers would be stretched out on the small rug in our two room flat of C-3 Janakpuri, as our father spoke in his even gentle voice, unfurling the story of India, reminding us of our role in it. He told us of the death of Vallabhai Patel, of the Liberation of Goa, about the new temples of modern India- the Bhakra Nangal Dam, of the declaration of Hindi as the national language, of the gold medals we won in hockey, of the stick wizardry of Dhyan Chand, of the voice of Saigal, the poetry of Tagore. He told us the meaning of the term Socialism, the importance of Secularism (though it took me years, if not decades to truly understand the concept). He taught us about Democracy in the best way possible. By going to the election booth every Election Day, dressed in spotless white, my mother in a new sari by his side, and returning with a dab of ink on the index finger of his left hand to show that he had cast his vote. I don't think I learnt the lesson of democracy too well. All my life I have never once cast my vote.

I wonder what my father would think if he saw me herein jail now? Like all fathers he held great expectations for all his sons. And now here I am in jail, accused of murder, awaiting trial. If he saw me in my under trial clothes, I wonder how he would feel. He too spent a month here at Tihar Jail didn't he? Would he have looked up to my act of murder as the crowning achievement of my not-so-glorious life?

As for our nation, well, he would have looked upon it with mixed feelings. Oh, he would have savoured the heady days of our economic success story; he would have been saddened at how we threw it all away. He would have exulted in our cricketing triumphs; he would have bemoaned the demise of our hockey. He would have followed our nuclear tests, our space launches, and our growing technological prowess with pride. He would have been saddened by the insurgency in Kashmir, in Punjab, in the North East, by the Naxalite movement. He would have been shocked at the levels of corruption that our politicians had stooped to. But the old man would have still remained optimistic at the end of it all. He would still see the silver lining. He would still be sure that India's Tryst with Destiny, its destiny as a great power, was just in the midnight around the corner.

# A STILL-BORN DEMOCRACY

## Pakistan, 1948 to 1958

Shahryar Khan never could recover those hours lost on the road to Srinagar. The lost hours cost him the valley of Srinagar and with it all of Kashmir. The lost hours altered the geography of the sub-continent, the very future course of the two nations.

He thought of Mahavir quite often, remembered his blood-smeared, lifeless face. He wondered how many of his own men were fighting on the opposite side, how many friends and brothers and cousins faced each other on opposing sides, now that a line on the map divided the two nations. There were many, he knew. He did not blame himself for Mahavir's death, they were soldiers doing their duty towards their nations, but in private, he grieved the loss of his friend. In any case, there was little time to think about it in the days that followed. The Indian army poured in. For a year the campaign continued, through the long winter of 1947, the following spring and autumn. It was winter once again when the guns finally fell silent on 31 December 1948.

Shahryar was there in Kashmir all throughout. He was there when the Indians poured in. He was there throughout the long campaign of 1947 which went on for over a year till December 48. He helped conduct the operations skillfully, holding back the Indians, minimising their own casualties. His actions earned him the *Hilal-e-Jurat*, Pakistan's second highest gallantry award, which was pinned on him by none other than the President, Jinnah himself, on 14 August 1948, Pakistan's Independence Day.

Shahryar would remember that day for years thereafter. The photograph of a stooping Jinnah, fur cap in place, bending to pin the medal on his immaculately starched uniform would always occupy the pride of place in his study. The photographer was a seasoned one and had caught both Jinnah and Shahryar at their most flattering angles. Even then, the gauntness of Jinnah's face and the frailty of his features showed. His body was by then riddled by tuberculosis and the effects of fifty cigarettes a day, and it finally gave way on 11 September 1948. With his passing, Pakistan lost not just its founding-father, its *Quaid-e-Azam*, it lost the only leader who had the charisma and the iron will to guide it through its turbulent founding years.

Shahryar heard the breaking news in his office at 08.45 am that morning. He did not break down as millions of Pakistanis did on the streets. He merely sat silently as the news came in over Radio Pakistan. Then he stood up, placed his cap on his head and saluted the flag of Pakistan and the photograph of its President, which was so prominently placed in his office. It seemed the only way pay tribute to the man who had created his nation.

Shahryar returned from Kashmir only after the guns had fallen silent in December 1948. Well, not really silent. Indian and Pakistanis kept firing at each other from the positions they held – the jagged Line of Control dividing the two sides. His exploits in Kashmir earned him a promotion to a Colonel's rank. It also got him a posting to General Headquarters, Rawalpindi, as the Military Assistant to none other than the Chief of the Pakistani Army – the redoubtable General Ayub Khan.

## II

Shahryar's move to Rawalpindi was possibly the first 'cushy' posting in his career- if you don't count Abbotabad that is. This time he welcomed it. More than him, it was Nazneen who was elated at the prospect of being together. She had changed over the past year, had blossomed with her new-found motherhood. Shahnawaz had become the focus of her life now and as she opened herself to her son, she unfolded even more to her husband. She joined him at Rawalpindi with the excitement of a new bride, took charge of the sprawling bungalow allotted to them, and made a home for the three of them. Their love-life too soared. They made love often, with great tenderness and passion – not the marathon, adventurous sessions of yore, but the slow, comfortable love-making that comes with years of companionship. All in all, Shahryar mused, as he lay smoking a cigarette after another languorous round of love-making, it was good to be back home.

He loved his job too. As Military Assistant to the Chief, he held one of the most sensitive posts in the army. He had a ring side view of history, but all he saw was not pleasant. He saw the political set-up in turmoil, he saw the economy flounder, and he saw the law and order in his nation deteriorate. And with the nation falling into chaos, the only organisation that seemed capable of putting it back on the rails was the army – under its brilliant, mercurial Chief, Ayub Khan. And as his Military Assistant, Shahryar would help him take control of the nation.

## III

Shahryar looked at his watch. Another ten minutes to go. He did not want to move prematurely – everything had been synchronized to the minute. He was in full uniform, not his usual ceremonial uniform, but battle fatigues, complete with the pistol in his holster. It had been years since he had used it, but liked the comforting feel of its rough, corrugated metal. Not that he expected to use it. He had been told repeatedly, "No firing, no violence, no noise, no fuss'.

That little knot of tension was building up – that quivering tension that always came before an action. He liked that feeling too. He would be back in action after almost a decade and actually missed its adrenal fuelled high.

His men were in position. Most waited in small squads along the leafy boulevard that led to the President Iskander Mirza's palatial bungalow. Others were poised near the Police Headquarters, the radio station, the Central Bank, the offices of *Dawn* and the other leading newspapers, and at the airport and railway station. They were all personally selected by him and knew what was to be done. And they were disciplined Pakistani Army soldiers, not the tribal rabble he had led in Kashmir. They would follow orders explicitly. This time there would be no mistake.

Shahryar waited. Smoked a last cigarette. Then at ten dot, he eased his staff car towards the gates of the Presidential House. The guards did not stop him. They were in the game as well. As were the President's Military Assistant and the Aide de Camp. As army officers they had been appointed by the Army Chief and owed allegiance to Gen Ayub Khan. They had faithfully relayed each activity of President Mirza and helped them formulate their plan. Now everything was perfectly in place.

Shahryar's car glided across the long driveway towards the porch. The door was open, none of the civilian staff were around, all that had been coordinated earlier. He walked in through the huge ornate doorway, crossed the chandeliered drawing room, as large as a basketball court; climbed the plush, carpeted stairway leading to the President's living quarters. He knew the President was there in his study; that had been coordinated too. He stopped at the door, paused, looked around, and lifted his hand to knock.

He lowered his hand. Damn. These years of military training. Here he was, all set to take captive the man within and he still wanted to knock and take permission to enter before doing so. He turned the door knob and pushed. The door swung in smoothly and he entered.

President Iskander Mirza was at his table. He was a handsome man, always had been, and prided himself on that. But now his face was taut with tension. He did not look too surprised when Shahryar entered. Perhaps he had been expecting this late night visit.

He cut a dignified figure in his silk dressing gown. And in spite of the visible tension he was in, he mustered up enough authority to stand up and turn a cold stare towards Shahryar, "How dare you come here like that? Get out".

Shahryar did not remove his weapon. He did not need to. He saluted – military instinct again – and announced, "Mr President, I hate to say this, but you are under arrest".

### IV

*The drama which played in the Presidential Palace on that night of October 1958 was the first military takeover in Pakistan. Two others would follow later. With this coup, General Ayub Khan took over and appointed himself President.*

*The army take-over was initially welcomed by the Pakistani populace. Pakistan had been floundering, its political structure corroded, its economy stagnating. Seven Prime Ministers came in ineffective procession from 1951 to 58. None could hold the nation together, none really bothered.*

*When the Army Chief, General Ayub Khan took over with the 'bloodless coup' of that October night, it was initially meant to be a temporary measure. But, they were wrong. Once the military entered Pakistani politics. It would never really leave.*

### V

Shahryar's role in Ayub Khan's coup served him well. It was a brilliant coup, no doubt. Not a shot was fired. None were even aware of it till it was announced on radio next morning. The President was placed under house arrest and then promptly exiled to London. The self-serving politicians of his coterie were jailed – and then the army went about setting things right.

Oh, they were welcomed all right, greeted as heroes, the saviors of their nation. Perhaps they were, at that point of time. Only the medicines they offered were worse than the ills they set out to cure. The army's involvement in government was the start of a cancer. Like all cancers, it abated every now and then. Like all cancers, once it set in, it never really let go.

But yes, General Ayub – no, President Ayub now, and his army did do well. At least in the initial years. Black marketing and hoarding stopped. Prices came under control. Land reforms came about, roads were built, corruption was curtailed, law and order returned. Ayub's stock rose – and Shahryar rose with him.

When his promotion came, it was but inevitable. No one doubted it. No one was even surprised when he was given command of one of the strongest and most vital brigades of the Pakistan Army.

Shahryar could have got a comfortable brigade in comfortable Lahore or Islamabad. He chose otherwise. He chose to command an infantry brigade on the Line of Control, with the Indians eyeball-to-eyeball against him. From his command post, he could see their positions quite clearly. With binoculars, he could also see the same narrow road as it wound its way towards Srinagar. In his mind's eye he drove down that road many times. He travelled through the apple orchards and walnut groves, through pristine valleys and emerald meadows; past the shimmer of lakes and into Srinagar. He wondered if he would ever drive down that road to Srinagar and into the heart of Kashmir again. He would, he promised himself. He would. If not in his lifetime, then in Shahnawaz's. If not him, his son would drive down that road to Srinagar. If not his son, his grandson – if not him, the next generation. But, *Inshallah,* Srinagar would be theirs, and get Kashmir, they would.

## VII

And what of Shahnawaz? There is a saying in Hindi, "*Upar wala jab bhi deta hai, deta chappar phad ke*", – 'When the Good Lord gives, he gives it all'. The Good Lord, be it a Hindu or a Muslim one, or maybe both, did give Shahnawaz his all. It seemed that fate wanted to repay him for the trauma it had inflicted on the day of his birth. That cruel birth in the sugarcane field was something he obviously never remembered, nor was he ever told about it. To him, to the world, to Nazneen and Shahryar, he was their child, sole and true, their only son, their pride, their heir, their prince.

And prince he was. He grew up like one all right, living the rich, feudal life that he accepted as his rightful due. Nazneen had accepted him as her own unconditionally. Emotionally, biologically, in every sense of the term, he was hers. Shahryar took longer to develop that same deep bond. For him acceptance came after years, but when it did, it was with the same unquestioning love. Shahnawaz became the long-awaited son whom he taught how to shoot and ride, who sat in his lap as he drove around their sprawling estate, whom he showed off proudly at mess parties and family functions. He was the son whom he regaled with the stories of Pakistan's two thousand year old civilization, its heroes – Akbar and Babar and Ghazni and Ghori. He told him the story of its birth, how Jinnah had struggled to bring about their nation; about how Kashmir, the crown-jewel of Pakistan's map, had been stolen by Indian perfidy. He told him of his days in the army, of the ibex and antelope he had bagged on *shikar* expeditions, his ancestors, even bedtime stories at times. They were the stories a father shares with his son – and like all oft-repeated stories became larger than the events they portrayed.

Shahnawaz grew up a prince in that house, doted upon, pampered and well, actually more than a little bit spoilt. In his early years, his father would be away for much of the time, but when he returned the house was always full of friends and relatives. The drawing room always resounded with loud talk and laughter and Shahnawaz was always there next to him – trying to become part of the men talk, listening, trying to understand each word that was spoken. He remembered the animation in his father's features when he spoke about Kashmir, his thumb and forefinger coming close, just an inch apart, "This close, we were this close to Srinagar". And in his sub-conscious grew the thought – someday he would close that inch long gap, someday he would cover the yawing chasm they represented. Someday, he would help take over Kashmir.

Shahnawaz's arrival also seemed to bring luck to the family. Or so Nazneen always said. With time Shahryar grew to accept it too. But it was more than luck. Shahryar had been repeatedly performing brilliantly, wherever he was, and his efforts were rewarded. In October 1962, he received his General's baton. He remembered the date well. It was 20 October 1962. He was sitting in the Operations Rooms when the news arrived. First was the news of his promotion, delivered by a beaming aide. And even as the flood of visitors trooped in with their congratulations, even better news came streaming in over the radio. That day at 0600 hours, the Chinese had attacked India in a two pronged attack at Ladakh and Arunachal Pradesh. As a military man he knew the Indian preparations were no match for the Chinese. The Chinese attack would sweep through the thinly held Indian positions and inflict their arch-enemy it's most crippling and humiliating defeat.

"Cheers", he laughed, when he heard the news. "This calls for more than Scotch. This calls for Champagne". He was not referring to the news of his promotion, of course. He was referring to the Chinese attack on India.

# THE BLEEDING HIMALAYAS

**October 1962**

*When the Chinese attacked India, all along the disputed border in October 1962, the nation was shocked. It shouldn't have been. All indicators pointed to a coming Chinese attack. They were simply ignored.*

*India and China share the largest disputed border in the world, over 7000 kilometres of it running from Ladakh in the west to Arunachal Pradesh in the East. The Chinese claimed almost 67,000 square kilometres of Indian territory as their own. As the problem festered, Nehru ordered the Indian army to adopt forward positions all along the disputed border.*

*The decision, made under wrong advice, was a disaster. Ill-equipped troops, unprepared for the freezing high altitude conditions were sent to occupy isolated posts in virtually indefensible positions. When the Chinese attacked – still shouting, "Hindi –Chini Bhai Bhai" they swamped the Indian positions, isolated them one by one, decimated them and forced the shattered remnants to withdraw almost till the plains of Assam.*

*Over 7000 Indian soldiers perished in the onslaught, let down by their political and military leaders. It was a scale of defeat none could have imagined and the nation was benumbed with sorrow. Lata Mangeshkar – the Nightingale of India – best captured the mood, in her song, "Ae Mere Watan ke logo," a mournful tribute to the fallen that brought Nehru, and a grieving nation, to tears.*

## II

*"Ae Mere Watan ke logon,* (*Oh, the people of my nation*)
*Zara aankhon mein bhar lo pani,* (*Let tears fill your eyes*)
*Jo shaheed huen hain unki,* (*For those who have fallen*)
*Zara yaad karo qurbani"* (*Let us remember their sacrifice*)

Lata Mangeshkar's voice floated out from the Ram Lila grounds on 27 January, 1963. It was the day after our fourteenth Republic Day, but the nation was not celebrating. The country was still shaken by the tragedy that had overcome it.

It had been just two months ago that the Chinese had swept past the weakly held Indian positions. None expected them to attack so swiftly or so violently. None expected them to roll down across the Himalayas so rapidly; none expected them to overrun the Indian army with such ease. None expected such a disaster. None. Least of all Nehru.

Her voice carried over the radio waves and over the nation. It fanned a funeral pyre in Sholapur, Maharashtra, it soothed a grieving widow in Jhunjhunu, Rajasthan, it comforted an aged, uncomprehending mother in Bhiwani, Haryana. Its words played with a young sister skipping listlessly in her courtyard at Lucknow. It wafted over a child looking over his young mother's shoulder for a non-existent father in Jammu. It touched us all as it floated from the shores of the Arabian Sea and the Bay of Bengal, moved over the Deccan Peninsula, roamed across the deserts of Rajasthan, and the mustard fields of Punjab. It soared over the vast Indo-Gangetic plains and then began climbing towards the Himalayas.

Her voice hovered over the mountain tops, and wafted over the fresh new snow that concealed the bodies beneath its shroud of white. Did her voice reach the brave men who lay beneath? Did it move their ghosts to tears as it moved us?

They say thatghosts of Indian soldiers still roam these hills. Legend has it that at times they slap a sentry dozing on duty, or warn a post of a coming avalanche. What do these ghosts feel now? Those ghosts in pitiful summer uniforms with antiquated .303 rifles in hand and five or ten rounds of ammunition in their pockets. Perhaps her voice soothed them too and lulled them back to sleep.

But what did her song do to those who were responsible for this debacle. It moved Nehru to tears. But what of the other guilty ones? The Intelligence Chiefs who lied, the Generals who refused to see the truth, the politicians who pushed the army into a Himalayan blunder. I think her voice would haunt them too.

Lata Mangeshkar's voice rose higher still, as high as the Himalayas,

*'Jai Hind*
*Jai Hind ki Sena*
*Jai Hind*
*Jai Hind ki Sena...'*

It came to our homes where we hunched around the radio set. Masterji was crying unashamedly. Our mother stood by the kitchen door, *duppatta* twisted in her hand, biting her lower lip. My two younger brothers, too young to comprehend the tragedy that had befallen the nation looked at the rug beneath the feet. I looked at the floor too. The lump in my throat was bursting, my hands were twisted into tight fists and as Lata Mangeshkar's voice died away I made what was either the best or the worst decision of my life.

## III

I don't know whether the decision to join the army in that emotion-choked moment was a right one.

Things did eventually pan out right in the twenty odd years that I spent in uniform. It gave me a ringside view of our nation and the events that were shaping it. The decision also shaped my overall destiny – a destiny that had led me eventually to this prison cell.

I did not announce my decision to Masterji, my mother, or my brothers, at least not yet. I did my homework first, checked the recruiting offices, found out about the recruitment procedures and then went through the three day selection process at the Recruitment Center, Ghaziabad. I sailed through it. But, I need not have been so proud at being selected. In those days, the army was recruiting everybody. I then rushed home with a box of sweets to announce the good news of my selection.

Good news, like hell! My brothers looked at me with awe when I announced it, but Masterji looked shocked. My mother exploded, *"Pagal kutte ne kata hai tujhe? Kam se kam pehle hame bata dete."* (Has a mad dog bitten you, or something? You could have at least spoken to us before doing it) Masterji tried to talk me out of this with his usual sensible logic. "Look, what is your hurry? Wait for 2 years more. Finish your graduation and then join the army if you want. Then you will be able to join up as an officer."

Yes, they were right. I could have waited two more years. Just a year and ten months in fact, till I became a graduate. I would have been able to get commissioned as an officer then. Who knew how my life would have panned out then? But, I didn't wait, and that single impulsive decision saw me standing, tin trunk and bedding by my side, at Rourkee railway station on that hot afternoon of June 1963, all set for my recruit training at the Bengal Engineering Center, Rourkee.

I guess they put me in the Engineers because of my education. I was almost half a graduate. I was not too enthusiastic when they allotted me to the Engineers though. I wanted the infantry. The good hard-slogging, fighting infantry. In my mind's eye I often pictured myself holding on to my position heroically on a desolate hill-top pouring fire on attacking Chinese hordes; wounded repeatedly but holding out indomitably till I finally collapsed, but not before I had wiped out half the attacking force and gained enough time for reinforcements to come in and finish off the rest. Sometimes I even gave a nice little speech before my eyes glassed over. Oh, it was quite heroic and lovely and all that. The stuff of day dreams for an 18-year old boy who had set out to become a man.

All that would never happen. My army service would never be as heroic, or as glorious as I imagined. I would win no medals, get no honours. But perhaps in some small wayI contributed – or so I liked to believe.

## IV

I hated recruit training. Every moment of it. I hated waking up at four every morning. I hated the physical training at five, I hated the sadistic, barking instructors who hauled us up at midnight to roll and haunch and crawl our way across the games fields. I hated drill most of all. Firing was good though. I became a surprisingly good shot, one of the best in my batch. I was pretty good at academics too. Not surprising, since with two years of college education, I was better qualified than most of the instructors.

But what I hated most of all was the army's denial of my leave when I needed it the most. That perfunctory rejection of my pleas for just three days of casual leave to meet my mother in her last days. She had ignored her cough, hidden her frequent attacks from the rest of the family for a long time and when she finally collapsed, the doctor's diagnosis was damning. Tuberculosis, very acute and very rampant. She spent three weeks in hospital, three weeks when I was not permitted leave to meet her because some bastard of an instructor felt that improving my drill was more important. The telegram came, a second, telling me to come immediately, a trunk call from Delhi when it was near the end. And when I did get the leave I had requested, it was too late. She had gone by the time I arrived. And when we cremated her the next morning, the breeze carried away the wood-smoke and ashes. It also carried away a large part of our lives.

I could not say my good-bye to her, but she did to me. She had kept a box of '*pinnis*' for me, large balls of ghee, flour, sugar and dried fruits...each one an atom bomb of energy. On the last day of each of my periodic visits home, she always gave me a tin of *pinnis* to give me strength and energy for my training. With each box came the admonishment, *"Puttar tu kuch khata-wata nahin. Teri haalat dekh, kaisa ho gaya hai tu. Yeh leh aur kha."* (Don't they give you anything to eat out there? Look at your state. Here, take this and eat). She always made them in the last few days of my leave. I don't know why she had prepared it so much earlier this time. Maybe she knew the circumstances in which I would be coming home this time and had kept her farewell ready.

Each box I had invariably shared with my barrack mates – sharing was a norm when you live together. But this box I hoarded jealously inside my trunk. I ate just one every day and then just half as the quantity diminished. I kept them for a long time, savoring just one mouthful every morning....remembering her...remembering the feel of her hands, the magic of her fingers. And then it was down to the last morsel, just around a quarter of a *pinni,* which was all that was left of her. I ate it all, licked every crumb that remained in the box, and then broke down for the first time since she died. I broke down like a child who has lost his mother as I devoured the last offering of her love. And though I could never say goodbye to her, at the moment when the last morsel slipped in to my mouth, she said her last goodbye to me.

I carried her memory through the rest of the training; through most of my life in fact. And then the routine of the days took over. The days became more jam-packed as we approached the date of our passing-out parade, the day we finally graduated from being mere recruits to becoming soldiers. We practiced drill non-stop for weeks on end, polished our belts and boots till they gleamed, practiced our orders till our throats were sore. In a way, the maddening routine was a relief. It kept my mind off her. And when we finally did march out of the parade ground for the final time, and tossed our berets in the air in celebration, it was with quite a sense of achievement. Dammit! I had done it! I was a soldier at last.

# A Collision of Trajectories

## The Early 1960s

*In the first half of the sixties, the paths of India and Pakistan followed two widely contrasting trajectories. Under General Ayub Khan, who had taken over as President in 1958, Pakistan was on a roll. Prices came under control. Some measure of law and order returned. The economy flourished at a healthy 6 percent rate of growth. Pakistan was becoming the model for a new state.*

*The army too did well under Ayub Khan's tutelage. It got a flood of equipment and military aid – brand new Patton tanks, self-propelled artillery guns, Sabre jets and missiles. The army grew strong and confident – perhaps a little too confident.*

*On the other hand, India had a dismal half-decade from 1960 to 1965. The economy crawled at a pathetic 1-2 percent – the 'Hindu Rate of growth' that misplaced policies had led us to. Yes, Secularism and Democracy were in place. There was honesty and probity in government. And there was a false sense of benign, non-violent greatness till the defeat of 1962 shattered all illusions.*

*Nehru died soon after in 1964, the shock of the defeat in the 1962 Indo-China War taking its toll. In his place came Lal Bahadur Shashtri, a mild and unimposing successor. But his diminutive, five feet, one inch frame concealed a core of steel.*

*India's military and political turmoil was too good an opportunity to let go. Pakistan still harboured dreams of Kashmir. Now with a demoralized Indian Army and a weakened political leadership this was perfect moment to attack India.*

*They miscalculated. Their attack in the Punjab, led by their Armoured Division with spanking new tanks made impressive gains initially, only to be flounder in the water-logged fields which the Indians had deliberately flooded. Virtually the entire Armoured Division was bogged down in the flooded fields of Punjab. After twenty two days of brutal slogging the two nations agreed to a Ceasefire, but the problem festered. And the two nations remained separated brothers, hostile neighbours, and implacable enemies – just as they had been since the day of their conjoined birth.*

# THE FLOODED FIELDS

## Punjab – September 1965

August in Punjab is a terrible month. The rain comes down in torrents, pounding the earth, flooding the fields. It is as still as a grave then. There is not a gust of wind, not a wisp of breeze. In the still, heavy atmosphere, the rain comes down relentlessly, buffeting the trees, splattering the earth. The rains lashed down on the thick eucalyptus and *shisham* groves of the Chunga Munga Forest near Lahore. It splashed on the tanks that crouched there, hidden beneath camouflage nets. It turned the nets sodden, it penetrated between the tarpaulins and ground sheets, it entered the engine decks and short circuited the electrical circuits. It dampened the ammunition, decayed the batteries. It played havoc with men and machine alike. Oh no, the Chunga Munga forest was definitely not a nice place to be in at this point of time.

Major General Shahryar sweltered in his tent deep in the heart of the forest. As the Divisional Commander of the famed 1st Armoured Division, he was better off than his men. But like the rest of his men he hated the stay here, and the interminable wait. None of his officers or men knew what on earth they were doing here. Only Shahryar and his Brigade Commanders were aware of the true reasons and they had been sworn to secrecy.

His division had been moved to the Chunga Munga Forest near the International Boundary to be able to strike deep into India when the time was right. They waited for a month, then two, then three. They cursed the scorpions, the snakes, the weather and the men who put them there in the first place. But now, their long wait would soon be over. Their time had come.

The signal came late on the night of 9 September 1965. It was in a simple envelope marked 'TOP SECRET" 'For the Eyes of the General Officer Commanding Only' and contained just one line in heavily ciphered code. It was the signal for Shahryar to launch his Armoured Division into India.

# "BREAK THE BUND, YOU BASTARDS – THE TANKS ARE COMING"

### September 1965

I had thought that nothing could be worse than recruit training and that my lot would improve once I became a full-fledged soldier. I was wrong. I joined my regiment – 103 Engineer Regiment (or One Not Three, as we liked to call ourselves) at Ambala on that cold night of December 1963. I would be in that Regiment for the next eighteen years. I would grow into a man there, would fight two wars under its flag and spend half my adult life there. That regiment would be a greater influence on me than perhaps any other factor in my life.

And on that cold December morning, when I disembarked from my train, all this seemed far away. The five of us, all recruits, landed at Ambala railway station to a torrid indoctrination into unit life. We were greeted pleasantly enough by the NCO who had come to receive us, given tea and biscuits, told to place our trunks and bedding in a one ton vehicle and then told to start fucking running behind that vehicle all the way to the unit located 11 kilometres away.

That was just the beginning. Life in the unit was as busy and as meaningless as it had been during recruit training. I seemed to be doing nothing but cutting grass, peeling potatoes, cleaning the lines for an inspection, doing guard duty every night, doing everything but soldiering.

A year passed – that mandatory year of unit life after which a raw recruit is considered to have become a soldier. Not that it made any difference. I was treated the same, still did the same that I was doing before.

But now there seemed to be a change in the unit activities. We spent more time out now on training exercises. It seemed that we spent all our time out in the training areas laying dummy mines, clearing them, constructing bunkers, demolishing them, making tracks, laying bridges and lifting them again; firing, practicing radio communication – I enjoyed all that. It made me feel like a soldier.

Of course, we knew that there was something in the offing. The papers were full of the growing tensions between India and Pakistan and we kept on doing those idiotic mobilisation exercises. Ask any soldier, he'll tell you. When an army starts mobilisation exercises, there is something afoot.

That night in the first week of September when the code word "Surya Kiran" – that idiotic code word for mobilization which we were all supposed to memorize – was announced during another midnight fall-in, we groaned again in frustration. Another night ruined. We loaded stores, dumped our kit bags, packed up in the mandatory six hours and took our places in the backs of the trucks allotted to us. Usually for these exercises, we moved a short distance, halted and returned. This time when we moved out we did not return. Instead just after dark the convoy eased itself out on to the Grand Trunk Road and headed westwards towards the Indo-Pak border.

It seemed that the whole damned Indian army was out on that road. Jeeps, guns, trucks, tank transporters, civilian trucks with 'On Army Duty' emblazoned on their windscreen, Air Defence guns, all seemed to be crawling westward with their headlights off. By now, we knew it was no mobilization exercise. The news had even come in on the radio – we were headed to war.

We did not know where we were headed for. I don't think anyone did. We reached the Beas River Bridge, just sixty kilometres short of Amritsar, got off the Grand Trunk Road and moved along a series of *katcha* roads to a village called Asal Uttar. Here the road petered out, we dismounted, ran for another two or three kilometres and then slumped panting and exhausted on the banks of a wide, brick-lined canal. But, even as we tried to catch our breath a NCO rushed forward, passed out shovels, pick axes, crowbars, anything that could cut and barked out, "Break the bund, you bastards. The tanks are coming."

We didn't know where we were, what we were doing here or why were we doing it. We knew the war was on in full swing now, we had heard of the Pakistani attacks. But at that point of time, no one knew the truth, whether we were winning or losing or both. We merely began digging, breaching the banks of the canal till one of the NCOs came up and bellowed, "Not here, you sister-fuckers, the other side." Then we scrambled up the embankment on the other side – the side facing the enemy – and began digging again, cutting the banks, scooping out shovels of earth blowing up portions of the stubborn earth with explosives, trying to make the banks give way.

We had our first casualty of the war that night. It was Gurnam Singh. Gurnam, that huge, red-faced Sikh with his booming laugh and colourful language. Gurnam, the light heavy weight wrestling champion of our unit, who got two five litre tins of ghee from his village each time he went on leave and then shared it freely with everyone. Gurnam, who boasted of seven acres of land and twenty buffaloes in his village. Gurnam, our explosives expert. He was the first to go.

He had been working like a man possessed all night. Rushing to the explosive dump, rushing back with packs of plastic explosive, placing them in the sides of the embankment, fitting the initiators, detonating them – cutting into meter after meter of that stubborn earth; hacking the loosened earth, waiting for that damned bank to breach. He worked like a man possessed and for good reason. His seven acres of land and twenty buffaloes lay just twenty kilometres behind us – right in the path of the advancing enemy tanks.

It was his eighth or ninth charge that exploded pre-maturely when he was crimping the detonators. He wouldn't have even realized it when it happened. The force of the explosion shattered his face, his chest and abdomen, killing him instantly. Two others went with him. Sumer, his assistant, would die later that night on the way to hospital. Mahapatra, who was preparing the hollow in which to place the charge would die, very, very painfully three days later in Amritsar Military Hospital.

Gurnam, Sumer and Mahapatra died just doing what we all were. But they became heroes. In later years, their photos adorned the walls of our Quarter Guard and kitchen halls. Stories grew around them. Gurnam had died jumping on the explosives to save the others; Gurnam and Sumer had carried the burning explosives and ran for a mile to take it away from the rest. The three had hurled the explosives on the on rushing enemy. They had jumped with the explosives on an enemy tank, taking it with him. After a while, even those of us who were there when it happened, began to believe in these stories. After all, fiction sometimes embellishes the truth – and then that becomes the truth itself.

We didn't have much time to grieve their loss, or the luxury of mourning. We continued hacking away at the banks and slowly the breach in the canal banks formed and widened. Gradually the water seeped away from the breached banks. The earth moistened, formed a wet patch, became a slush, then a puddle. The loose red soil became sticky, gooey clay which clung to our boots and made our vehicle wheels skid and spin futilely in the slippery earth. All day and night we widened the breach and let the water pour across on the other side. The seep became a rivulet, the rivulets became a flood. Slowly the area became a water-logged swamp – an impassable death trap. Only we did not know it was so, nor did we know for whom the trap was being prepared.

# MAYHEM AT MILESTONE 38

Shahryar boasted of running a tight knit and efficient division and within two hours of receiving the signal, his tanks had already begun rumbling out of the Chunga Munga Forest and begun moving eastwards.

His tanks crossed the International Boundary around noon and fanned out inside India. From his helicopter above, Shahryar watched their well-rehearsed maneuvers. He watched their leading columns approach the small town of Khem Karan, saw them send out two pincers that encircled it in a ring of steel. He saw his infantry enter the town and capture it. He saw the Pakistan flag rise over the Railway station and then pushed his elements deeper into India. So far at least, everything was going like clockwork.

It was only early in the evening that they had their first serious encounter as his leading Regiment made contact with the Indian positions. He watched the regiment fan out and move cautiously forward. Even as Shahryar watched, an orange flash emanated from the Indian position and a second later a silver- blue flash as his leading Patton tank received a direct hit on its turret.

The Patton, juddered, slowed. And then amazingly moved forward again. The round from the Indian tank had been unable to penetrate its thick armour cladding. From his vantage point above, Shahryar could see the Indian tanks; they were Shermans, which were easily out-gunned and out-armoured by his more sophisticated Pattons.

The second Pakistani tank fired – missed an Indian Sherman tank hidden in its firing position with only its turret and gun visible. The Sherman fired and hit. The Patton shuddered, then like a behemoth after a punch on the jaw, began moving forward again. The Sherman's round had bounced harmlessly off.

The Patton's second round did not miss. It hit the Sherman on its exposed turret, and the armour piercing round sliced through steel, penetrated, ricocheted wildly inside the closed turret compartment, smashing through the gun cradle, sights, radio set, the gunner, loader and commander and theammunitionwithin.

The Pakistani gunner whooped with joy as the Sherman exploded. Viewing the battle through his binoculars, Shahryar cheered too. It was the first kill of his division and *Insha'Allah,* the beginning of many more.

The next one came almost instantly. Another Sherman went up in a muffled explosion as a Patton scored a hit – another cheer went up. One more kill for 1st Armoured Division.

His tanks were close to the Indian positions now and at closer ranges the Indian rounds could penetrate the armour of the Pattons. A Patton was hit, stalled, and exploded. Another Patton lurched as a round shattered its tracks, and exploded as a second penetrated its hull. Another Indian Sherman went up in flames. His Pattons were racing forward, firing furiously – much of it un-aimed, but at these ranges it really didn't matter- and then overran the Indian position with the force of a charging train.

They mowed through the Indian positions, churning the hastily prepared trenches beneath their tracks, machine guns firing. His own infantry followed close behind the tanks, clearing the pockets of resistance, mopping up the remnants of the enemy. And then the firing subsided and then a green flare arced upwards, then another. Green over Green. The success signal. His attack had succeeded in overrunning the Indian positions.

Shahnawaz stood up in joy and then raised both hands high in prayer. He had done it. By God's grace, he had done it. In the very first encounter with the enemy, he had defeated the Indians. He was now ready to take his tanks all the way to Delhi.

## II

Perhaps the ease with which they had won the battle, had inflicted a sense of over-confidence in his division. Yes, the first day had easily belonged to Shahryar, but the more bitter battles were still to come. And the Indians, though initially off-balance, had recovered to begin preparing their own little surprise.

They moved deeper into India over the next day, moving slowly now, as the Indian resistance intensified. It was on the third day of the battle that they received their first major setback. Shahryar was in his helicopter, as always, when he saw the area ahead of his left brigade suddenly erupt with tank fire. Even from his vantage point above, he could not see the Indian tanks. Then green yellow flashes emerged from the sugar cane fields beyond and two of his leading Pattons erupted.

From his vantage point Shahryar recognised the Indian tanks – they were Centurions, the heavy 50 ton behemoth that was easily a match for his Pattons. They had concealed their tanks inside the tall sugarcane. One was even disguised as a haystack. They opened fire when the Pattons were just around five hundred meters away and at these close ranges the impact was lethal. Then the Indian tanks opened up again and another Patton exploded.

It was not much better on his right flank. Here, his second Brigade had walked into another ambush. They had no indicator of it till the first tank lurched and crumpled forward, its left track blown apart by an anti-tank mine. The Indians had laid mines across the entire frontage and as the Pakistani tanks halted, Indian anti-tank jeeps closed-in, fired, hit a target, ran; Closed in again, fired, another one, ran, fired – , and again.

In the confused battling that continued all night, none realised that the tanks were being funneled into a narrow gap. The firing on the flanks, had deflected the entire force into a deadly killing area, an area that had been flooded and made virtually impassable.

For two nights the Indians had been breaching the canals covering the ground with ankle-deep water. The soil was now slushy and loose. A walking man could cross it with difficulty, a vehicle would sink in axle-deep; and a 48 ton tank would flounder and sink right up to its belly in the boggy earth.

The leading tanks ploughed their way through the water. In the dark, none realized the extent of the flooding. Most drivers simply assumed it was a wet patch that they would soon cross. It was only as they went deeper, that one by one they bogged down and stalled. The elements behind followed, oblivious to the danger ahead, to meet the same fate. Shahryar's tanks had literally ground to a halt in the flooded fields of Punjab.

There was no communication with either of his Brigades but Shahryar knew they had not moved all night. Yet the magnitude of the disaster only hit him when he lifted off in his helicopter at first light the next morning. From atop he could see both his leading Brigades irretrievably bogged down in the flooded fields. Here and there, smoke emanated from the stranded tanks, sitting ducks now for every anti-tank gun in the vicinity. A few tanks still returned the fire, but it was more a gesture of futility then defiance. Many of his tanks seemed abandoned – he could not see the commanders on the turrets.

Damn. No wonder they had not moved. How could they. And none of the leading Brigade Commander had spoken to him on radio since midnight. Perhaps the Indians had just jammed the radio frequencies. He had to get forward and help extricate his elements. And he had to do it on ground. His helicopter could not fly over Indian lines, by now even their Air Defence had become considerable. He landed, ran towards his waiting jeep and sped off in the direction of his trapped brigades.

Shahryar's vehicle, accompanied by two others sped forward towards the village of Asal Uttar where the bulk of his armour was trapped. And as he approached, his radio crackled.

"Qazi for Imam. Qazi for Imam. Over." It was one of his Brigade Commanders. He had finally established communication.

"Imam for Qazi. Where are you? I am coming to your location."

"Qazi for Imam. I am still south of the village Asal Uttar on the Khem Karan Amritsar road."

"Imam for Qazi. Wait there. I am travelling on the same road. I will meet you at Milestone 38."

This radio transmission, the last Shahryar ever made, was a mistake. A fatal mistake. Shahryar, the methodical perfectionist, had given out the position he was headed for. His transmission was intercepted by an Indian Signal communication unit which had been monitoring his radio frequency for days now and had identified who 'Imam' was – the Divisional Commander himself.

It took less than seven minutes to pass that information to every artillery battery in range. Imam was headed for Milestone 38 on the Khem Karan – Amritsar road. Imam himself – what a catch.

By the time Shahryar reached Milestone 38, twenty minutes later, Brigadier Ilahi, his brigade commander was already waiting for him – so were the Indians. As Shahryar's small convoy slowed down – the first artillery salvo opened up. The initial rounds landed almost on Ilahi's jeeps – killing him and his staff instantly. The shock of the explosion sent Shahryar's own vehicle careening off the road, throwing him to the side.

Another salvo came. The blast hurled Shahryar to the ground, the concussion rupturing his eardrums. Even then, deaf, partially blinded and dazed with shock, a small part of his brain still gave Shahryar the command, "The jeep. The map. The operational order is in there. Get it. Destroy it before the Indians come."

He stumbled towards his vehicle when the next salvo came – this time bang on his jeep obliterating his driver, his maps, his operational orders, everything. He still stumbled forward uncomprehending, past caring, when the next round exploded.

The high explosive air burst detonated twenty feet above the ground. Jagged shards of shrapnel sprayed downwards, shredding the trees, gouging into the earth, tearing through vehicles and men. One penetrated

Shahryar's helmet, another knifed through his left shoulder, pierced the aorta and exited through his chest. He didn't even feel it. He was dead before he hit the ground.

The Indian patrol reached the site eight minutes later. They were all dead except for a staff officer who survived miraculously when his jeep overturned on him, shielding him from the rain of shrapnel. The officer leading the patrol saw the carnage around him, saw Shahryar's mangled body, noticed the General's epaulettes on it and whistled. They wrapped the body, and that of the others, with a white sheet. It would be taken to the Military Hospital at Amritsar, given the respect it deserved, and then be ceremoniously handed over to be buried with full military honours.

The offensive halted after Shahryar's death. None could give the direction or the momentum to continue. Ninety seven tanks remained trapped in the flooded fields. The Pakistani offensive had literally ground to a halt in the flooded fields of Punjab. Perhaps it was fortunate that Shahryar did not live to see it. That would have been more painful than the shrapnel that claimed him. The old warrior was gone. His torch would now be passed to another generation – his son, Shahnawaz.

## V

I can't believe what I see. As I can see, is a flood. And dotting these flooded fields are dead and dying tanks. Some are destroyed completely; others are damaged, with just their tracks and bogie wheels blown off or their turrets askance. But most are intact, merely abandoned by their crew in the Punjab fields.

I had seen some of the fighting, or rather heard it. For two days the tank fire went on. But it is quiet now. There is a cease-fire now and we waded out to the abandoned tanks, danced on their hulls and slapped each other's shoulders as though we were personally the victors of the battle. But then, we may not have fired ourselves, but in a small way we did contribute, didn't we?

The ceasefire also brought a rare and distinguished visitor to our location. He was a small man, dressed in a spotless white *kurta* and dhoti, a Gandhi cap perched delicately on his head. He smiled and waved and folded his hands in a humble '*namaste*' as he passed – driven around the battlefield by the Chief of the Army himself. That small unassuming man was none other than our Prime Minister, Lal Bahadur Shashtri, himself. I saluted as he passed and he waved back at me.

Prime Minister Shashtri died a few months later, in January 1966 during the India-Pakistan talks at Tashkent. It was a heart attack perhaps caused by the tensions of the preceding months, but rumours of poisoning circulated. I heard the news on the radio and the image of that man with his open smile and humble 'Namaste' came back to me. That small man was a giant amongst Indians and I am glad that I could salute him.

The cease fire also brought me a spell of much needed leave a few months later. I returned to my home a hero. Can you imagine it? Me, whose only contribution was breaking a few feet of a canal embankment. I exaggerated quite shamelessly, and by the time my stories finished, it was as if I had virtually won the war on my own. You will pardon me that though. I was just a young, excitable twenty something then – and the imagination of a twenty year old does tend to run riot.

My imagination was running riot in a lot of other fields as well. There was that buxom Rashmi in the next building who took up a lot of my imagination – and was the heroine in many of my fantasies. So, with my hormones raging, when Masterji suggested that perhaps it was time to find somebody suitable, I first pretended to be shocked, then outraged and then agreed with a great show of reluctance.

And so began my wife-hunting. Masterji, my two brothers ribbing me on the sides and Me, reeking of after shave, in my only ill-fitting blazer and regimental tie. Masterji had spread the word around and had already shortlisted some prospective brides. We saw two of them the first week, and then I saw Nivedita – the daughter of Masterji's old friend from his teaching days. I wouldn't say I was smitten. Oh no. That would be far too romantic. I just looked at her, shyly pouring tea in to my cup, in her new sari, and knew that I would like to spend the rest of my life with her. I didn't know what she felt then – all I knew is that when I confided to Masterji that it was 'Yes' – her father came over that evening with a packet of sweets.

*Bas*, that's it. That's how romance was in our times. That's how we met, that's how Nivedita and I became Man and Wife and began the next – and the most beautiful – phase of our lives.

# Between the Wars

*The aftermath of the 1965 war brought greater instability in both India and Pakistan. In India, the diminutive Lal Bahadur Shashtri passed away after a massive heart attack during the post-war negotiations at Tashkent. Jawaharlal Nehru's daughter, Indira Priyadarshini Gandhi took over, as Prime Minister and a new era began.*

*In Pakistan, the years after 1965 brought about even greater instability. The image of the army was shaken with the reverses of the war. And in the wake of its discomfiture rose Zulfiqar Ali Bhutto – a hard, ambitious man whose family would play the same role in his nation that the Nehru family did in India. The country itself was in bad shape; the economy was in shambles; the army was weakened and sectarian riots were erupting across the country. What were most ominous though were the murmurs of dissatisfaction emanating from East Pakistan – its distant wing located at the other extreme of the sub-continent, separated by 1600 kilometres of hostile Indian territory.*

*The two wings of Pakistan were miles apart- and not just geographically. Religion was a weak glue that could not hold them for long. The Bengalis were different from their West Pakistani counterparts – in appearance, outlook, political beliefs, culture, in every way. Why the two wings were not even siblings. They could well have been separate entities.*

*Politically, the Awami League, the East Pakistani Party under Mujibur Rehman, was gradually gaining ascendancy. It had emerged as the largest political party in the General Elections of December 1970, and it now meant that he would become the Prime Minister of Pakistan. President Yahya Khan did not acknowledge the results of that election. He just declared it null and void.*

*This was not only unconstitutional, it was unacceptable. Mujibur's supporters and the students poured into the streets in violent protests. With the situation in East Pakistan getting out of control, the Army launched a violent crackdown. Troops were flown in, Mujibur Rehman was arrested as were most political leaders, protestors were shot, students and intellectuals rounded up, eliminated and then disposed in shallow pits, Bengali soldiers and police were disarmed and taken in to custody. The carnage continued for months, forcing a stream of refugees into neighbouring India.*

*The refugees streaming in to India gave Indira Gandhi the excuse to launch an attack in East Pakistan. In December 1971, the Indian armed forces attacked, racing through almost up to Dacca in just 14 short days. On 16 December, the Pakistani army in the East, led by General A K Niazi, surrendered unconditionally, laying down their arms at a surrender ceremony at Dacca Race Course. Bangla Desh was created. A new nation was born.*

# THE DIARY OF SECOND LIEUTENANT SHAHNAWAZ KHAN

*19 December 1968,*
*Pakistan Military Academy, Kakul*

*Abba jan. You should have been here today. You would have been proud of your son.*

*I passed out from the Pakistan Military Academy today. And I won the Sword of Honour.*

*In each step which I took throughout the parade, my thoughts were of nothing but you. I turned my eyes heavenwards at the end of the parade, because I knew that you would be up there in the jannat of warriors, watching me below, guiding me, like you have always been doing.*

*Amma jancried as she put on my epaulettes for me. They were tears of pride. But the deeper tears were for you. She felt just as I did. You should have been here to put on my epaulettes on me.*

*I join my Regiment next month. I have been allotted 4 Frontier Force, one of our oldest and most decorated units.*

*Wish me well, Abba jan, as I start my new life in the army. Guide me, give me strength, give me courage to become even one tenth of the man and the soldier that you were. I need it now to help me do my duty.*

# SCHOOL OF WEAPONS AND TACTICS

**Nowshera, Pakistan, December 1969**

Shahnawaz was drunk. Outrageously, rip-roaring, boisterously drunk. The bell that announced the closure of the bar had gone off fifteen minutes ago, but Shahnawaz had wisely signed for six more drinks before it rang and the drinks were lined up on the bar counter. Most of his course mates had weaved out unsteadily for dinner and there were just he and Sid there. Just the two of them and the aged bartender gazing disapprovingly at them.

Sid, or Lt Anwar Siddique, his course-mate, buddy and best friend was equally high. The drinks were on Shahnawaz though. He was the one who was celebrating.

The two friends downed their drinks, reached out for another, clinked glasses and drank.

"We better get some dinner soon. Else even the Dining Hall will close."

"Forget it," Shahnawaz laughed, "We'll go for *kababs* at The Mall. I am quite sick of mess food in any case. Let's celebrate."

Yes Shahnawaz was celebrating. He had won the Best Student award at the School of Weapons and Tactics, narrowly edging out Sid, who was the prime contender and his rival. But the victory he was celebrating seemed a little tarnished, his rejoicing slightly forced.

His victory did not feel so sweet just because he had trumped over his best friend. His victory felt marred because deep down he knew it was Sid who deserved the award, not him.

Sid was the brains of the course, always had been. While the rest slogged all night memorizing their manuals, he would glance through them and then be able to instantly recall the ranges of weapons, the organization of a battalion, dates of History, the working mechanism of a carbine, the infernal lore of military paraphernalia they were expected to remember. His marks were invariably higher than the rest, yet when the Best Student award was announced, nobody was really surprised that it was Shahnawaz who had clinched it.

He blurted it out, 'You know, Sid, I thought the award would go to you. Maybe my briefing in the final outdoors exercise swayed it in my favour". He added the last a little lamely.

"Shahji", Sid slurred, "Ye*gal nahi. Ye na wasta duuja si"*. (That was not the case, the reasons for that are more). He spoke in Punjabi, his heavily accented Punjabi, which he rarely did. His choice of language was telling and Shahnawaz knew it.

Shahnawaz chose to ignore the statement. He knew Sid's speaking in Punjabi was to highlight the fact that his Bengali roots had denied him the award he deserved. Discrimination against the Bengalis, not just in the army, but everywhere, was an unspoken fact, rampant but never acknowledged.

"Forget it. It's just a medal and a certificate in any case. *Chalo*. Let's go for dinner. I'll find you a place where we get some good fish".

Sid laughed. That moment of tension between the friends passed, "Fish. What do you know of fish? You come with me to Dacca one day. I'll give you *Hilsa* made in mustard that you'll die for. And when you see some of the beauties of Dacca University, you'll fall in love, believe me."

Shahnawaz laughed back, '*Na*, the beauties will talk about poetry and music and high sounding culture, and it will all go over my stupid head."

"Yes, my friend, but they will do it in Bengali, the world's sweetest and most melodious language. You'll fall in love, take it from me. Now let's get some *kababs* and *tandoori* chicken. For good fish you'll have to come with me to Dacca."

The two friends staggered out, the disapproving eyes of the ancient barman following their unsteady steps. Sid would leave the next week to join his unit in Dacca. Shahnawaz would join his own unit in Sialkot. But he would go to Dacca soon. But he would not have any *hilsa* with Sid, nor would he flirt with any doe-eyed Bengali beauties. He would go there when the divide between West and East Pakistan had already become too wide to cross. He would go to Dacca University, but as an oppressor. He would meet Sid, not at his home but in a desolate field; not as a friend or a course-mate, but as an enemy. And when they met again, they would be from two different countries altogether.

# ANOTHER DIVISION, ANOTHER NATION

## The Creation of Bangladesh, 1971

If mine and Nivedita's courtship- if you could call her serving me a cup of tea and me nodding in assent a courtship – was brief, the road to our marriage was much longer, at least by the standards of the time. Those were the days of "*Chhat Mangni, phat byaha*", – Quick engagement, faster marriage. It took a year more before our marriage, because Masterji insisted that she complete her graduation before plunging in to marriage. I chaffed at the delay, but unlike me, she waited and graduated. Then on 01 December 1967, a date when the stars and the two of us were in perfect alignment, we walked around the fire, exchanged garlands and became man and wife.

Our time together was tortuously brief. We spent a month together during my leave when we got married – then another 10 days sometime later – another month in the later part of the year. Small periods of leave and then long absences. Fortunately Delhi was just a few hours from Ambala and if nothing else, psychologically we felt we were within touching distance of each other. But even that proximity came to an end as in early 1970 our unit moved to Barrackpore, near Calcutta – literally at the other extreme of the nation.

In any case, other events were building up that put my own little problems of a love-lorn marriage on to the back seat. Once again things were heating up between India and Pakistan. This time it was not Kashmir. It was East Pakistan. In March 1970, Pakistan had cracked down on the East, smothering their calls for great autonomy. As the protests intensified so did the crack-down. A flood of refugees from East Pakistan poured into India, bringing back stark images of the traumatic partition of 1947. Another partition of the sub-continent was underway. Another nation was being created in a similar holocaust.

Along with the refugees also came the Mukti Bahini fighters – the East Pakistani militia that had been waging their own long resistance against the Pakistani army. Many of them were trained fighters from the Army or the police. Many of them had been victims of the carnage the Pakistani army had unleashed – had seen their families killed, their friends disappear, their homes burnt. They came in with their faces hard and set, with eyes that had seen too much. They came with their *lungis* and vests, with captured rifles and grenades in hand, with hatred in their hearts that they channelised viciously against their West Pakistani oppressors.

I was the explosives instructor for the Mukti Bahini around 1970. I had just done a course in explosives and was considered something of an expert in handling them. It was easy enough to teach them how to make improvised bombs, how to blow up a culvert, how to make a timer, how to set off charges in tandem, how to blow up a railway line or demolish a building. We taught them to patrol, to shoot, to raid and snipe and they became experts at it. We accompanied them on forays inside East Pakistan to raid a Pakistani camp or ambush a patrol. I went with them quite a few times too, dressed in a vest and *lungi,* just like them. And as the months passed the Mukti Bahini and the Indian Army became closer – training, raiding, fighting together, working in tandem for the creation of Bangladesh which by now was inevitable.

Everybody knew that war was about to break out. I think we were only waiting for the opportune moment and the time came soon enough. On 03 December 1971, the Pakistani Air Force attacked Indian airfields across Northern India. That same evening we were ordered to move into East Pakistan. We were going to create Bangladesh.

# THE DAIRY OF LIEUTENANT SHAHNAWAZ KHAN

*26 March 1970*

*Islamabad Military Airfield*

*Amma Jan,*

*Please pardon this rushed letter to you. I have literally not had a moment to myself in the past few days.*

*I know I had promised that I would be home this week. In fact, my leave was even sanctioned, when everything was cancelled yesterday. In fact, even those on leave have been recalled.*

*My unit is flying to East Pakistan tonight. Don't worry, it is nothing much and we should be back within a month or so. I'll trunk call you when we reach and will write as often as I can.*

*Look after yourself and don't forget your medicines. Keep away from sweets. You know it's not good for your diabetes.*

*Will write again soon, Khuda Hafiz,*

*Your loving son,*

*Shahnawaz*

II

Shahnawaz was part of a large contingent of Pakistani troops that were air lifted to Dacca in March 1970 to put down the protests. The situation in East Pakistan had deteriorated. Students and political protestors were out in the streets demanding independence for East Pakistan. The Pakistani army was ordered to clamp down and they did it with absolute brutality. It was thought that these high-handed methods would curb the uprising and nip it in the bud. Instead it fuelled further protests and heightened the clamour for an independent nation.

The call for Bangladesh was growing louder.

*

*15 April 1970,*

*Dacca*

*I am writing after a month. Have not had the time to take off my boots, leave alone pick up a pen.*

*We have not been told much, just that we are to put down these rebellious Bengalis. Hopefully that should not take much.*

*We are patrolling every day. There is a curfew on, and we have been ordered to shoot at sight. I tried not to fire initially, but they fire at our columns and once even threw a fire bomb at us. I fire now whenever I see something suspicious, but try not to kill.*

*Hopefully, it will be all over and we'll get back soon*

*Lt Shahnawaz Khan*

*

*30 August 1970,*

*Somewhere in the Chittagong tract*

*Another operation last week. It never ends.*

*We had to attack a village where Bengali militia, the Mukti Bahini fighters were holed up. There were twelve of them* inside. We got each one of them and then burnt the village for sheltering them.

I didn't like doing it, but I have to do what I am ordered

*

27 September 1970

Somewhere in the Chittagong Tract

A bad day.

We were attacked by the Mukti Bahini. Six of our men became shahids. Two were captured. We found their bodies, badly tortured, hanging from a tree.

The Mukti Bahini are attacking very often now. We know there are many Indian soldiers with them. We captured one of them last week. He was wearing a lungi and vest, but he couldn't speak a word of Bengali. When we interrogated him, he finally confessed that he was from someplace called Trivandrum in South India.

*

19 November 1970

Hili

Great news. I have been promoted. I am a Captain now and have been made a company commander.

We have moved to a place called Hili. It is near the border with India. Have been really busy preparing our defences here. Our Commanding Officer keeps telling us to get ready for a war with India.

Those bastards. I'll show them.

*04 December 1970*

*Hili*

*War has broken out. But we have been expecting it for weeks now.*

*The Indians have attacked all across East Pakistan. I am expecting an attack on my company any day now.*

*Good. Let them come. We'll throw them out.*

## III

The life of a Sapper is actually quite terrible. The Infantry is bad too. They do nothing but walk, walk, walk, and when they stay still, just dig, dig, dig. They always get the brunt of it, whether they are attacking or beating it off. The Armoured Corps is the best off. They have smart black dungarees, wear their beret at a cocky angle, move around in jeeps and their big tanks, and even carry their beddings, camp cots and stools on the huge basket trays on the tank turrets. The artillery is not too bad either. They fire big guns which are terrible on the ears, but atleast they don't have to walk so much. It is the Infantry, and us the Sappers who really get it bad.

The worst off are actually we Engineers. We walk as much as the infantry, we accompany them when they attack or when they hold defences, we clear the mines, we lay them, make tracks for them to move, create bridges where none exist – just to keep them moving. And yet, more often than not, we have none of the glory and share all of the pains. The glory goes to the infantry and the tank-men. We just get remembered when a mine goes off or when the pin of a hastily made bridge comes loose.

We marched with our Division into East Pakistan. We trudged through the paddy fields, across the thatched villages, across the thousands of streams and rivulets and miles of marshland. We moved deeper into Bangladesh, guided by the Mukti Bahini. They guided us through the fields and the groves, through the gaps in the enemy defences till we reached Hili, a small, insignificant village, on a clump of hillocks. It would be the first objective to be captured.

Hili proved to be a hard nut to crack. The Pakistanis had prepared well, their defensive layout was almost perfect.

The first assault went in on the first night itself. From where we were, we could hear the sounds of firing, see tracers lighting up the sky, and hear the crump of artillery shelling which went on all night. That attack failed. The Brigade halted, pulled back, and next night launched the second attack. Again the attack failed.

An attack on an enemy position is a very, very major event. Its success or failure can make or mar the reputation of a unit for generations. The failure of two consecutive attacks had shaken us and we half expected another attack to go in the next night, but nothing happened. Instead, we picked up our weapons and belongings and simply bypassed Hili. We marched around it in a wide circuitous detour, leaving a battalion to continue engaging it. The rest of us simply moved on.

We trudged on through the green fields of Bangladesh. We just walked and walked, day after night, night after night, till our feet were blistered and bleeding, our hands and hair caked with dust, our faces buried beneath a week of stubble. But then when an army wins, as we were doing then, the soldiers don't feel pain or exhaustion, or hunger or cold. The heady intoxication of impending victory overcomes all that. And so we marched, made roads along the way, cleared mines and booby traps, splashed across *nalas* and often just swam across rivers. We moved, on foot, in trucks, on bullock carts, on tractors sometimes even on buffalo back. But we moved.

They call Bangladesh the Land of Rivers. Indeed it is. It is crisscrossed by over 3000 large and small rivers and their distributaries. I think we must have crossed all of them till we reached the banks of the Meghna River, the mile wide swath that meandered its slow course to the Bay of Bengal. At its banks that we halted, removed our shoes; put our feet in gratefully in its muddy, tepid waters and peered across to the other side where lay Dacca, the Headquarters of the Pakistani Command, the seat of government and the future capital of a new nation that was in slow chrysalis.

## IV

We stayed at the banks of the swollen Meghna River for three days and two nights when I was pulled out and given, what I always feel was the assignment of my life. I don't know why they chose me for that job, but I am not complaining. Maybe my expertise in explosives helped or maybe, it was just the luck of the lottery. Whatever be the reason, I was selected to be part of a squad of thirty, who were hastily taken off from all other activities, put inside helicopters and told that we were headed for Dacca.

Dacca? Wasn't it still held by the enemy? All we were told was that we had to check and sanitize an entire area for mines or explosives before a major event. A major event? Inside Dacca?

We flew low over the paddy fields, along the railway line, across the suburbs of Dacca and then in to its heart. There were anti-aircraft guns on some of the roof tops but none of them fired. We could have been over flying Calcutta for all we knew. We hovered briefly over the circular amphitheater of Dacca Race Course and slowly dropped down into a wide clearing in the centre that had been converted in to a makeshift heli-base.

There were two other Indian helicopters there, Alloutes, with a platoon of Indian soldiers standing guard over them. Even more amazingly, a company of paratroopers – Indian paratroopers – were actually practicing drill in the centre of the race course. The only concession to it being a war zone – if it was war any longer – was that the soldiers were in combat fatigues, not ceremonial uniforms.

I would realize later that it was not a war zone after all. Indian representatives were already in the Pakistani Headquarters drafting out the terms of surrender with General Niazi. It was all decided by now. All that remained was the formal surrender ceremony that was to take place today – on 16 December at this very Race Course.

That is where we came in. We had been hurriedly called in to check the entire area where the surrender ceremony was to take place. Even a minor blast, be it by the vengeful Bangladeshis or the resentful Pakistanis could mar the entire ceremony. And in the six odd hours we had we did the best we could, checking, prodding, and digging for any hidden device. Our metal detectors pinged often, but they only revealed a few brass cartridges beneath, some strips of metal, even three horseshoes. No mines. No explosives. It was safe.

And then the people thronged in. They came in their thousands, waving the green and red flag of Bangladesh, waving the Indian tricolor, cheering "Joi Bangla" and "Jai Hind". The crowds streamed in, filling the race course way beyond capacity. Then the convoy of jeeps entered the course and moved towards the dais placed in the centre.

The leading jeeps halted. Two men got out, one a tall, very dignified looking Sikh officer in the Olive-Green of the Indian Army, the other in khaki brown, equally tall but with that little heaviness around the face and midriff of someone who likes the good life. They walked to the dais together and stood ramrod stiff at attention as a guard of honour – the same paratroopers I saw practicing earlier – presented a ceremonial salute. In the decorum of the army, no event is complete unless it is ceremoniously done. Then they sat at the table placed in the centre of the dais, other senior officers flanking them.

I edged my way closer on to the dais – in that throng no one really noticed me. I elbowed my way inwards, towards the table where the Generals were sitting. Close enough to see the table, the coarse green blanket covering it and the parchment on it. I saw General Aurora, the Indian Commander, pass it on to General Niazi. He barely glanced at it, picked up the pen on the table and signed on the right bottom corner. His face was impassive, but I could make out the resigned stoop of his shoulders. He passed the document to General Aurora, who signed it in one swift motion. Perhaps he did not want to prolong the moment for his vanquished opponent.

The two Generals stood. Niazi reached in to his holster, removed his pistol and handed it to General Aurora. In the background, the "*Joi Banglas*" rose to a crescendo, yet around the dais there seemed to be a wall of silence. General Aurora accepted the revolver, passed it to his aide, shook hands gravely with Niazi. "It's okay, Abdullah," I heard him say, "You did the best you could".

The photo bulbs were flashing away and this iconic photograph of the surrender ceremony would become one of the most famous photos of Indian history. Did you see me in it? I am there, in the extreme right corner and just around three fourths of my face is visible. Very often it is air-brushed out, but in some I can be seen. I brag of it endlessly. Yes, I was there when history was being created. Yes, I was there when a new nation was being born. I was there in one of the most significant moments of history. I was there. And in some infinitesimal way, I contributed.

## V

Captain Shahnawaz and his men lined up. He was ahead of them, his company in three files just behind him. He was glad his men could not see him, could not see the tears in his eyes, could not see him biting his lip to prevent a sob escaping.

He knew there were a lot of wet eyes behind him as his men lined up to surrender. Surrender, and to the damned Indians. Why?

But that radio message had come last night from none other than his Brigade Commander himself. It was quite clear, "Brave soldiers of Pakistan. You have fought well, and courageously. The nation is proud of you. But the Pakistani Army has surrendered. Wherever you are, you will surrender and hand over your weapons to the nearest Indian army unit by 0800h on 17 December."

The transmission had been repeated thrice. It was the only radio message that they had received in the past ten days. The Indians had simply jammed their communications before that.

Even now he could not believe it, nor could his men accept it, 'Why, Saab, why? The Indians have been unable to dislodge us for two weeks. They will not be able to do it even now. Why surrender?"

It was true. He and his men had held steadfast at Hili. Beaten back two full-scale attacks, held on in spite of all the Indians threw at him. So why surrender?

There was no answer to that. He was not aware of the surrender ceremony that had taken place at Dacca Race Course. All he knew was from that impersonal radio message crackling on the waves, telling him that all officers and men of the Pakistani army were to lay down their arms at 8am. Period.

And now at 7.30, his men lined up behind him weapons in hand, waiting for the Indians to arrive. They were silent and resentful, but once ordered had prepared well for the surrender. They had spent all night, breaking the firing pins, damaging the breech blocks and chambers. The weapons they handed to the Indians would be mere skeletons – unusable and worthless.

Through his misted eyes, he saw the Indian Major walk up towards him, a platoon of heavily armed soldiers on either flank. He barely heard him say,

'I am Major Karunakaran. You and your men have fought well. But your army has surrendered. You will hand over all your weapons and will be in my custody." His voice softened, "Don't worry. You and your men will be well treated."

He nodded, then slowly opened his epaulette, that newly acquired Captain's epaulette he was so proud of, removed the lanyard beneath it, loosened his holster strap, removed his pistol and handed it over to Major Karunakaran. Behind him, he heard the clink of metal on earth, as his men placed their weapons on the ground. He took a step back. The two officers saluted. But it was not the salute of equals any longer. It was a salute between the vanquished and the victorious.

But Shahnawaz did have a small victory. The weapon he handed over was not his. His own weapon had been thrown into a well the night before. The weapon he handed over was a rusted, unserviceable .38 revolver which had lain unused in the company armory for months. It was a futile gesture, but it gave him a small, if insignificant victory.

But his defeat was still not complete. Even as his soldiers stood there, small clumps of Mukti Bahini warriors slowly closed in on them. Some wore camouflage jackets and dungarees, but most were in their traditional *lungi* and vest. They all carried weapons, though, most of them unslung and ready for use. There were over a hundred of them and there was menace in their approach. His men were unarmed and defenceless, easy prey for the Mukti Bahini whom they had fought for over a year and who craved revenge. It was a situation that could soon turn ugly.

Shahnawaz watched the Mukti Bahini leader – he was in a camouflage uniform and wore dark sunglasses – approach. He had a Colonel's epaulettes on his shoulders and the distinctive snarling tiger insignia of the Mukti Bahini on his beret. He saw him go up to Karunakaran and engage in intense conversation. Though he could not hear what was being said, the body language and gestures – as did the actions of the men – conveyed it all. They were demanding that the Pakistani soldiers be handed over to them.

Karunakaran prevailed. The prisoners were in Indian custody, under their protection as per the terms of surrender. Eventually the Mukti Bahini Colonel shrugged, turned around, made a motion to his men and then walked towards the Pakistani soldiers lined ahead, heading directly for Shahnawaz.

Shahnawaz knew who that Colonel was, of course. It was Sid. No, this was not Sid. This was 'Tiger' Siddique, the dreaded commander of the area, who was known for his brilliant tactical acumen and his daring raids, who was known for using captured Pakistani soldiers as bayonet practice. He removed his sun glasses and looked directly at Shahnawaz. There was no recognition, not the faintest sign of remembrance. His face was stony-hard, his eyes like pebbles. He did not smile, he did not say anything. He merely looked directly at Shahnawaz and the column of his soldiers standing in surrender behind him and the message in his eyes was unmistakable. It said, "This time I have won".

# PRISONER OF WAR CAMP 107

### India, Barrackpore, 1972

I couldn't believe it. I was a hero. And this time in the acknowledged sense. My photograph – or rather the photograph of the historic surrender ceremony went on to become one of the most famous photographs of India's post-independence history. It was there in the newspapers, in magazines, in the Army bulletins and newsletters – everywhere. And there was me in it.

I may have stolen my celebrity moment, but it took little time to bring me back to what I was – a nondescript NCO, doing a nondescript job in an Army Engineer Regiment. And with the war over, we were back. Less than two months after the photo bulbs flashed at the Dacca Race Course, we were back to our own lines at Barrackpore.

Own lines? It was not our own lines any longer. The barracks had been cleaned and white-washed, and it looked better than I ever remembered seeing it. It also had a new ten foot high perimeter wall of double layered barbed wire, with high observation posts at each corner. It also had new inhabitants. The freshly white-washed lines were now occupied by Pakistani soldiers. It was now Prisoner of War Camp Number 107. As for us, well, we were told to pitch up tents and then just look after the administration of the camp and its new occupants.

We hated it of course. Those damned Pakistanis were treated better than we were. First, they were put in our barracks while we were consigned to tents. To make it worse, they had even taken our cots and furniture. Why, they were even given a Quran on each bed. And worst of all. At a time when we were all hoping for leave – me especially – all leave was once again halted.

I was made the NCO in charge of the Officers lines – a single barrack where around twenty Pakistani officers were billeted. They were not too bad actually, quite polite and well-behaved. It was amazing how much like us they were. Why, they could have been Indians lounging around in a village courtyard. But they were not. Thiers was a different nation, a different religion, a different mind-set. And every so often, as I gazed at them, images of the mobs at Sheikhupura rose unbidden in my mind and the divide between our two nations and its people came out once again.

I became quite friendly with the Pakistani officers and men in the camp. After all I was in daily contact with them for over a year. I saw the Commanding Officer's hair turn pre-maturely white, I saw one of the officers' die of jaundice – or maybe it was just the deep depression that I had seen consuming him for months. I gave them their monthly allowance on the first Saturday of each month, which they always accepted with an air of indifference and resentment. I saw them take their walks around the perimeter of the small compound, saw their cheeks hollow and their shoulders slump as the period of captivity increased. I watched them crowd around the radio every morning and evening. Saw them in their group reading of the Quran during the evening prayers. That was one ritual they followed unfailingly. For all of them, religion became their only solace and strength.

But actually a deeper support came from the letters and small parcels they received from home. It was my job to collect the heavily censored letters from the Camp Adjutant and give it to them at the evening roll call. I could see the gleam in the eyes of those whose names I called out, and the dull disappointment of those passed over. There was this young Captain Shahnawaz. He was one of the fortunate ones. He seemed to get a letter almost every other week.

There was something about Shahnawaz, I never could trace. He must have been three or four years younger than me, though he looked younger than his years. We were as different as chalk and cheese; the two of us, he an officer, me a NCO; he from his vast farms around Lahore, me from my middleclass home in Janakpuri. And yet, there was something in the way he cocked his head, the way his hands moved, the manner he laughed at times, when I saw something strangely familiar – something that seemed to be me. But it couldn't be. There could be nothing in common between that quiet, aristocratic officer and a crass, uncultured NCO like me. That resemblance, if at all it existed, would have been only in my imagination.

But yes, the fondness developed for that young Pakistani officer with his grave manner and courteous ways. I got him eggs, milk, sometimes even a chicken or so – which he always paid for almost immediately. And once, I smuggled in a bottle of whiskey for him. He took it the way he accepted everything else, with his usual grave smile – though his eyes lit up when he realized what was inside that paper wrapped package. I didn't accept the money he offered though. This one was on me. I was celebrating, I had become a father.

I had been waiting for the news a long time. Remember, those were not the days of the mobile and today's communications. There were no instantaneous calls and the news when it did arrive came by telegram – the standard instrument to convey messages of deaths and illnesses and births. It was from Masterji and said simply, "Nivedita gave birth to baby boy on 06 June. Mother, child both fine'. And in the telegraphic language on the coarse, yellowing paper, I got to know of Gaurav's arrival in our lives.

I was not there when Gaurav was born as I have not been there in so many momentous events of his life. But even in that moment I was there in thought. And I think that I had been a good father to him in the brief time we were to share together. Because, Gaurav would not be with us long. We would lose him soon. He would be with us for just 26 years; 26 years and 129 days to be exact. And in that brief time he would fill our world.

When that telegram came, none of this was known. A week later came the photographs. Three of them. One of Nivedita holding him in her arms, another of him swaddled in blankets, sleeping on his cot and the third of him awake now; hand uplifted, head tilted, mouth open in a wide, demanding "O". God, I had never seen anyone so adorable.

I showed off the photographs to all who wanted to see – and to all who didn't. I even carried them with me when I went to Prisoner of War Camp Number 107 that evening along with that bottle of whiskey I had smuggled inside.

I showed the photographs to Shahnawaz. His eyes smiled, almost twinkled as they lost their usually grave demeanor. He laughed out loud, clapped me on my shoulder and spontaneously reached out in a tight embrace, "*Mubarak Ho*", he said, "May Allah watch over him and give him a long and happy life."

How ironic is fate. Even in that moment when the two men – one a Pakistani officer and a prisoner of war, the other an Indian NCO and his custodian – embraced each other, they would not know, then or ever, that they themselves were brothers torn apart by the division of their nation. They would never know what linked them together, in the past or in the years to come. Perhaps there was an evil, malicious bird that hovered overhead as Shahnawaz wished a long and happy life for his nephew. His wish came from deep within. It was a sincere and honest thought. Yet, he himself would be the man who would bring about Gaurav's death. Twenty six years later he would nod his head once atop a desolate windswept peak. And that nod would consign his nephew to death.

But in that moment none of this was known. In that moment it was just two men in an intimate moment of shared happiness. And when the moment passed, beyond the spontaneous embrace, the two men withdrew and faced each other once again as what they were. Adversaries from two different nations; linked in blood maybe, but adversaries just the same.

# The Diary of Captain Shahnawaz Khan

*Prisoner of War Camp 107,*

*Barrackpore, India, 15 February 1972*

*These have been the worst days of my life.*

*We have moved to this Prisoner of War Camp here in India. God, the humiliation of it all. Being a prisoner, and that too of the Indians.*

*They have not treated us too bad actually. We are all in barracks and have a bed and a small cupboard to ourselves. The food is terrible. Just dal, some vegetables, rotis and rice day in and day out. Would have liked meat more often.*

*They have placed a Quran on the pillow of my bed. I read it every day. I press it to my heart each morning, and every day I say the same prayer. "We will avenge the humiliation of 1971"*

*Prisoner of War Camp 107,*

*Barrackpore, India, 02 May 1972*

*Another day. The same as before.*

*Got up. Attended the morning roll call at six, some light exercises, breakfast of puris and sabzi as always, some classes - basically the indoctrination shit that these Indians try to feed us with;, lunch, afternoon roll call, volleyball in the evening, evening roll call, dinner, lights out and into our cots at nine.*

This senseless routine is driving me mad. I don't feel like a soldier any longer. What I hate most is the damned pay parade when we line up every month to receive our prisoner allowance of 180 Rupees. I hate taking the money from the Indians. It cheapens me.

Prisoner of War Camp 107,

Barrackpore, India, 06 June1972

Another letter from Ammajaan along with a parcel of clothes and dried fruit.

Wish she had sent some books though. The library here is full of unreadable thrash. Most of it seems to be propaganda. We asked for some Pakistani newspapers but they refused.

We hear the radio continuously. I believe our government is in talks with India for our release.

I hope it happens soon. I want to go home.

*

Prisoner of War Camp 107,

Barrackpore, India, 15 June1972

I got drunk last night. Frankly it felt good.

Our Camp NCO had got it for me. He is a decent guy and he treats us with far more respect than most of the others. He also talks far more than the others.

He showed me the photographs of his new son and his wife yesterday and was beaming all over. I couldn't help but share in his happiness and wished them well.

He also gave me that whiskey bottle last night. As a

celebration, he said. I shared it with Atif, Shabbir, Mushtaq and Imran after lights out. Luckily we didn't get caught. It hit us quite bad though. After all it has been ages since any of us have had a drink.

Wish I could have given a small present or so for his son. I have nothing though. But as Ammajaan says, sometimes even blessings are enough.

*

17 Dec 1972

Today I spend a year in captivity.

It has been the worst year of my life. I should have fallen at my post itself, instead of being taken prisoner.

No news of our return.

*

15 Jan 73

I don't want to write it down. What if it doesn't come true.

After all we have heard it so often before. Only to have our hopes dashed.

But this time the Camp Commandant himself has announced it. He said that we are being sent back to Pakistan.

I hope it is true. God, please don't let this be a rumor like all others. .

*

28 Feb 73

We are on the train at last. It is a Military Special to take us back to Pakistan.

There are armed guards all around. But who will try to escape now. We are all so excited. We are going home. At last.

*

24 March 73

Lahore

I met Ammajaan today after a year and a half. How aged and frail she has become.

She has kept my room exactly as it was before I left. But I still feel somewhat strange being back.

My friends and relatives have been coming to meet me. I know they mean well, but I try to avoid them.

There seems to be a lot of shame. I feel it too. People look away when I walk past in uniform. It is not like it used to be. The army has lost the respect it once had.

But it is good to be back home. It is good to be back in Pakistan.

*

# AFTERMATH OF WAR

## 1972 to 1974

*As Shahnawaz and his nation reeled in the aftermath of the defeat, momentous changes were sweeping Pakistan. The sheer scale of the defeat, the loss of the entire Eastern Wing was not something that could be condoned. And the blame for the debacle lay squarely on the army.*

*General Yahya Khan, the President and the Commander-in-Chief of the army had to go. On 20 December 1971, he resigned and handed over the Presidency to Zulfikar Ali Bhutto, ushering in another era. Bhutto was a Machiavellian figure – handsome, brilliant, charismatic and deeply ambitious. He used the disgrace of the army to slowly ease their influence and consolidate his own position in Pakistan.*

*The most pressing problem was the release of 93000 Pakistani Prisoners of War. At the Shimla Conference held in July 1972, between him and Mrs Indira Gandhi, he deftly negotiated their release, offering few concessions in exchange. Yet, it would still take a year or so till the last Pakistani prisoner crossed over back in to his homeland.*

*And when Shahnawaz and the thousands like him came back it was to a different Pakistan. The army was out of power. It was discredited and had lost its aura. And Bhutto was on the rise. He took over as Prime Minister and began tightening his own grip on Pakistan.*

*In India, Mrs Gandhi was on a roll. She had just attained the most comprehensive victory of an Indian army in over 1500 years and was hailed as none other than the goddess Durga. In the national euphoria of the victory it was not surprising that she and her Congress Party were swept in to power in the national elections of 1972. By 1974, she was at her peak – all-powerful and seemingly invincible.*

*Her growing prowess and strength seemed to find expression when she ordered India's first nuclear test, completely defying world opinion. On 18 May 1974, India conducted its first nuclear test, deep in the deserts of Rajasthan near a sleepy village called Pokharan. That test, codenamed "Smiling Buddha", would give rise to a nuclear race between India and Pakistan and bring another dimension to the already tortuous relationship between the two neighbours.*

# THE SMILING BUDDHA

## Pokharan, May 1974

*Chinkaras,* the small gazelle that once roamed in huge herds across the Rajasthan desert, are nervous animals. But this herd seemed even more so. They skittered nervously across the dunes, tails bobbing furiously, eyes darting, ears flicking for any whisper of danger. There was none. The desert was as calm and as placid as it always had been. In the village of Pokharan beyond, the animals were tethered and the men folk were inside their huts. There was no danger but the desert seemed alive with signs of impending menace.

In Pokharan, the village of five mirages on the ancient trade route between Jaisalmer and Jodhpur, the villagers knew that something was afoot. Just the night before, military persons from the adjoining camp had driven up in their jeeps and politely but firmly told them that they were to remain inside their huts for all of the next day. They huddled inside their mud huts, stoked their *chullahs,* and waited for the moment they sensed was coming.

The *chinkaras* skittered towards the village, some God-given instinct telling them that a powerful force was coiled beneath the earth, waiting to be unleashed. They huddled closer, then in one heart-stopping moment, Time seemed to stop. A smothered roar seemed to emanate from the depths of the sands and then the earth quivered, shook violently for a moment. A small plume of dust and sand arose from the direction of the army camp two kilometers away. Then the dust settled, the earth stopped quivering and the *chinkaras* turned and fled mindlessly towards the deep desert. It was now 8 05 am on 18 May 1974, and though neither the startled deer nor the huddled villagers inside Pokharan would know it, 'The Buddha had smiled'.

## II

We moved back in to our own barracks in early 1973 or so, when the last Pakistani POW had left for his own nation. But we would not enjoy the comforts of our own barracks for long. Barely two months later we were ordered to move out of Barrackpore to a god-forsaken place in the middle of the desert called Pokharan.

There is a saying in the army that if you have not heard the name of the place you are posted to, it is a bad one. No one had heard of Pokharan and it was worse than anything we had imagined. There was nothing there – nothing. No barracks, no lines, no roads, nothing. It was just empty, desolate dunes within which we had to set up a new camp.

But move in we did, set up tents we did, grumble we did, and slowly we established our own routine of army life there. Barracks came up. Roads and tracks were developed. And a huge, triple layered barbed wire fence came up all along the perimeter.

In the first few months there, we did little out of the ordinary. We played a lot of volleyball, did a lot of dozer training, camouflaged our tents and barracks – nothing much, just the usual. And then in early 1974 we were told to begin digging two slim shafts deep in the warm, yielding earth.

At first we assumed we were digging a well for our own supply of water in this dry, God-forsaken place. The shafts were just around 10 feet in diameter and it could be nothing but that. We dug deeper, thirty feet, then forty, deeper still. And when we bored our way 90 feet deep, we were told to start digging horizontally and made a small room sized structure deep in the bowels of the desert sands.

By then, most of us had realized that it was not a mere well that we were constructing. It was far more. After all, an innocuous well would not draw so much attention. We often had people coming in to visit these shafts – not just army officers – but civilians. Civilians in army uniforms all right, but any fool could tell that they were not military men. They came in sandals, were at times unshaved and had none of the mannerisms that we associated with army officers. They came and went in brief visits till they finally arrived in strength – around 20 of them – in March 1974 and then stayed put permanently in our camp till that full moon night.

Moonlight in the desert is a beautiful experience. The moon hangs like a large, silver coin in the velvety darkness of night. Its light reflects off the dunes, painting them silver. And the night of 18 May 1974 was an exceptionally beautiful night. It was the night of Buddha Purnima – the full moon night on which Lord Buddha had taken birth 2500 years ago. It was the night in which India's first nuclear test would be completed. The peaceful Buddha with his philosophy of tolerance and non-violence would not have been smiling then. But ironically, the code word for the test was 'The Smiling Buddha."

I remember that night well. The scientists – because that's what they were, nuclear scientists in army garb – gota large crane, fitted a long cylindrical device on it, and moved it over one of the shafts. Then each one of them removed their shoes or sandals, folded their hands in prayer, placed a dab of vermillion on the device, broke a coconut at its base and then reverentially lowered the device in to the shaft.

Two scientists were winched down to connect the nuclear bomb – that is what the device was, a nuclear bomb, nothing more, nothing less – in its place at the base of the shaft. They emerged two hours later with long wrist thick black cables trailing behind them. They led the cables to the control room, and then signaled to us to seal the shaft.

That was where we came in. We had been rehearsing it for weeks now. Two dozers rumbled into position, lowered their blades, scooped out a dozer-blade full of sand and loose earth and poured it down the shaft.

It took four hours to seal that shaft completely, burying the nuclear device within. When the dozers stopped we finished the work with shovels making sure that the precious black cables emanating from beneath were not touched. Then for good measure we made a small mound of sandbags over it to seal it completely.

Even though we could not see what was happening inside, I could feel the tension and feel the nervous excitement of the scientists and the senior army officers inside the control room as they adjusted their instruments and made their final connections. We vacated the area and moved to a vantage point some distance away. And then it happened. At 0805 in the morning of 18 May 1974, the scientists activated an electrical circuit and 90 feet below the earth the impulse detonated the nuclear warhead buried deep within.

We felt the tremor, felt the earth quivering beneath our feet. It reached the village of Pokharan and cracked the mud walls of some of the hutments. It startled a herd of *chinkaras* and sent them hurtling, panic-struck, towards the deep desert. A small, muffled blast seemed to emanate from the bowels of the earth – the mound of sand bags collapsed as the earth around the shaft shook. Then as the quiver subsided, we saw the scientists shedding their stoical, scholarly demeanor, whooping and jumping like schoolboys, hugging each other, as they watched the small plume of dust in the vicinity of the shaft rise and then slowly subside.

India's first nuclear test was a success. The Buddha had smiled. Or had he?

# The Throttling of Democracy

## India, 1974

*The nuclear test was one of India's and Mrs Indira Gandhi's major successes. She was at the height of her popularity, the unquestioned leader of her party and the nation, adored by millions. Her fall, when it came was sharp and sudden.*

*It began in 1975 when the Allahabad High Court found her guilty of electoral malpractices during the elections of 1972. Her election was declared void and she was banned from contesting elections for six years. What it meant was that she had to resign and step down as Prime Minister.*

*Resign, she would not. Instead, citing a threat to national security, she imposed a state of Emergency on 12 June 1975, bringing Democracy to a grinding halt.*

*What followed was the throttling of India's democracy, human rights and personal liberty. Under the draconian Maintenance of Internal Security Act, she granted herself extraordinary powers, jailed thousands upon thousands of opposition leaders and protestors, suspended human rights, imposed censorship and began a rule by decree.*

*Other forces also rose with her, the most notorious being Sanjay Gandhi, her ambitious younger son. Although having no rank or official position he became one of the foremost figures of the Emergency and set about imposing his own agenda. Over 8 million Indians were sterilized, most of them forcibly, in pursuance of a birth control program. On the garb of beautifying Delhi, entire slums were dozed to the ground, and their terrified occupants evicted. It was no longer a democracy. It was feudalism at its worst.*

*This had to stop, and it did. In January 1977, confident that with the opposition in jail and in disarray she would be voted back in to power Mrs Gandhi revoked the Emergency and ordered elections. The Indian populace responded in the only way they knew. In a crushing mandate, the Congress Party was voted out of power. Mrs Gandhi and Sanjay Gandhi both lost their seats by massive margins and the curtain came down on the bleakest phase of Indian democracy.*

# THE DRIVE THROUGH TURKMAN GATE

## Delhi, 1975-1977

The saving grace of spending two years in remote Pokharan – not counting the fact that it enabled us to participate in one of the epochal moments of Indian history – was that our unit was due to move to a good location after that tenure. And in early 1975 our orders to move came – guess where – none other than Delhi.

I was elated. Delhi was home. Delhi was where Nivedita and Gaurav were, my wife and three year old son, whom I had seen only in patches during my short spells of leave, Delhi was also where my father was, alone in the same small flat at C-3 Janakpuri. He was alone now. My brothers had moved out. Vishal, the elder was in his final year at the Indian Institute of Technology, Gorakhpur. Kunal, the younger was away at the Indian Institute of Management, Ahmadabad. Both were carving out their own destinies – destinies that were large and strong. Masterji remained alone in his flat with his memories, the occasional visit, his newspapers and his loneliness.

Delhi would be the first time we would be together as a family after our marriage. And when Masterji asked us to move in with him, we accepted gratefully.

In those two years, I realised for the first time the pleasures of family life. I returned each evening to my wife and son, to my father; I watched my son take his first steps, then held his hand as he walked. I watched my wife in the routine of the day, a simple pleasure which I had not experienced in our years of separation. I saw her in the kitchen, on the dining table, in long, animated conversations with Masterji; I saw her laughing with Gaurav gurgling by her side. She was with me in the walks we took after dinner; she was naked by my side as we made long, slow love at nights. I saw her for the first time in the different shades and moods of her womanhood. We had been married five years now. This was the first time we truly became a family.

Within a year the twins came, Vikram and Supriya. They emergedwithin minutes of each other (Supriya, the older by eight minutes, something she never let Vikram forget all his life) at Military Hospital, Delhi Cantonment. And, our family was now complete. And with Masterji there, a father and grandfather to us all, we couldn't have asked for more. I think he was happy too with the house bustling with sound and laughter, with the dining table full, with someone to talk to at the end of the day, to discuss the headlines and tut-tut about the state of the country.

He still had his old habit of poring over the papers and making his little clippings. But now he turned more and more to the small black and white television we had got him for Diwali. We were in the age of television now. There was only one channel – Doordarshan, not the multitudes that we have now – but it was enough. He lapped up the news reports, the musical shows, the talk shows, movies on the weekend, even the weather reports. I think the TV helped fill the emptiness of the hours that he always felt ever since our mother passed away. In many ways, it both numbed and fulfilled him.

It was on television that he –and the nation as such – got to know of one of the most momentous happening in our nation. At 8 am on 25 June 1975, over the radio and television waves came the voice of the Prime Minister, Mrs Indira Gandhi, announcing reassuringly, "The President has proclaimed Emergency. There is nothing to panic about."

### II

The declaration of the Emergency left us stunned. Yes, we had been following what was happening in the nation, frankly I gave it little heed. Yes, I knew that Mrs Gandhi had been told to resign by the Allahabad

High Court, because of malpractices during the 1972 elections. I knew that she had been steadfastly refusing to give up her chair in spite of nationwide protests. But frankly, I dismissed it all as political shenanigans which would soon blow over. But declaring a national emergency? No one expected that.

On the first day the declaration of the Emergency had been announced in big, banner headlines, but there was nothing more. No condemnation, no comment, nothing. It was as if it was not happening at all. It was as if there were no arrests of political leaders taking place outside, it was as if there was no clampdown on rallies and protest, it was as if Democracy was functioning as always and censorship had not been imposed at all.

There were clues. An obituary column in the Times of India, simply read "D E M O'cracy, beloved husband of T Ruth, father of L I Bertie, brother of Faith, Hope and Justica, expired on 26 June 1975." Masterji's astute eyes picked it up. He encircled it in black, cut the column and preserved it. Just as he did the blank, black- bordered editorial of another newspaper that protested silently against this dismemberment of democracy.

But Masterji couldn't protest silently, could he. He marched out in his immaculately starched white *kurta* and pyjamas, with his Gandhi cap perched defiantly on his head. He spoke at student rallies, he marched with protesting students, he harangued against the Emergency at tea stalls and in park benches. He saw his students disappear, many simply picked up from their homes or colleges and not be seen again. It did not seem to deter him. In some part of his mind he seemed to be reliving another struggle for freedom he had participated in thirty years ago.

As the long months of Emergency passed, actually it did not seem too bad at all. Trains ran on time, persons attended offices, there seemed to be law and order, and there were definite signs of progress. But all this was on the surface. I would see the real face of the Emergency very soon.

They picked him up sometime in March 1976. He had gone out that morning in his usual white *kurta* and pyjamas, his face set as always and then did not return. Not for lunch, not for tea, or at night, or the next day, or the next week, or the next four months.

They picked him up at a student rally in the lawns of Delhi University. He was making a speech there, reading out an open letter he had written to the Prime Minister, when the police came. They burst upon the gathering of clerks, students, lawyers and professors with a viciousness usually reserved only for the very criminal. They did not fire, but their *lathis* flailed, breaking arms and ankles, shattering skull bones, tearing ligament and sinew. Masterji continued his speech even as the police waded through the small crowd. He continued as the policemen charged up the dais, he continued as they advanced towards him with *lathis* upraised, he continued even as the *lathi* came downward and then broke off with a sharp cry as it smashed on to his hand, raised instinctively to protect his face. It was his bent left hand – the one that had been broken facing similar *lathis* during the "Quit India" movement of 1942. It hit almost the same spot, broke the fragile hand once again, sending the old man crashing to the ground. Then it came down on his exposed back.

## III

I had been pacing up and down the lane outside our home for an hour now. It was eight in the evening and Masterji had not yet returned. Damn. How many times had I told the old man to forget his pointless protests and meaningless speeches? He never listened. Where on earth was he now?

"*Puttar, kya ho gaya. Bade pareshan lag rahe ho*," (Son, what has happened. You look very upset) a tall, bearded figure in a white flowing kurta approached.

I knew who he was. He was Baba Randhawa, our Sikh neighbour, who lived next-door with his sprawling brood. He was the owner of the thriving Randhawa garage and one of the more prosperous, and the most large-hearted persons of the locality. How many evenings had we spent at his place, how often had meals come over from their house after my mother passed away.I bent and touched his feet.

He placed his hand on my shoulder, walked by my side, "Yeh *Masterji ki purani aadat hai. Unhe yeh speech-weech band karna chahiye. Yeh bure din chal rahe hai.* (It is an old habit of Masterji. He should stop his speeches and all that now. These are not good days.)

He paced by my side, saying little, but his calm imposing presence, comforted my agitation. We walked in silence along the darkened lane and then from the bushes came a low whistle – then another one.

It was Jagmohan – one of Masterji's old students, hiding in the shadows there. He swayed uncertainly, his shirt stained with blood, his forehead crudely bandaged.

Randhawa went up to him, *"Kya ho gaya hai tumhe. Ghar chalo, tumhe chhot lagi hai. Malampati lagwate hai" (*What has happened to you. You have been hurt. Come home, we'll treat you)

Jagmohan refused to come out of the shadows. He was fearful that the house was being watched. The aura of fear and suspicion was everywhere those days.

He told us what had happened. He was at the rally when Masterji was making his speech at Delhi University. He saw the police come in, he saw Masterji being hit, he saw him being taken away with the other students. Where, he could not tell, it could be anywhere.

Such was the power of the government machinery in those days. Thousands could be rounded up and simply made to disappear merely because they dared to speak up. But I had underestimated its power. I would see it at close quartersthat very night.

I was glad that Baba Randhawa was there with me that night. It was he who suggested that I put on my uniform. It was he who took me on his scooter, to the nearest police station.

No police patrol stopped us on our way to Janakpuri Police Station. But there it was a wall. My army uniform opened no doors, elicited no answers. It took two hours before the Sub-Inspector even deigned to listen to me. He wrote down nothing, registered nothing. He just gazed indifferently at me with bored, listless eyes.

"Name?"

"Not yours, *chutiye,* the missing man's?"

"Where was he?"

"A rally? What type of rally?"

"What was that *behenchod* doing there in any case?"

"How do you know the police took him? Who told you?"

I got nothing from them. Nothing, but a sneering condescension and a vague suggestion to go to the Jama Masjid Police Station, because that was closest to the spot where Masterji was supposedly picked up. The entire outlook was, "We know nothing about it, but maybe the bastard got what he deserved".

Baba Randhawa put his arms around me, *"Chalo waha chal te hai. Shayad Jama Masjid Police station me kuch pata chalega"* (Okay let's go to Jama Masjid Police Station. Maybe we will find out something there).

We had no way of knowing whether my father would be at Jama Masjid Station at all, or whether he was in some other bleak station, or in hospital, or the morgue, or merely dumped on a roadside somewhere. But it was the only lead we had. We scootered through the congested lanes of Old Delhi, past the ramparts of the Red Fort, through its squalid underbelly at Turkman Gate towards Jama Masjid Police Station. And there I saw the true face of the Emergency.

The Turkman Gate area was just a shanty colony, one of the many eyesores dotting Delhi. Here, the homeless migrants; the rickshaw drivers, the sweepers, the ayahs, gardeners, masons and carpenters, the whores and pimps; lived. They had descended years ago, set up small hutments and made the place their own. With time, the hutments became brick houses, regular stone and wood structures. They got water and electrical connections sanctioned, then ration cards and with it the legitimacy of an address. A generation had lived their humble lives here, dreamt their small dreams here. Yes, it was an eyesore, but a home just the same.

And nothing could hide the fact that it was after all, still a slum. It had no business to be here. It had no business to an eyesore in the heart of Delhi; a Delhi which was being beautified to showcase the achievements of the Emergency. Why such a place did not belong to the India that the perpetrators of the Emergency had envisaged.

There was a dozer there. Four of them in fact, rumbling impatiently in the side-lines. There were lines of police too, complete in riot gear and barricades. There were politicians – it was easy to make them out, they were the ones in white with safari suit clad bureaucrats hovering besides them. They were all there, poised to unleash the power of the State on its hapless citizens.

And there were the occupants, lined up in front of their homes. The mothers with children balanced on their hips, the aged with the despair of time in their eyes, the children sucking a biscuit to keep them quiet. Most were squatting on the pavement, forming a human barricade in the path of the dozers that were to demolish their homes. Beyond them, I could see their elders, talking with the politicians and their bureaucrat cronies. One of them, obviously their leader was in the forefront, gesticulating wildly, pointing repeatedly to a sheaf of paper he held in his hands. Perhaps those documents were pathetic proof of ownership, some kind of legal sanction to the homes they had occupied for ages.

We knew about these 'beautification' drives of course. We had heard of forcible evictions, the overnight displacement of thousands, the razing of homes with one stroke of a dozer blade. None of it appeared in the papers, but the stories had spread from mouth to mouth, embellished with facts, interwoven with fiction. I had not paid much credence to these stories. I was now to see one of them at close quarters.

The negotiations would have gone on for perhaps an hour or so. I saw the politicians wavering, discussing amongst themselves. I saw the leader of the slum dwellers spread out his papers, point out to them with greater assurance. The dozer engines idled, a little less menacingly now. Then the white Ambassador car with its red domed light glided up. The door opened and a white clad figure stepped out.

I knew who it was. Who did not? His handsome face with the thinning hairline, the bushy sideburns and horn rimmed glasses was there everywhere. It was there in the papers, on Television, emblazoned on banners across Delhi, everywhere. Who could not know who it was? It was Sanjay Gandhi, Mrs Gandhi's younger son, the heir apparent and the major force behind the Emergency.

The crowd of politicians rushed towards him. Sanjay Gandhi did not like to be kept waiting. He was a man in a hurry. A man used to doing things his way. The Delhi beautification drive was his brain child, and by God, a few thousand protestors were not going to stop him.

He couldn't have spent more than ten minutes or so there. It was enough. I saw his face cloud with anger. I saw him wave dismissively, saw him nod, get in the car and drive away.

The idling dozer engines revved up again, roared. Some additional companies of the police moved in to position around the barricades. The politicians and bureaucrats waved. Then the dozers moved in.

They came in with the slow, inexorable force of Government machinery. Ahead of them, the police moved in, flailing *lathis* clearing the path, scattering the protestors, driving them out. I saw a *lathi* smash down on their leader, a gloved hand remove the pathetic sheaf of paper from his hand, saw the *lathi* crash down again on the supine figure and as the dozers moved in, the terrified crowds scattered.

The blades ripped the walls of the simple huts in just a single swipe. The caterpillar tracks crunched through the broken walls, flattening them in an angry diesel-fuelled roar. The tracks crushed underfoot the beds, the tables, radios and television sets, utensils, a prized tea-set got as a dowry, photo-frames and tin trunks. It crushed underfoot the humble lives of its occupants and trampled the very fabric of our Democracy.

That's when I saw that man. He couldn't have been more than twenty, that man in his pale blue shirt and faded trousers. That brave, or foolish, or just desperate man, who stood in front of his home, barring the approach of the dozer. It did not even pause. It continued its slow crawl forward, knocked him to the ground with the ease of a hand swiping a fly and then its left track rolled over him, mangling him in to the debris.

I think the stoning began then. I saw a *burqa* clad woman pick up a piece of debris of her crumpled home, hurl it towards the lines of police beyond. More stones. Then the shots rang out in retaliation. More screams. More shots. And all the while the dozers rumbled unstoppably forward.

Baba Randhawa held my hand, "*Chalo puttar. Ham chal te hai. Yeha rehna ab theek nahi hai.*" (Come. Let's go. It is not good to remain here any longer)

We left after that. Weaved our way back home on his scooter through the back streets. Thankfully, no police picked us up for questioning. I was too scared to even speak out against what I had seen. And to whom could I protest in any case. Randhawa and me went to the police station again the next day looking for my father. I went daily to the police station, to the adjoining ones as well. They did not even acknowledge my presence. An old man picked up? Who knows? Go to the next station, you may find something there.

## IV

Masterji came home four months later. His body did not carry any of the cigarette burn marks, his wrists had not been crushed, his ankles had not been broken. It was only his left hand – the one that was broken the second time over with a police *lathi* – that was strangely afflicted. It seemed to have shriveled and hung limply at his side. He lost use of it completely. That hand would never heal, the pain would always remain.

But my father had been wounded in other, deeper ways as well. He never spoke of it. He never told us what happened in his months of imprisonment. But I knew it. I sensed what had happened. They did not beat up my father in prison, perhaps because of his age. But his age could not save him from another indignity. In jail, my widowed, 65 year old father had been forcibly sterilized.

But my father would get his revenge. It came sooner than we expected. On 21 March 1977, Mrs Gandhi announced the lifting of the Emergency after 20 months and 20 days. She also announced General Elections, sure that she would win. An astrologer had assured her that.

Masterji went out to vote, of course, in his usual white *kurta* and pajamas. He came back with a dab of black paint on the index finger of his left hand. And I think for that day at least, I saw his hand move, saw some strength in that shattered hand. I saw it twitch by his side as he remained glued to the television for the next few days. He watched wordlessly as the results of the elections come in. He watched Mrs Gandhi being voted out of power, watched a new government being sworn in. Perhaps that brought him a sense of closure. The Emergency had passed, an era had ended. It was just for him and me and for each one of us, for India and Indian democracy, to continue moving on.

And what of the inhabitants of the Turkman Gate shanties, the thousands who were evicted? I went to that place again a few years later. There were no shanties there now, no congested lanes, no open gutters and ugly shacks. In its place was a well-laid out Delhi Development Authority colony with neat three storied houses, wide roads, parks and benches alongside. The pavements are clean, the walls white-washed. Did those who were evicted from here look upon this as the symbol of a new India or do they merely see in it the debris of their small, shattered dreams? In the center stands a bust of a handsome face with bushy sideburns and wide horn-rimmed spectacles. A plaque beneath pays tribute to the man, "whose vision and determination made this dream come real". I could not help but notice the irony. The bust stands at the exact spot where the dozer ran over an insignificant man in a pale blue shirt and faded trousers.

# PAKISTAN

## 1974–1977

"We will eat grass. Even go hungry if we have to. BUT WE WILL HAVE OUR OWN NUCLEAR BOMB"

Prime Minister Zulfikar Ali Bhutto's voice thundered over the radio. It resonated over a nation still reeling in the aftermath of a defeat by its much larger neighbour, a neighbour who now had a nuclear bomb.

Shahnawaz switched off the radio as the signature tune of Radio Pakistan faded, "Those Bastards". He swore. Like all other Pakistanis, to him the Indian nuclear test was something that could not be allowed to go unchallenged. Once again, the memory of the cruel dismemberment of his nation and the year he had spent in Indian captivity came to the surface. That memory rankled. It always would.

Yes, Pakistan would build a bomb of its own. It would develop a nuclear program, surreptitiously and swiftly. Then, in May 1998, when India detonated five more nuclear devices once again in the sands of Pokharan, Pakistan would respond with six tests of its own. The nuclear cloud would hang like a specter over the two antagonistic nations thereafter.

But that would be many years down the line. At that point, in the early 70s, both Shahnawaz and his nation were still trying to find their moorings. The nation was in transition. The army was out of power. Bhutto was elected and seemed to be doing a good enough job of running the country. The image of the army had been hit hard by the defeat of 1971 and for Shahnawaz and hundreds like him, that sense of failure gnawed.

Then in 1977, came the turning point – both for him and his nation. In 1977, he got his next promotion, became a Major. In 1977, he also gave in to the incessant persuasions of his mother and agreed to get married.

He knew the girl – Shazia; Shazia Abbas then- a distant cousin. She had been coming over very often, on visits cleverly engineered by his mother. And Wow! Shahnawaz had to admit that she was a beauty. In her jeans and T shirts, which she preferred over the staid *salwar kameez* of most other girls, she set his heart and other parts of his body racing. He loved her laughing, vivacious ways and her carefree exuberance was the perfect foil to his own quiet, grave manner. He loved her voice, the way she sang, the way her music flowed out so easily and effortlessly. She was a gifted singer, had trained under one of the most renowned masters of Pakistan for over ten years, and sang often on radio and TV. She loved movies, especially the Indian ones, and Shahnawaz loved holding her hand in the darkened movie hall. He loved the smell of her hair, the touch of her body. He loved her younger brother, her college, her scooter, the bench where she sat, everything about her. Why – if she had a parrot he would have probably loved it too.

In other words, he was simply besotted.

He had probably fallen in love with her during their third or fourth meeting and when he blurted it out to *Ammajan*, she was not surprised. His wizened old mother had planned it all throughout, but feigned surprise and cocked up her eyebrows in mock astonishment.

"*Wah*", she laughed, as she came forward, embraced her son and kissed him lightly on his forehead. "*Bilkul sahi choice hai. Kya pari le aye ho tum hamare ghar me*". (Youhave made just the right choice. What an angel you are bringing home)

And so it was that in June 1977, Shahnawaz and Shazia joined their lives together at a simple *nikah* ceremony in their farm house at Lahore. His life, and he himself, changed with her arrival. He spoke more easily, laughed more often and there seemed to be a new meaning to life. The two were obviously and clearly, deeply in love with each other, and their abiding love would sustain them all their lives; from the passion of their youth, to the stability of their middle years and in the turbulence of their later ones.

As his own life changed, so did the destiny of his nation. In June 1977, (just as the Emergency was being revoked in India) Prime Minister Bhutto was removed by the Army Chief, General Zia-ul-Haq, in the second coup of the country's history. Zia took over as the President of the country, jailed Bhutto and later had him hanged.

The country's brief tryst with Democracy was once again over. And yet, other changes were taking place in the neighbourhood that would impact the course of their nation – and Shahnawaz's life – for decades to come.

# The Death of a Prime Minister: The Wounding of a Religion

### India, 1980-1984

*When Mrs Gandhi and her Congress Party were swept out of power in the elections of 1977, the elections brought in the Janata Party, a hastily cobbled coalition of opposition parties into power with Morarji Desai as the Prime Minister*

*The Janata Party eventually collapsed with its own internal squabbling. Unable to deliver either on the economic, political or social front it was voted out by a disillusioned people in the next elections of 1980. Mrs Gandhi was re-elected by the same people who had rejected her four years ago.*

*The Iron Lady of Indian politics was back.*

*But her next stint from 1980 to 1984 was even more turbulent than the previous one. The law and order situation was deteriorating, there were communal riots in Assam, and the economy was slowing. Worse, in Punjab, India's richest and most prosperous state, the demand for Khalistan – a separate land for the Sikhs- was being increasingly raised by Jarnail Singh Bhindranwale. Bhindranwale had been cultivated and propped up initially by Mrs Gandhi herself. But he had broken away and now from his base in the Golden Temple at Amritsar, the holiest of Sikh shrines, he unleashed a wave of violence that threatened to tear Punjab and the nation apart.*

*Mrs Gandhi dithered in acting against Bhindranwale. By the time she decided he was well entrenched inside the Golden Temple with hundreds of well-armed militants. The shrine had been virtually converted into a fortress.*

*On 06 June 1984, the Indian Army stormed the Golden Temple. It took over 24 hours to clear the temple and that too after bringing in heavy tanks and artillery. Over 800 Sikh militants and 200 army personnel fell in the intense battle inside the temple. The gold-gilded Harmandir Sahib was pocked with shells, its interiors raked with machine gun fire. The Akal Takth, the seat of temporal Sikh power was virtually in ruins by damage caused by High Explosive tank shells. Yet that was only the visible damage.*

*A deeper damage had been caused to the Sikh psyche by the attack on their holiest shrine. Sikh personnel in the army mutinied; Sikh peasantry marched towards Amritsar when they heard news of the attack. Raids on villages and gurudwaras, conducted in search of hidden weapons and militants, further infuriated the Sikhs. And they claimed revenge.*

*At 9.12 on the morning of 31 October 1984, as Mrs Indira Gandhi was walking from her home at 1 Safdarjang Road towards her office, she was shot dead by Beant Singh and Satwant Singh, her Sikh bodyguards. Mrs Gandhi, her body riddled with over 20 bullets, died that afternoon at the All India Institute of Medical Science.*

*That same evening anti-Sikh riots broke out. The riots, allegedly engineered by local Congress leaders, raged across Delhi and spread across much of India. Over 2700 Sikhs perished in the carnage that followed. It was a communal divide, not seen since the partition of the nation in 1947. And to many who had witnessed the horrors of 1947, it seemed to be a partition once again.*

*Rajiv Gandhi – her elder son and now heir apparent, after the death of Sanjay Gandhi in an air crash – said in a chilling retort to the news of the rioting, "When a great tree falls, the earth is bound to shake". The earth shook. It shook the nation to its very foundations.*

# The Attack on the Temple

### Amritsar, Punjab, 1984

My tenure in Delhi came to a close in 1979. It seemed a brief one, but that is how it always was with army postings. Put us in a good place and they would move us out in two years dot; place us in a God-forsaken hole and the tenure would invariably extend to around three. But brief or not, I was grateful for the time we had as a family.

In that time I saw Gaurav grow into a somewhat precocious nine year old. I could see many of Masterji's values, even that sense of lofty idealism, slowly seeping in to him. I saw our twins grow into hyper-active six year olds, inseparable but always at logger heads with each other. I saw the first streaks of grey appear in Nivedita's hair and mine, felt the little heaviness build up on both of us. I saw Masterji become stooped and cantankerous. He was not the same person after his imprisonment and I think a sense of impermanence had crept in upon him. I was glad for the time we shared together and the bonding we developed then.

My brothers, Vishal and Kunal, too came often, though their visits were gradually reducing. They were pursuing their own careers and lives – careers that would be rich and glittering. With time and distance we were drifting apart. We were all becoming different persons only we did not realise it till it was way too late.

And when we moved out of Delhi, it was not to too bad a place. It was to Srinagar. Kashmir, in the early 80s was not the conflict zone that it would soon become. It was still the land of blue waters and emerald meadows, of tourists and film shootings, of traffic policemen at Lal Chowk trying to get some semblance of order in its chaotic roads. When Nivedita,

Gaurav and the twins came to visit – as they did often – we walked the streets with thousands of tourists, haggled with shopkeepers, rode the *shikaras* of Dal Lake and the sleds at Gulmarg, with no fear, except that of being cheated by the local touts.

That Kashmir would soon change. From 1987 onwards the beautiful valley would be wracked by an insurgency that would tear it apart. There would be no tourists for the *shikaras* at Dal Lake or the sleds at Gulmarg; the streets would be patrolled by heavily armed soldiers, the streets deserted, the nights curfewed. The traffic policemen would be replaced by sand–bagged bunkers at each cross road. There would be graffiti on the walls shouting, "Indian dogs, Go Back". There would be suicide attacks and sniping, there would be raids and cordons and the Paradise on earth would be irrevocably despoiled.

I am glad that Nivedita and I saw it when it was still at its most beautiful. I would return to Kashmir eighteen years later, but then it would be a different Kashmir. It would be a war zone and I would lose my son on its soil.

## II

We left Kashmir in late 1983. The first snows were just falling over the Pir Panjal Ranges when our Regiment convoy moved out of Srinagar and headed for our next posting – to Jullandhar in Punjab. And when the convoy crossed the Jawahar tunnel, the sole tunnel that links the Kashmir valley to the rest of India, I felt a pang at leaving. There was something in the beauty of the place that evoked a sense of sadness. Was it the Mughal Emperor, Jehangir, who had said, *"Ger Bar Ru-E- Zaman Ast; Hami Asto, Hami Asto, Hami Asto*". 'If there is Heaven on Earth, it is here, it is here, it is here.' That's what I mean. Its beauty could make poets of us all – or maybe just killers.

Our convoy rumbled into Jullandhar Cantonment late one evening in the middle of November 1983. I was in one of the leading jeeps. I had been promoted now – was a Naib Subedar, a Junior Commissioned Officer. And well, I enjoyed my new rank and the responsibilities and the privileges that came with it. It meant I could be sitting in a jeep, and not in the back of a rumbling, swaying truck as we rolled into Jullandhar.

We were coming back to Punjab after our last outing in 1965 and it carried fond memories for most of us. It was home to many. But now in these days of 1983- 84 the simmering unrest brewing in the state was about to spill over. None really realized how fast it would go out of control.

Yes, the papers were increasingly filling up with news of Jarnail Singh Bhindranwale,. Holed up inside the Golden Temple in Amritsar, the militant Sikh leader had been increasingly raising his demand for an independent nation – Khalistan. But then nobody gave it much credence. Not when Bhindranwale and his militant followers virtually converted the Golden Temple in to a fortress. Not when Hindus were pulled out of buses and shot, not when the Deputy Inspector General of Police – himself a Sikh – was shot dead by militants inside the Golden Temple itself. Not till it was too late. By June 1984, the situation had reached the point of no return. That's when Mrs Gandhi gave the signal to the army to attack the Golden Temple.

## III

I remember that night well. It was the 5th of June 1984. The papers had been full of speculations of a likely attack by the army on the Golden Temple. And when we moved out with complete weapons and equipment towards Amritsar, we knew that the operations had begun. We were embarking on Operation Blue Star.

We knew that the Army would be storming the Golden Temple to flush out the militants within. Honestly, we hoped we would not be part of it. We would do it if ordered, we were soldiers after all. But our heart was never in it.

Fortunately, we were not part of the force that actually assaulted the Temple. Ours was more a supporting role. We were to help cordon the routes leading towards the Golden Temple to prevent angry Sikhs from rushing to protect their holy shrine, at least till it had been cleared of militants.

We reached Amritsar just before nightfall and slowly took up our positions around Lawrence Road and Hall Bazaar, along the warren of narrow roads that led towards the Golden Temple. From the distance, I could see its gilded dome and could even hear the *kirtan* from its minarets. A curfew had been imposed and the streets were deserted. Nothing moved besides the incessant columns of army trucks moving towards the temple. Yet, from behind the barred doors and closed windows, we felt eyes, hostile and angry, boring down on us. In spite of the constant rumbling of trucks, what struck me most was the silence that seemed to hang over the night. Not even a dog barked in that sullenresentfultown.

We took up positions at the Hall Bazaar crossroad, the old-town road, that led to Jallianwala Bagh – the site of another historical tragedy – and then to the Golden Temple complex. There were Sikh soldiers amongst us. Our Company Commander, Major Ravinder Pal Singh Bedi, himself was a Sikh. They would have gone through mixed feelings that night, but what they felt remained within them. No emotions showed as we set up our barricades on the roads leading to the Golden Temple.

We were around three kilometres from the Golden Temple and heard the assault when it went in at ten that night. We heard the staccato of machine gun and carbine fire; the screams of the wounded and dying and the silence that followed after the initial assaults failed. Then came the even more menacing sounds of the squeal of tank tracks and then the crack of a 105 mm tank gun. Then another. The sounds reached us in muffled roars, rolling in waves. Then came another roar, closer and far angrier. Along the road were hundreds of Sikhs marching down the road for the defence of their shrine.

They were armed with nothing but staves and axes, small *kirpans* and ceremonial swords, literally anything that they could get their hands on. Their chants of *"Bole So Nihal, Sat Sri Akal"* rose to a crescendo as they advanced down the road only to be halted by our barricade and the tall figure of Major Bedi standing ahead of it

He was in full uniform, his olive green turban tied impeccably over his head, as always. His beard was full and luxuriant; he never trimmed it as many others did. I noticed he did not carry his weapon. He just stood there in the centre of the road, cross-armed and faced the oncoming mob of angry villagers.

I moved towards him. He indicated slightly, motioned me to stop. I moved back, took my own position behind the barricade. He would handle this alone.

He waited till the villagers came closer and then spoke. He spoke in Punjabi and his voice was soft, almost compassionate, but it carried the implacable firmness of a direct order.

"Go home now. All of you. Everything is under control."

"What control. Your army is attacking our temple. Let us pass. We will not allow them to touch the Golden Temple."

"The temple is unharmed, believe me. It is only a small operation against the men inside. There will be no damage done to our Temple."

"Small operation. They are firing inside it. Our temple is being destroyed."

Even as he spoke we could hear the sound of machine gun and tank fire building up. The army was launching another attack on the temple and the militants fighting doggedly inside.

The villagers surged forward as the sounds of firing built up. From where we were, we could see tracer bullets streaking through the night sky, see the flash of explosions reflected off the gold plated dome of the temple. I cocked my weapon and pointed towards the villagers now moving dangerously forward. In the barricades adjoining me I saw the others do the same. This was going to get ugly.

Major Bedi gestured towards us, motioning us to drop our weapons. He continued standing there, unarmed, unwavering, speaking in chaste Punjabi, reasoning with them, placating them. Slowly the villagers stopped trying to surge forward, but stood beyond our barricades in small, sullen groups. They remained there for much of the night, singing their prayers, breaking out into '*Bole SoNihal – Sat Sri Akal"* but fortunately did not try to break through our barricade and go to the defence of their Temple.

In the distance the sounds of firing still continued, but it was largely small arms fire now. The infantry had entered the complex and the tanks and artillery had halted their fire for fear of hitting their own. The staccato of automatic fire slowly reduced in intensity, but the cracks of single shots and carbines continued for a long while thereafter. We stayed there all night, keeping the crowd at bay, watching the smoke rise from the direction of the temple. Even from this distance, I could see that the gold-plated dome of the Akal Takth was badly damaged, one of the minarets of the *parikrama* had been virtually blown off. The exact damage I would never really see, nor would it be accurately reported.

We were there the next day, when All India Radio announced the successful operation against the militants in the Golden Temple and BBC described its widespread damage. We were still there next week, when the news of the immense casualties began seeping out. By then the damage to the Temple had become widely known and the wound on the Sikh psyche was deeper than anyone could have imagined. But the story was not yet over. The consequences of the attack and the next act of the tragedy was still to come.

## IV

It was 31 October 1984 at 9.12 am. The time stands outs clearly, like a clock whose hands have been permanently frozen. It seems etched in my mind.

I was at Jullandhar Railway Station that morning, on my way home to Delhi for a small spell of leave. The Shan- e- Punjab was late, unusual for it. Maybe it was because of the early winter fog that enveloped the tracks on its route from Amritsar. It should have been at Jullandhar by 8.05. It reached almost an hour late.

As I climbed in to the unreserved second class compartment at Jullandhar Railway Station, at the other end of the line in Delhi, Prime Minister, Mrs Indira Gandhi was walking from her residence at 1 Safdarjang Road towards her office. She was immaculate dressed as always, dressed in a simple saffron sari with just a hint of make-up. At 9.12, as the train whistle shrieked and the train pulled out slowly from Jullandhar station, Mrs Gandhi smiled at Beant Singh, the Sikh Sub-Inspector in duty. As she did, he removed his .38 revolver and fired five rounds at her. Satwant Singh, the other Sikh guard on duty there, unslung his carbine and emptied its entire magazine of 25 bullets on Mrs Gandhi's fallen form. Almost every bullet penetrated and by the time her frail, bleeding figure was taken to the All India Institute of Medical Sciences, it was already too late.

The first news came in on a transistor radio held by a passenger at around eleven that morning, as the train was crossing the wide Sutluj River Bridgejust beyond Ludhiana. It only said, "The Prime Minister, Mrs Indira Gandhi was shot by her bodyguards at 9.12 this morning. She has been taken to the All India Institute of Medical Sciences."

In the swaying, jostling train, with the green fields of Punjab passing across the windows, the news struck like a bombshell. Then came the rumours, reinforced at each station we halted at during the interminable journey. She was wounded. She was recovering. She was dead. Then at 6 pm came the dreaded pronouncement on All India Radio, "The Prime Minister, Mrs Indira Gandhi, was shot by her Sikh bodyguards this morning. She died at the All India Institute of Medical Science at 2.20 pm this afternoon." And the finality hit us.

It was also when I sensed the shift in mood. It turned from bewilderment to sorrow, then anger. I saw eyes turn accusingly at four young Sikhs, silent and defensive in a corner. Nobody spoke for a long time. Then a voice rang out, "*Madher chodho*" – the mother fuckers.

We knew who the mother fuckers he was referring to were. We all knew. It was not only Satwant Singh and Beant Singh, it was them all. Nobody said much after that, but the message was clear. The guilty had been identified. The judgment had been sounded. And now retribution and punishment would fall on the entire Sikh community.

## V

It was almost ten by the time the Shan-e-Punjab chugged desolately in to New Delhi Railway Station. There was no line of taxis or auto rickshaws in the taxi stand outside. The stand was empty. Only a few damaged rickshaws and a single taxi stood there, windscreens shattered, bonnets broken, damaged and abandoned.

I walked most of the way home. Crowds were gathering in the streets. The mood was already turning ugly when I reached C -3 Janakpuri. Anti-Sikh violence was just rising.

I rang the bell. Once, twice. No answer. I rang again. Called out Masterji's name, called out to Nivedita, saw her draw the curtain from our room above. Then the door opened. She rushed into my arms, pulled me inside and bolted the door behind her.

'My God. I was so worried". She held me tight.

Masterji came over. Checked the door, bolted it again. He put his hand over me as I bent to touch his feet. "You should not have travelled today. Thank God you have reached here safe. "

From behind, Gaurav came in. Then Vikram and Supriya, bounding into my arms like they always did each time I came home.

Even in their relief, I could sense the tension in the room. And as I turned in to our own room, I understood why. Inside the small room were the Randhawa family. The white-bearded patriarch, his three sons, his two-daughters-in-law, his two grandchildren – all eight of them.

The Randhawas were more than just neighbours, they were almost family. Old Baba Randhawa had been with me on that night of the Emergency during our futile search for Masterji, as he had always been whenever we, or anyone else, needed help. The old patriarch had come over in the trauma of Partition, uprooted from their vast fields and homes at Sialkot. They had rebuilt their lives from scratch, starting off with fixing punctures from a pavement, then a small cycle repair shop, then a scooter repair shed, and then a small garage which went on to become the largest and most prosperous one in the area. Their home next door had expanded from a single room tenement to a small bungalow, a loud, noisy home which was always open to all, and their kitchen, almost a communal *langar.*

I bent to touch his feet. *"Fikr mat kijiye, Randhawaji. Aap ko yaha koi haath nahi lagayega. Kal subah tak sab theek ho jayega"* (Don't worry Randhawaji. Here nobody can harm you. By tomorrow morning it will all be okay)

Randhawa nodded, but my reassurance sounded hollow, even to me. By now anti-Sikh riots were raging across the city. Sikh homes and families were being targeted by their own neighbours and friends.

The mob came for them at two that night. They gathered around the Randhawa house, pelting stones. The small wooden gate was ripped aside, the doors smashed. I saw their new Maruti car smashed, their scooter pulled out and burnt.(The same scooter on which Baba Randhawa had carried me looking for Masterji on the night of the Emergency, ) Then the mob poured in; came out carrying television sets, curios, rolled up carpets, paintings, even an ornately framed photograph of the Golden Temple. They did not find any member of the family inside and turned to the next place where they could be. Our own home.

The crowd began baying outside the door. The pounding began. Masterji walked up to the door. I followed. Between the two of us there was nothing we could have done if the mob decided to come in, find the Randhawas and wreak their perverted vengeance.

Masterji opened the door. He was always a small man, and seemed to have shrunk even more with time. But his small frame covered the entire door. I stood behind him, in my uniform – my army uniform that I had donned automatically, more as a symbol than for any of the security it could have provided.

There were so many in the crowd whom I recognized – the Guptas, the Ahujas, the Sharmas, the Bansi Lals – so many who had exchanged sweets and played riotous Holi with their Sikh neighbours ; who had exchanged plates of *daal* and *saag* with them; had come over for *Divali* and *Gurpurab*. They were no longer neighbours and friends now. They were the hunters and the hunted.

There was another amongst them. I did not know him, but I had seen his pictures on election banners – hands folded, a servile ingratiating expression on his face – asking for votes. He was Bharat Haladi, the local MLA – a small time goon who was slowly climbing up the political ladder. He was the one, providing direction, inciting, adding the fuel to the already volatile situation.

It was he who spoke up first, "Where are the Randhawas? *Kaha hai saalon*?"

Masterji did not reply for a while. He merely continued standing by the door. When he spoke, it was addressed at the mob, "*Raat ke do baz gaye hai. Band karo yeh paagal pan. Ghar jao*" (It is two in the morning. Stop this madness and go home)

Someone from the mob roared. *"Ghar jao? Hamare desh ki Maa ka katal kiya hai in behenchodo ne. Unke nahi chhoden ge. Ek ek ko pakad kar bhun lenge. Kahe hai woh Sikh behenchodo"* (Go Home? They have killed our mother. We won't spare them. Where are the Sikh sister-fuckers?)

Bharat Haladi spoke. There was a menace to his voice, a confidence of one who knows he can do what he wants and get away with it. "*Yeh Sikhs ko hame de do. Ham tumhe chhod denge.*" (Give the Sikhs to us. We will spare you)

Masterji's voice never rose. He still spoke in the calm inflexion of a patient school master addressing a particularly difficult student, "There are only Indians in this house. I have told you. Now go."

They crowded around for another twenty minutes or so. But no one crossed the threshold of that door.

I wonder if my presence in an army uniform behind Masterji made any difference. Maybe it did marginally, but what held them at bay was more the iron strength of character that barred the door. The mob muttered amongst themselves, turned back, threw some more stones at

Randhawa's house, and began moving back down the road, looking for other prey to vent their senseless, meaningless anger.

The Randhawas stayed with us all week till the violence finally subsided. Army vehicles patrolled the streets now to bring some measure of secular calm. The houses and shops still smoldered though. The wrecks of cars and scooters still littered the streets. But the blood had been washed off the pavements. The bodies, those horribly mutilated bodies with their hair and beards hacked or burnt, had been removed and the fallen turbans gathered and disposed.

But the Randhawas left Delhi soon after. They went to Kapurthala, Punjab and the sanctuary of kinship. They returned five months later, re-occupied their home, rebuilt their burnt and vandalized garage. They rarely spoke about what had happened and refused the compensation of One Thousand Rupees which the government offered for the damage they had suffered. Over the years when the inquiries finally took place, they went to court as witnesses. They testified. They identified Bharat Haladi at the head of the crowd that destroyed their home. "Yes, it was him. Yes, I saw him. Yes, I am definite." Their testimony and that of the hundreds who spoke out made no difference. The case lingered on interminably, till it was finally buried in the complexities of legal jargon. Bharat Haladi rose in his political career, became a Member of Parliament, then a Minister of State, then a Minister. Why, that bastard would have even become the Prime Minister. Oh, he prospered all right.

The Randhawas picked up their shattered lives – as did the thousands of Sikh families. Their garage expanded and in their simple hard-working manner they re-built their lives. The incidents of the nights of 1984 were not a defeat for them – that they could overcome. What they could never overcome was the knowledge that Haladi and hundreds like him still walked free. They remained unpunished, continued to smile ingratiatingly from election banners, became MLAs and MPs. 1984 was slowly forgotten and eventually it was almost as if it had not happened at all.

# THE RE-RISE OF THE PAKISTAN ARMY

## 1977 Onwards

*While India was in the throes of one of the most tumulus periods in its history, Pakistan seemed to be recovering its equilibrium. General Zia-ul-Haq had taken over as President in 1977 and the army was back to its previous ascendency.*

*Then in December 1979, the Soviet Union invaded neighbouring Afghanistan. Suddenly Pakistan became the front-line state in the battle against the Soviets in Afghanistan. Propped up by the USA, it became the conduit through which aid and arms were funneled in. Pakistani officers and men began training and equipping Afghan Mujahidin- the resistance movement comprising of dozens of separate groups. In return, US largesse flowed in, boosting the Pakistani economy. Pakistan seemed to be prospering, its army once again in full control.*

*Under Zia-ul-Haq their involvement in Afghanistan and Kashmir intensified. They had long term aims in Afghanistan. Even while helping the Mujahidin groups there, they wanted to use them for Pakistan's own battles in Kashmir later. Pakistan would pay a very heavy price for its policy of befriending the Afghan Mujahidin groups. It would bounce back on them with disastrous results in the years to come. But all that was not foreseen then. For now it seemed to be on a roll.*

# BEFRIENDING THE MUJAHIDIN

### Afghanistan, 1979 -87

Major Shahnawaz Khan had a long, uncomfortable journey on the flight from Washington DC to Islamabad. It was a long journey, almost 14 hours, and he could have done with a stiff whiskey to break the jet-lagging monotony. But Pakistan International Airways had stopped serving alcohol on their flights some time ago. Their food, in any case was never too good, so there was nothing to do but eye the pretty air hostess, and just bear it.

They landed at Islamabad airport late at night. It did not take him much time to clear customs and immigration. These days, army officers were spared these tedious formalities. He was waved through, collected his baggage and strode out in to the warm Islamabad night.

Shazia and Salim were there, waiting just outside the lobby. She looked stunning as always, in a perfectly cut maroon and white *salwar kameez.* Salim was in her arms – almost two now, old enough to recognize his father and reach out gurglingly towards him. He hugged Shazia. Nowadays, with so much emphasis on Islamisation that President Zia-ul-Haq had introduced, public display of affection, even between husband and wife, was frowned upon. But to hell with it. It was good to be back home.

It had been a long separation this time, almost three months. He had been sent to attend the Company Commander's course in the USA, at Fort Polk, Louisiana, with officers of the US army. This was the second course he was doing there this year. The next visit he would try to take Shazia and Salim with him as well.

But he would have little time with Shazia and Salim. Because the very next day, even before he had given his report on the course at General Headquarters, Islamabad, he was handed over a signal. It said quite simply, "You have been deputed to the Directorate of Inter-Services Intelligence with immediate effect. You will report to Headquarters ISI on 01 July 1982."

Shahnawaz looked at the signal with surprise. A deputation to the ISI – Pakistan's powerful intelligence agency? Who would have expected it? He knew about the ISI, of course, who didn't. It was virtually an autonomous authority that coordinated all intelligence activities in the country and the neighbouring ones. The best and finest officers of the three services were usually selected to be attached with them on deputation, and more often than not they rose rapidly thereafter. He would miss his regimental life, but this would not be too bad. He would be in civvies, travel extensively, have immense power and resources, and well, the job would be different.

He reported to the Jinnah Building at Islamabad Avenue at 0900 hours sharp on 01 July. From outside, the building did not look like the Headquarters of the nation's spy agency, it looked more like a college. He waited in the Reception outside, till a NCO came in- in civvies, just as he was- and escorted him through a warren of corridors into the heart of the building and to the office of Brigadier Mohammed Yusuf – the Deputy Director General of the ISI and the head of its Special Activities Division.

## II

Brigadier Yusuf sat behind an ornate rosewood table, his office providing an open view of the lawns and fountains beyond. At first glance, one could not have imagined that this scholarly looking man held one of the most important jobs in the country – that of looking after the intelligence and counter-intelligence of the neighbouring countries, mainly India and Afghanistan. Yet, his greatest strength lay in the virtual anonymity with which he performed the role.

Nobody entered the office throughout the hour which Shahnawaz spent with Brigadier Yusuf. There were no bearers bringing in cups of tea, no aides entering with files, nothing. It was just the two of them and Yusuf's first words indicated why.

"Congratulations, Shahnawaz, on being selected for deputation with ISI. The first rule we follow is that whatever we say, hear and do will not be mentioned to your colleagues, your friends, your wife, not even to other members of this organization. You will report directly to me and what transpires between us is to remain purely between the two of us. Understood?".

Shahnawaz nodded. The secrecy of the ISI was legendary. Everybody knew about them, nobody knew anything they did. They had been blamed for everything, from assassinating political dissidents, to fomenting insurgency in India, to trading in arms and drugs, everything. But nothing had been proved – ever.

"Tell me what do you know of Afghanistan?"

The question took Shahnawaz by surprise. What he knew about Afghanistan was only what he had read in the papers. He knew that the Soviets had invaded it in 1979 and had installed a puppet government there. He knew that different resistance groups, popularly known as the Mujahidin were fighting the Soviets there. He knew that the USA was supporting them in their battle and that Pakistan itself was supplying the US arms to the Mujahidin on their behalf and was getting increasingly involved in the battle.

It took a minute to compose his thoughts and blurt out what little he knew. Yusuf let Shahnawaz ramble for a while and then interrupted.

'And what do you know of the Mujahidin?'

Here Shahnawaz was stumped. He knew of the Mujahidin groups, all right, but sketchily. That was a different turf.

Brigadier Yusuf did not wait for his reply. He continued, "There are around 24 different Mujahidin groups operating in Afghanistan, most of them headed by local tribal chiefs. For them fighting the Soviet invader is a *jihad*, a holy war. The Americans want to use them to defeat the Soviets. They cannot help them directly, so they have to do it through us. You will be the link now between us and the Mujahidin groups. You will cultivate them. You will understand their requirements. You will make sure that the arms and equipment they need reaches them. You will supply them, train them, and make friends with them. And you will do so without telling a soul about your activities. Do you understand?"

The last line was spoken even more slowly and with chilling emphasis. Shahnawaz understood all right.

Brigadier Yusuf continued, "You are to leave next week for Afghanistan. You will meet one of the heroes of the Mujahidin movement. He is recovering from wounds he has suffered in a Soviet attack. You will deliver to him something he sorely needs. Meet him, and understand him. He is a difficult man, but he can become a valuable ally for Pakistan."

He tossed down a small dossier with the photograph stapled on one corner. The photo was of a middle-aged Afghan, pale and sun-burnt, with that rugged handsomeness and hint of Mongoloid features that most Afghans have. Though the face was expressionless, the narrow hooded eyes revealed a shrewd, animal cunning and a capacity for great cruelty. It was the face of a man who could be a dangerous enemy, and maybe a loyal friend. The name on the dossiersaid 'Baitullah Wazir'

**III**

The view from his window of the Khyber Hotel in Peshawar was quite spectacular. Shahnawaz could see the old Khyber road beneath, meandering towards the foothills of the Hindu Kush Mountains and then begin its steady climb towards the historic Khyber Pass at the crest and then rolling down to the other side in to Afghanistan.

Yet, Shahnawaz was not admiring the view. He was concentrating more on how he would tackle the man he had been sent out to meet. He would have to cross over into Afghanistan, drive for over a day across its rugged mountains and then meet him at his village in Qula Wali Khan. Normally, it would have been impossible to meet Wazir. He never met outsiders and it had taken weeks of persuasion from ISI agents in Afghanistan to agree to the meeting.

Shahnawaz finished his cigarette and tossed the butt out of the window. No one would have recognized him now. His hair was long, he had grown a full, thick beard; he was dressed in a black Pathan suit with a flat felt cap on his head. In that attire he did not look like an Army Major, he looked like a local contractor. Which is exactly what his papers identified him as – Name – Muzamil Afridi; Place of Residence – Quetta; Occupation, timber contractor.

No one knew who he was or what was he doing here. No one, except Brigadier Yousuf and Naik Suleiman Tarmizi; Suleiman, his driver, orderly, buddy and bodyguard all rolled in one, who would accompany him for this mission. In the two months or so that they had been together, Shahnawaz had grown to rely more and more on this silent, resourceful Corporal. He was glad that he was here. In this hostile land he needed someone he could depend upon.

Suleiman was waiting by their Toyota pickup truck. He was ready, the truck packed, engine warmed up, the fuel, oil and tire pressure checked. He was in a similar Pathan suit, only in light blue. He did not salute when Shahnawaz approached – that would have been a dead giveaway – but his body stiffened involuntarily in reflex. He opened the door for Shahnawaz, got in to the driver's side, revved up once or twice and then smoothly glided the pickup truck on to the main road and towards the Khyber Pass beyond.

The pick-up truck moved slowly across the Khyber road. Armies had marched along this same route for centuries. Alexandra's army had ridden across it, Babar's Mughals had used it to establish an empire in India, the British had marched over it in their ill-fated campaigns to subdue Afghanistan. Each step was marked by History, and Shahnawaz's own journey too, in a very small way, would help shape the course of this country, and his own.

The truck began its slow climb up the mountain range, descended, and then reached the check point on the Afghan-Pakistan border. The border guards made a great show of checking their documents, but did not ask to open their luggage or inspect their vehicle. They had been paid off well, by the local ISI agents there, much in advance. They waved the truck through, crossed the Durand Line and entered Afghanistan.

They drove six hours through the rugged mountains, till they reached Qasim Khan Village, their immediate destination. Here they made contact with the ISI representative – Brigadier Yusuf had coordinated it well. They spent a long, cold night there and next morning began the long drive towards Qula Wali Khan, Wazir's village. There were four more men in their vehicle when they drove off; young, taciturn Afghans with black turbans, Kalashnikovs slung across their shoulders. They drove across the featureless landscape all day, along dirt tracks and non-existent roads, and when night was just falling, they reached Qula Wali Khan. Baitullah Wazir's village, his sanctuary.

The mud and stone village had been frozen in time, unchanged for centuries. There were no roads here, or electricity, forget about running water. There were no women to be seen, only a few swathed in *burqas* with water pots delicately balanced on their heads. No children played in the streets. The village, like the hundreds across Afghanistan, lived in a different world. But its very anonymity made it an ideal refuge for a wounded warlord.

Shahnawaz was guided to a mud hut, larger than the others perhaps, but otherwise not much different. An armed guard frisked him again and then escorted him over a flight of stairs on to the terrace where Baitullah Wazir waited. There Shahnawaz would meet the man with whom he would be associated for the next fifteen years. A man who would become a friend and then a sworn enemy.

But Shahnawaz had no inkling of this. He had also no inkling of the past that bound them together. He did not know that this Mujahidin warrior was the son of Rahimtullah Wazir, the shaggy bearded tribesman who had been with his father during the advance to Srinagar in 1947. The past of the two men was interlinked; their future about to be intertwined.

*"Salaam Aliekum,"* Shahnawaz bent his head, raised his open palm to his forehead in the traditional Afghan gesture of respect. "We have heard so much about your courage in fighting the Soviet occupiers. It is an honour to meet you in person."

Wazir waved dismissively. The two young Afghans flanking him left. "And what brings you here, all the way from Pakistan to our humble village?"

"I come with an offer of help. I can provide you assistance in your war against the Soviets."

Wazir laughed derisively, "And what help can you Pakistanis, who have never won a war, provide to us Afghans, who have never lost one?"

Shahnawaz paused, let the insult ride over. "We know the Soviets have the men, the tanks, the guns and the helicopters. They are no match for your courage. But you need weapons to match your courage. We can provide you with that."

"And what do you want in return?"

"Nothing. It is just an open hand of friendship that we extend to you. When the time comes perhaps you may be able to repay the favour. And we have what you need to defeat the Soviets."

Wazir roared, "We are more than a match for the Soviets. I have killed twelve of them myself. Three with my bare hands. We have attacked them in their camps, We have lured their tanks to our passes and blown them with grenades. We can defeat them on our own. But what is it you have to offer?"

Almost on cue, Shahnawaz heard a hum in the distance, like the flutter of a bumble bee. The hum grew louder as two Soviet MI-24 Attack Helicopters appeared, made a low swooping pass along the valley, climbed, made a second pass along the adjoining mountain crest, jinked and then turned away.

Wazir stiffenedat the sound, as did Shahnawaz. Shahnawaz knew the power of the Soviet gunships. The heavily armed helicopters could swoop out of nowhere, unleash a deadly barrage of cannon and rocket fire and disappear before anyone could retaliate. Wazir himself had been injured in a gunship attack just three months earlier.

Shahnawaz waited till the sound of the gunships receded and they became blips in the horizon. "You and your men fear no man. But even one as fearless as you needs help when Death comes from above. I have what you need to counter it."

He led Wazir to the courtyard where his pickup truck was standing. Nodded to Suleiman who removed the tarpaulin to expose a line of boxes neatly stacked beneath. Shahnawaz pulled out one of the boxes, unhinged the lock and removed the small, sleek tube that nestled within.

Shahnawaz unhooked the optical sighting system of the shoulder fired, surface to air Stinger missile launcher. He raised it to his shoulder and traversed it in a wide sweep across the sky, towards the direction where the Soviet gunships had disappeared over the horizon.

'With this," he said, handing the Stinger missile launcher to Wazir, "You can bring down your enemies even when they come from the air."

## IV

Shahnawaz shifted uneasily in his position atop the mountain. Suleiman was there crouched by his side, equally cold, equally uncomfortable. From where he was he had a dominating view of the valley below. He could see the dust trails of the two pick –up trucks patrolling below; he could see the range opposite. Most importantly, he could see the horizon in a 360 degree arc all around.

Baitullah Wazir was in position about half a kilometre to his right. Both men were in camouflage fatigues, US army issue; both carried their personal weapons and both had a deadly Stinger missile launcher and a box of two missiles by their side.

They had been taking position atop this mountain range daily for over a week now, their ears straining to hear the angry bumble bee sound of a Soviet Helicopter gunship, their eyes aching from peering at the horizon. None appeared. Then Baitullah hit upon the idea of using two pick-up trucks to drive up and down the valley below. That would be the bait to attract the big birds.

It was in the morning of the eight day that their bait worked. The gunships usually struck early mornings or late evenings when visibility was best, and these two swooped out of nowhere as they usually did. Even though they had been expecting them, their sudden appearance took them surprise. The two helicopters raced above them and lined up for their first strafing run on the Mujahidin vehicles below.

They were at the start of their run when Baitullah fired. His Stinger missile raced towards its target, about 40 yards ahead of it – it seemed to pause in mid-air, seeking a heat signal, didn't receive any, and then sped ahead and slammed into the valley.

Shahnawaz adjusted his optical sight. Lined it to the rear of the leading helicopter. Held his breath, fired, and watched the missile move almost in slow motion, it seemed to be sniffing the air and then it caught on to the heat exhaust emanating from the helicopter and homed unerringly towards it.

The missile struck the MI-24 attack helicopter just below the engine. It was a heavy aircraft, designed to withstand machine gun and cannon fire, but it was no match for a Stinger missile. The stricken helicopter seemed to hover, tried to gather height, and then plummeted in to the valley below.

Shahnawaz loaded the second missile, saw Baitullah doing the same. But the second helicopter was too fast. He jinked sharply, picked up height and rapidly disappeared over the horizon.

Shahnawaz whooped – ran towards Baitullah who was staring at the retreating helicopter, still pointing his launcher towards it. Below he could see the pickup trucks rushing towards the downed copter. He embraced Baitullah in a burst of exuberance and said, "Congratulations. You have downed your first enemy helicopter."

Suleiman joined in. Playing on Baitullah's vanity was the surest way to win him over completely. "*Mubarak ho janaab. Aap ne to pehle hi missile se dushman ko uda dala*" (Congratulations. With your first missile itself, you have destroyed a enemy helicopter)

Other Mujahidin were converging towards them. Baitullah stood up, lifted his launcher over his head like a triumphant boxer. Shahnawaz put down his own launcher, took one step behind Baitullah and then shouted in triumph as the Baitullah's warriors closed, "Your leader has destroyed a Soviet helicopter."

## V

After that it was easy. Shahnawaz won them over. He spent the next two months there training the Mujahidin, explaining to them the nuances of firing a Stinger missile – aim at the tail, not the nose, launch when the target was around two kilometres away, that was the most effective range; fire in a 30 degree cone and the missile would home in by itself. They were fast learners, these Mujahidin and he was a good teacher.

He returned to Pakistan two months later and briefed both Brigadier Yusuf and the US CIA station chief in Islamabad on the outcome of his mission. When he returned a month later, he had with him a team of twelve ISI and CIA operatives and another consignment of 60 launchers and 300 missiles.

Yusuf repeatedly emphasized before his departure, "Meet all the Mujahidin leaders. Get them all on our side. Remember, we have long term plans for them."

And meet them all he did. Over the next two years, he travelled across all of Afghanistan, meeting each Mujahidin leader, providing weapons and sleeping bags, first aid kits and radio sets, emergency rations, boots and satellite phones. He got their wounded in to Pakistan, arranged safe houses for them. He planted a team of Pakistani officers and men with each group. He developed ties between the Mujahidin groups and the Pakistani government that would last a decade, even though the ties would sour and the same groups turn against them in later years.

The course of the war slowly began turning. The Stinger missiles neutralized the Soviet army's most potent weapon, their gunships, forcing them to fight on ground. Faced with steady attrition, the Soviet army became increasingly demoralized. The stage was slowly being set for their eventual retreat and Shahnawaz would have played a big role in it.

### VI

In 1984, Shahnawaz had two major turning points in his life – one on the personal, one on the professional front. In June 1984, the twins, Aftab and Mehtab, arrived at Islamabad Military Hospital. It was a joke between him and Shazia as to how they managed to produce them at all. After all, in the past two years, they had barely spent two consecutive nights together.

But he was there when they came. He was there to hold Shazia's hand, he was there to scoop little Salim, now all of four, to see his new brothers, he was there when Shazia gave them their first feed. He was there to take them home, five of them now, and proudly present them to *Ammajaan*, lying in her bed.

Old age had not been kind to Nazneen. Her diabetes and chronic arthritis had left her bed-ridden for over a year. She stayed with them – or rather with Shazia, since he was away most of the time – and spent her days in the most airy and sunlit room of their house, lying propped up on pillows, reading her Quran, watching her television. Her long illness had taken its toll, but when Shahnawaz bent over her with the two babies cradled in his arms, her eyes shone. She reached out for them, placed the Quran lightly over their tiny heads and blessed them

'*Yeh to chand ke tukde hai. Kitne sunder hai yeh. Dono tumhare Abbajan par gaye hai*". (How beautiful they are. They have gone just on your father) She glanced sideways at Salim standing sulkily to a side, resentful that he was no longer the centre of attention.

"*Lekin mere Salim jaisa to koi nahin hai. Id ka chand to wohi hai*". (But. of course, there is nobody like my Salim.)She reached out to her eldest grandson and drew him to her.

For Nazneen, the arrival of all her grandchildren completed her cycle of life. She saw her own husband in the twins, she saw her own dimples in Salim's (Shazia too had very pretty dimples, but she conveniently ignored that fact – she was a mother-in-law after all). It did not matter that Shahnawaz was not their biological son. Maybe she had even forgotten the fact that Shahnawaz had been found abandoned in a field, his true parents unknown. That did not matter. Neither did it matter that Shahnawaz was not their blood. It made no difference. After all, he was their heart.

She died in her sleep three months after the twins came home. She had a small smile on her face – as though she was seeing her husband in the distant light that was coming closer. Perhaps she had a premonition of her death. The Quran was open, resting on her chest and the page opened to the first lines of the Muslim prayer for the dead.

## VII

In 1984, Shahnawaz also received another assignment. This time he was sent to Lahore to interrogate a group of Sikh militants who had crossed over from India to Pakistan.

There were six of them – young, hot-blooded and angry. Shahnawaz looked at the boys. For a fleeting instance memories of the Mukti Bahini – the Indian trained Mukti Bahini – in East Pakistan came back to him. The memories of the year in a prisoner of war camp returned and the pent-up bitterness resurfaced. He knew how he could use these boys.

And so the first training camp for Sikh militants came up at a village called Bedian, near Lahore. Shahnawaz supervised the initial setting up himself. He helped Sikh youth cross over, trained them, sent them back to India with weapons and explosives, briefed them in conducting raids and ambushes. By the end of the year, the second camp came up, then others. By 1987, over 2000 Sikh militants had been trained and sent in to Punjab, to launch vicious terrorist strikes there and bleed India's most prosperous state.

By 1987 also, the Soviets had enough in Afghanistan and announced their intention to leave. The Soviet withdrawal would eventually be completed only in 1989 and it would be a major victory by the Mujahidin over a superpower. A victory in which Shahnawaz's actions had played a major role.

And so, it was no surprise that in 1987, Shahnawaz received an out-of-turn promotion to the rank of Lieutenant Colonel. And he was called for a congratulatory cup of tea in the office of none other than President Zia-ul-Haq himself.

President Zia peered at him through his hooded eyes, the dark rings around them accentuating the sense of menace and intrigue they contained. But when he spoke, his voice was gentle and courtly, almost like a kindly uncle, not at all like the military dictator of a country.

"I have been briefed about the good work you have been doing in Afghanistan. It is a great service to our nation. But remember, the ties you have developed with the groups must be maintained. I have long-term plans for them"

He prattled on for a while, talking of Afghanistan, of the USA, of Kashmir, of Islam, switching between topics randomly, as was his wont.

"And how is your wife? I have heard she is a good singer. Of course, one should spend more time in prayer than in singing."

Shahnawaz did not reply to that. After all, when your President expresses an opinion, you don't contradict him.

Then he said abruptly.

"I think we should start focusing on Kashmir now. The time has come to get it back from the Indians." He gave a hard, bitter smile, "We have to pay them back for 1971, don't we?"

# YEARS OF CHANGE

## 1987-1992

*In the last years of the 1980s, the course of both nations were changing. Pakistan had spent almost a decade under President Zia-ul-Haq – a decade which saw greater Islamisation in the nation, and also growing involvement with the militant groups in Afghanistan. Both policies would have disastrous consequences in later years.*

*In Afghanistan, the Soviets were forced to withdraw in 1989. And now the Mujahedeen – trained, funded and cultivated by the Pakistani Army and ISI – were unemployed. They would be put to good use in Kashmir.*

*In August 1988,President Zia-ul-Haq was killed in an inexplicable air crash near Bahawalnagar. Conspiracy theories abounded, but none could be fully proved. In the coming General elections, Benazir Bhutto, – Zulfiqar Bhutto's equally charismatic and ambitious daughter took over as Pakistan's first lady Prime Minister. Pakistan went back to civilian rule, but there was no change to its policies. With the war in Afghanistan winding down, the focus shifted to Kashmir. In the unrest of Kashmir, Pakistan funneled in the Afghan Mujahedeen to wage another 'jihad' in the troubled state.*

### II

*India too, was going through its own process of change. With the assassination of Mrs Gandhi in 1984, her pilot-turned-politician son, Rajiv took over as Prime Minister. Much was expected from the young, charismatic Rajiv Gandhi, and yes, there were initial signs of change. But the hopes dissipated soon enough.*

*Promises of a clean, honest government were washed away as his government got embroiled in wide-spread corruption. In his short spell, Rajiv Gandhi had sent the Indian Peace Keeping Force into Sri Lanka in 1987 to maintain peace between the Sri Lankan government and the Tamil rebels. The deployment was a blunder. The LTTE turned against them, and after two inclusive years, the force was finally returned with little to show.*

*In 1987, India faced another watershed moment. Elections were held in Jammu and Kashmir elections which were allegedly rigged to enable the Congress Party to win. The rigged elections sparked a wave of protests – and soon degenerated in to an armed movement demanding 'Azadi,' or complete freedom from India. The movement escalated in to a full-blown insurgency, abetted and supported by Pakistan. Pakistani trained militants crossed over to wage a bitter conflict within the state. For over a decade, the insurgency raged, tearing Kashmir, claiming over 60,000 casualties and once again destroying relations between India and Pakistan.*

# JULLANDHAR – JAFFNA – JAMMU

## 1985–1992

1984 was perhaps the worst year in the history of our nation. After the attack on the Golden Temple, the assassination of Mrs Gandhi and the Anti-Sikh riots, another tragedy struck before the year closed. On the night of 2-3 December, the poison gas, Methyl Isocyanate, seeped out of a malfunctioning Union Carbide plant in Bhopal. It spread over the sleeping town like a specter and when it finally wafted away, it took over three thousands with it. It claimed thousands, except those who were truly responsible for it.

Perhaps the nation was being punished – only the punishment was being meted out to innocents, as always – just as the innocents had been punished during the Anti-Sikh riots. The scars on the Sikh community would take years to heal. But heal they did, fortunately.

I saw the slow process of healing and reintegration in the years that followed. Nivedita and the children remained behind at Delhi at Masterji's insistence as I sojourned through my different postings. Masterji's home was the mooring to my family now. And the home which had accepted me within its walls and its heart as its own, also became the home for my wife and children.

And I was glad that Gaurav, Vikram and Supriya had the stabilizing influence of Masterji during my frequent absences. My father, with his quiet strength was the greatest support system that we had. But without knowing it, I was losing two equally strong support systems, two people I loved intensely – my brothers. We had drifted apart, like so many brothers, each following our own lives. Vishal was in Mumbai now, a rising nuclear scientist with the Bhabha Atomic Research Centre. Kunal, a lecturer at the Indian Institute of Management, Ahmadabad, with two published books to his name was already being recognized as a modern day management guru. They came to Delhi rarely, and with each visit I realised even more how our relationship was fraying, and the difference between us. Here was I, a JCO in the army, nothing much to speak of, and there were they, rising stars with glittering careers, living in a different world altogether. They never did or said anything to show it, but the difference hovered in the background, like unspoken words.

But the growing distance between me and my brothers was more than just the social divide. It had more to do with our presence at Masterji's home, the house here at C-3 Janakpuri. That aspect would come to the surface at a time when I would lose the man I loved most – my father. Then I would also lose my two brothers. And their loss would hurt even more.

## II

The years between 1987 and 1992 were not very happy ones. In July 1987 we moved out virtually overnight to Jaffa, Sri Lanka, as part of the Indian Peace Keeping force there. For two years we remained there, fighting a Liberation Tigers of Tamil Eelam, the bitterest and most dangerous opponent we had ever encountered. We were sniped at virtually daily and attacked with bombs and Improvised Explosive Devices by an enemy we rarely saw. It was a dirty, cruel war and what made it worse was the hostility we faced from some of our own people. I still remember the slogan shouting crowds at Chennai, jeering at us, taunting us, calling for us to leave Sri Lanka. In a difficult war in a hostile nation, the fact that a segment of our own people was against us, hurt. It really hurt.

And when we finally moved out from Sri Lanka in 1989, it was with sense of absolute relief. We moved to a familiar zone, the town of Jammu, the winter capital of Jammu and Kashmir. Jammu would have normally been a lovely place to be in. This city of forts and temples, nestled on the banks of the Jhelum River was not yet affected by the insurgency that was now raging across most of Kashmir. But it was definitely singed by its flames.

We saw the effects of the insurgency in Kashmir while in Jammu. We saw it in the refugee camps filled with Kashmiri Hindu families who had been forced to flee the valley. We saw it in the increasing number of casualties that began trickling into the military hospital. We heard about the cousin killed in a bomb blast at Srinagar, a newly married brother-in-law crippled in a rocket strike at Anantnag, a dear friend blinded in a grenade attack at Gulmarg. And these were only the casualties on one side.

The actual casualties of the war were the thousands of Kashmiri civilians – those misguided youth who crossed over to Pakistan, only to be shot when they returned, the innocents trapped between the security forces and the militants, those who disappeared, taken away by militants or security forces to God-knows-where. The nameless casualties of Kashmir ran in to thousands. And the Indian government's lack of sensitivity perhaps prolonged the insurgency by years.

They were not very happy years, the years I spent there between 1990 and 1992. And 1992 was unhappy in more ways than one. That was the year I lost Masterji. It was also the year when I fell out with my brothers. 1992 was also the year when I retired after 25 years in the army. My last year in uniform would be one of the saddest ones I have ever had.

# CARRYING 'JIHAD' TO KASHMIR

## Afghanistan-Kashmir 1988-92

Shahnawaz looked around at the harsh, desolate landscape. It was as bleak as always, harsh and fierce, cold and uncompromising as the people who inhabited it. There was nothing to break the monotony of the land. It was just lines of grey-brown mountains rolling away from crest line to crest line. The only signs of movement and human activity came from the Soviet military camp tucked within the valley.

Shahnawaz turned his binoculars towards the camp. It was almost dismantled now, the tents folded, the barracks stripped of their fitments, the generators and water purifiers packed in crates. From the distance, he could hear the sounds of heavy diesel engines revving up, see the exhaust belch from the Kraz and Tatra trucks lined up there. Then the line of trucks moved out of the camp, crawled on to the dirt track and began heading westwards.

Baitullah was next to him, surveying the scene with his own binoculars. His men were there too, weapons in hand as always. He hoped none of them would fire. Not even in the air in celebration. He did not want any incident at this juncture.

Shahnawaz beamed, turned to Baitullah, "So my friend. You have done it. You have defeated the Soviets. They are leaving."

Wazir laughed out loud, clapped one heavy hand across Shahnawaz's back, "The fools. No enemy has been able to occupy Afghanistan. No one can tame us Afghans. No one."

Shahnawaz laughed back, "None can defeat you. You have won this *jihad*." He paused. "But, my friend, for a great *jihadi* like you, your battles are not over. There are other places where the *jihad* must continue."

Wazir narrowed his eyes. The shrewd warrior knew what was coming.

Shahnawaz continued, "Across the world, Muslims are being oppressed. In Kashmir, the Indians have trampled over our Muslim brethren. The Kashmiris have been waging their *jihad* for freedom for years now. They need brave, strong soldiers of Islam to help them in their battle. And we will pay you very well for your help."

Wazir stood up, gesticulated towards the long line of trucks moving slowly towards the west, "We have defeated a superpower. We are now ready for another *jihad* in Kashmir."

## II

Shahnawaz returned from Afghanistan for the final time in early 1990. His task there was a complete success. His next role now lay in Kashmir.

Kashmir had been on the boil for some time now – since 1987 when the Indian politicians rigged elections and set off a wave of protests amongst the local population. And when they clamped-down on the protests with their usual heavy handedness they played in to their hands even more. Hundreds of angry, disgruntled Kashmiri youth, streamed in to Pakistan, had been welcomed there, trained, equipped and sent back in to India. Now was the time to add fuel to the fire. And the fuel would be provided by the same Afghan Mujahedeen that Shahnawaz had carefully cultivated.

Shahnawaz had returned to the army after five years of deputation with the ISI and it felt good to be back in uniform. To his uniform were now added the epaulettes and red tabs of a Colonel. He had been promoted just a few months ago and had taken over an infantry battalion on the craggy peaks along the Line of Control in Kashmir. Opposite him were the Indian positions, in posts as craggy and barren as their own and beyond that the tantalizingly close road to Srinagar.

Shahnawaz walked around the perimeter of his battalion defences. He always did that, but today he wanted to be doubly sure. Today was important.

His men were ready, he had briefed them personally and they knew what to do. His mortars were located centrally, from where he could control their fire himself, the heavy machine guns were armed and cocked. He looked at his watch. 8.45 now. It was dark already, but he would wait another hour. In this moonless night, the inky darkness would provide the cover he required.

From the shadows Wazir emerged. He was in his usual *firhan*, a flat Afghan cap on his head. Yet beneath that rugged clothing was a Kevlar bullet-proof vest, and in one hand was a M-16 assault rifle, a satellite phone in the other.

"Ready, old friend," he clapped him on his shoulder

Wazir nodded, "Yes, we are. But I hope so are your men."

"They are. As you leave we will open fire on the Indians with all we have. We will fire all night and keep their heads down. That will give you cover to get across, enter India and do what you have to do."

Baitullah nodded again, "We know what we have to do. And we will do it well. Don't forget, we defeated the Soviets. The Indians will be easy."

Shahnawaz smiled to himself. The confidence of this man was amazing. Here he was, all set to cross three lines of Indian defences, infiltrate in to Kashmir, wreak havoc there, and come back the same way. Yet, on his face there was only the tension of expectation. No fear.

He put both his hands on Wazir's shoulders, "We have an hour to go. Try and get some rest, you have a long night ahead. May God guide you and give you success in this jihad as well."

## III

Shahnawaz waited till it was ten, when night was inky black, and then gave the signal. And every weapon in his battalion opened up at the Indian positions opposite. It began with automatics and mortars, then even the carbines and rifles opened up. The Indians responded vehemently. After the first few minutes of confusion, they returned the fire in far greater volume than he anticipated.

That was good. It meant that their soldiers were in their bunkers and firing from the sanctuary of their defences. They would be none out in the open now.

He signaled again. Wazir emerged, along with twenty of his men. He gestured, they filed out. They did not have to say much. They had been through the plan repeatedly. Wazir and his men would cross the Line of Control in groups of twos and threes while the Indians were distracted by the fire, link up with another group who would hide them inside and then spend the next three weeks launching a series of strikes inside Kashmir.

Shahnawaz intensified his fire for the next hour or so till he was sure Wazir and his men had crossed the Indian positions. At around four in the morning, he got the radio signal. One word, "Jehangir'. Wazir had linked up with the group awaiting him on the other side.

He returned three weeks later on another moonless night. There were sixteen now, five killed in encounters with the Indians. But they carried with them the flush of success. They had attacked a CRPF post at Pulgaon, wiped out two Hindu families in a village near Anant Nag, blown up a culvert on the road to Srinagar and ambushed an army patrol. Their first mission was a success and they got a grisly memento to prove it.

"Here," he laughed, as he embraced Shahnawaz near his command post, "We have got something for you."

One of his men opened the draw string of a canvas kit bag, turned it over, shook it and let the contents roll out.

Shahnawaz stared at what had fallen out, tried hard not to let the nausea overcome him. There on the hard ground, rolled three heads, purple and putrefying. One had his eyes partly open, another an expression of sheer terror permanently engraved upon it, the third face was surprisingly serene. He gave another shake to the bag. Two metallic hemispheres clattered out. They were Indian helmets, blood-stained, but complete with chin straps and camouflage webbing.

Wazir laughed evilly, kicked one of the helmets, "How do you like the present I have got for you from India?"

# ORPHANED AGAIN

## March 1992, New Delhi

I call the call sometime around noon. How could I forget the date, it was 02 March 1992.

It was the day Prime Minister Narsimhan Rao announced the new economic policy for India and the economy liberalized and came out of its shackles. It was the day the Indian economy began its slow climb upwards to take millions out of poverty.

I could imagine Masterji sitting at the table, newspaper in hand, smiling in approval as he scanned the headlines, then going through each line, word by word, starting with the front page, then the editorials hailing it, then the Op-ed page with its objective commentary, then the sports page where Pakistan had just beaten India in another one day international at Sharjah, and then page three where he would linger longer than he would have liked known. He was fond of filmy gossip, the old man, though he would never admit to it. Then he would have folded the paper neatly, placed it carefully to his side and said, "*Chalo, yeh to theekh hua hai*".

In fact, Nivedita told me that was exactly what happened that morning at eight. He did all that, stood up, and then fell back to his chair coughing violently. He asked for a glass of water, took a few small sips, mopped his perspiring forehead and then slumped backwards, just like that. By the time the ambulance arrived and a frantic Nivedita and Gaurav put him in it, it was already too late. The attendant had pulled the white sheet over his face even before the ambulance reached Ram Manohar Lohia hospital.

I reached the hospital late in the evening. And it took just one look at Nivedita's face, that crumpled face with Gaurav trying manfully to console her, to know what had happened. No words were necessary. In any case no words could convey the magnitude of our loss.

Vishal was already there when I arrived. Kunal flew in from Ahmadabad around midnight. We huddled together, three bereft brothers, sharing a common legacy of memories and loss. Kunal cried openly, he was always the emotional, sensitive one; Vishal and I held on to him in silence.

We took him home one final time from the hospital the next day – no, from the morgue, that's where he was. His face was still set and severe, perfectly shaved, his few thin strands of hair combed neatly back. He was in his usual spotless white *kurta* and *pyjama* and one eye was partially open. I tried to close it, it didn't.

I performed the last rites. Led the prayers at the cremation, got the ashes back home, immersed them in the Yamuna the next day and tried to hold us all together in our grief. I was the eldest of the family now.

The eldest in the family? Oh no. My position in the family unraveled just two weeks after his death, almost immediately after the thirteenth day ceremony. That's when I realized that I had not just lost my father. My brothers were lost to me as well.

Vishal broached it first. There were just the three of us, him, Kunal and me sitting in the small courtyard with the huge sense of emptiness hanging around it. The two of them must have discussed it amongst themselves many times before. The words seemed rehearsed.

He cleared his throat, paused and then blurted, "Now that father is not here. You won't stay in this house, will you?"

I started. It was something that had not even struck me. I had never even thought about it. After all Masterji would be there forever, wouldn't he?

He continued. "You will have to leave the house. Our father has made no will. So the house will go only to his legitimate heirs – no?"

I still didn't comprehend. Then Kunal interjected cruelly, cutting me with the most hurtful words I had heard in the forty odd years I had been their brother.

"After all, you are not his legal heir. You are not really part of the family, you were adopted. You don't really have any right over the house."

And for me, I now became orphaned the third time over. The first time when my father died way back in 1948. Then two weeks ago when Masterji left. And now with these words.

I did not know what to reply, but my eyes filled with tears at the sorrow of a greater loss than just Masterji. I reached out to my brothers, embraced them, felt their bodies stiffen beneath, but they did not withdraw.

"The house, everything in it, was Masterji's. It is yours now. That's how he would have wanted it. I want no part of it. I am not his legal heir, I was only his son. I have no stake in it. It is yours."

I looked around our small one-storey home with its little courtyard running around it. The home which had embraced me when I came to it from another land. The home where I grew up in; where my mother and father brought me up as their own. Was that home mine? Did I truly belong here all these years? I think I did.

I looked at that house again. The house which would soon come under redevelopment and be replaced by a seven story building. The house for which a builder would pay a small fortune. That house was not mine. It belonged to Vishal and Kunal. All I had of that were its memories. And memories are either priceless, or worth nothing, depending on how you look back upon them.

We moved out the next month. Found a small two room tenement which we tried to make a home. A home without Masterji. I handed over the keys of the house to Kunal, and gave away a major part of my life. But then that house was never mine, I was never the legal heir, remember. But that home always was, I was always the son and always would remain.

# Out of Uniform

## 1992

I checked my uniform one last time, smoothened the creases on my trousers, adjusted my belt and pulled down my beret. I thought I looked okay. A little heavy now, a little bald and grey, but okay. But then the uniform always made me look good and feel nice about myself.

I saluted and walked in to Colonel Bedi's office. He was commanding the unit now. It would be the last day I would enter his office. It would be the last day I would be wearing this uniform

Colonel Bedi smiled, reached out to shake hands. It was an old custom, this farewell interview and a cup of tea with the Commanding Officer when a person retired. But it was more than just a ritual. There was genuine warmth and concern.

"So," he smiled. "Twenty six years. It has been a long journey. How do you feel now, leaving after all these years? And what do you plan to do."

Twenty six years. I was leaving after twenty six years. I could not really imagine a life without the army, and actually the thought frightened me. I don't know how I felt, or even what I planned to do. There would be a pension coming in, but not much more. I was just forty five, the army retired its people young.

And in twenty six years, what had I really achieved. Yes, I had become a Junior Commissioned Officer. I had seen the wars. I was there in the corner of the photograph of the surrender ceremony at Dhaka. But beyond that there was really nothing to show for all these years. Again, as it did so many times, the pang of regret of not joining as a officer hit me.

Perhaps my life's achievements would have accounted for something then. I think I was the 'Almost there' man. One who almost reached his destiny, only for it to remain forever unfulfilled.

But I did not say all these things to Colonel Bedi. How could I? I merely parroted the standard, time-tested lines, "Sir, I have been lucky to have had all these years in the army."

## II

And so it was, that in September 1992, I came back in my civvies to our small tenement in Delhi. Back with two trunks and a suitcase, old uniforms, mementoes, new hopes and fears all stuffed in them. I came to a way of life that was alien and intimidating, but it was all that I had now.

In the base of one of the trunks nestled another deadly memento. A .38 Pistol which I had purchased from the stock of surplus obsolescent weapons, which the army sold to servicemen. I had applied for it, brought it for a princely Rupees 112/ and then forgot all about it. It would lie in my cupboard for another ten years, cleaned and oiled regularly, but never used. I would use it only once in my life in what would be the culminating moment of my life.

In these fears and uncertainties of my new life, there was Nivedita to give me strength. With Time, there was that little heaviness around her hips and waist and in her hair were flashes of grey. But her face remained as unlined as ever, her eyes still sparkled, her laughter was still ready and spontaneous. She had that rare quality, which I could never attain – contentment. In the little that we had, she created a world for us, a small, compact world. And her calm and happiness spread its wings over the five of us who lived in that world.

Her stability had percolated down to Gaurav, Vikram and Supriya. She gave the focus to each one of them, the strength to choose their destinies and then follow it to the hilt. Gaurav was appearing for his Indian Military Academy exams – the decision was his, not mine, but my own little urgings would have helped in some measure. He gave the exam, went through the long interviewing process that followed, and just sailed through. We were all there at the station that June 1993, when he jumped on to the train taking him to the Indian Military Academy at Dehradun. He would pass out of the Academy a year and a half later, toss up his cap in celebration, have his mother and me pin the stars on his shoulders and become an officer. It is strange how we look to our children to fulfil our own ambitions. My son had attained all I never could, and in the short life that he had ahead of him he would achieve more than most ever did.

1993 was also the year when I received the call from Kunal, sometime in August.

It was the first time he was calling after father's death and the events that followed. His voice was strained, almost apologetic, and I knew his gesture was in part to atone for what he had done.

"*Bhaiyya*," he began. It felt good to hear the '*Bhaiyya*' again. He paused, "What are you doing these days."

I would have normally launched in to my usual litany of how great everything was, and how I was loving every moment of my time – you know, the usual façade I put up. Instead, I blurted out, "Nothing, I am fed up with doing nothing."

"Would you be interested in a job?"

A job? You bet. I had been stagnating for over six months and needed something to do.

He continued, "One of my students is starting his own Company at Delhi. He is looking for a Security and Administration Officer – preferably ex-Army – I thought of you."

Kunal, as a lecturer at the Indian Institute of Management was already a recognized Management guru. Some of the best management graduates in the country had gone through him. It would have taken just one call from him to clinch it.

And so in June 1993, I reported to the office of Accent InfoSolutions at Gurgaon, in my ill-fitting suit and best tie. My role was not much, just looking after the administration and security of the office complex, but it was something I had been doing all my life. And I found it surprisingly easy after a while. I enjoyed the role. I liked the financial security it provided. I liked the easy informality of the office and the sense of routine. And after all, I had finally become an officer.

# ISLAMABAD

## 1992-1999

Shahnawaz smiled as the sounds of a *ghazal* floated over his study. It rose gently, the voice climbing, testing its own limits, then dropped and flowed like a calm, melodious river through their home.

He was back in Islamabad, after a grueling stint along the Line of Control, this time posted to General Headquarters. It felt good to be back home again with Shazia, Salim, Aftab and Mehtab.

He put aside the file he had been working on and let the music go through him. This was the best part of the day, these early morning sessions, when he worked in his study, and Shazia practiced in the music room. Her voice rose, clear and strong, blending perfectly with the harmonium accompanying it. The sheer beauty of the music made the hair on his forearms stand on end.

It always did that, Shazia's songs. Her songs of lost and found love, her ballads of longing, mystical Sufi songs, ghazals, each one of them. He was glad that she had continued with her music even after marriage. In the years when it was frowned at for a woman to be seen in public without her husband, she sang unescorted at concerts and shows, appeared on radio and television (with her hair demurely covered by a impeccably selected scarf). Her first album had been released last year. It was not really a runaway hit, but got her noticed as an emerging new talent in Pakistani music. And now she was preparing for the next.

The harmonium picked up another melody and Shazia's voice intertwined effortlessly with it. The river followed another course, this song was a nostalgic tune of a happy childhood memory. Her practice would go on for another hour, and then she would emerge, radiant and exhausted, downstairs.

Salim walked in to his study, father and son high-fived each other and he whispered.

"I am going to Imran's place this morning. He is going for his graduation to the US. We are having a farewell party for him."

They didn't have to whisper. Shazia's room was tucked away from external sounds. But it was a family ritual. When she practiced, they kept silent.

Salim continued, "And most probably, Zaheer is also leaving next semester. His father has got him admission in Berkeley."

The implications were clear. Salim was hinting when his own father would start the process to send him abroad as well.

"I don't know why your generation is so fixated with going abroad. What's wrong with our own universities?"

Salim snorted; the derisive snort of a strong-willed teenager, "*Pah*. There is no future here. We have to go abroad to make our lives."

"You mean the girls are prettier there. Anyway we will see about that when the time comes."

They had this conversation quite often before and Shahnawaz could not really understand the obsession with today's youth to leave their own country and pursue their dreams elsewhere. But then there was a disillusionment in the country, especially amongst the youth. The politicians, as always were too obsessed with their petty feuding and money-making to do anything about the country.

But even as his own nation seemed adrift, Shahnawaz's own career was well and truly on course. He was a brilliant soldier, a proven war veteran with an impeccable record, and yes, he did know the right people at the right places. His Brigadier's epaulettes were but a matter of time, and something he undeniably deserved.

The promotion to Brigadier came on 28th May 1998, at a time when the streets of Islamabad were filled with celebrating, flag-waving crowds. What a day it was. What a great day for Pakistan.

It was the day Pakistan had just conducted its nuclear test – six of them – in response to the five tests that India had conducted a fortnight earlier. They conducted one more – a point had to be made, didn't it. And the point was made. The two antagonistic nations were now possessors of the deadly bomb.

Shahnawaz, like millions of other Pakistanis, cheered at the news. And the same thought that dominated Pakistani thinking, crossed his mind as well, "We have the bomb. Now we will show the bloody Indians what we are."

He would get a chance to show the Indians soon enough. Just a month later, in July 1998, he put on his Brigadier's epaulettes and took over a famous, battle hardened brigade located at Skardu. His brigade was located on the Line of Control, directly opposite the Indian positions at a place which would soon grip the imaginations of both nations.

The name of the place was Kargil.

# "WE HAVE THE BOMB"

## New Delhi, 13 May 1998

*"Bharat Mata ki Jai"*

*"Vande Mataram"*

"We have the Bomb. We are a world power"

*"Parmanu bomb Zindabad"*

*Parmanu bomb Zindabad?* Long live the Atom Bomb? How ridiculous the slogan was. But though the English was not correct, I could understand the sentiment behind it all. I could share the joyousness of the cheering, slogan shouting crowd that thronged the Delhi-Gurgaon highway. Even though the crowds stalled traffic, this time I did not mind the delay.I too shared the euphoria and sense of triumph that gripped the nation.

India had just detonated a series of nuclear tests – five in all – deep in the subterranean shafts of Pokharan on the 11 and 13 of May 1998. I smiled with pride each time I read the news. I remembered my own role at creating the shafts at Pokharan during the first test, way back in 1974. Mine was a small role then, but my brother Vishal – so what, if now estranged- had played a greater, far more vital role in this one. I saw him in the photos of the site, standing with the team of nuclear scientists, dressed in an ill-fitting army uniform, hand upraised, hisfingers forming a triumphant 'V'. Dr APJ Kalam, the unassuming leader of the team was there in the centre. He would become one of India's best Presidents and Vishal himself would rise to be one of India's top nuclear scientists. Masterji would have been beaming with pleasure when he saw the same photographs in "The Celestial Times" up there.

I was smiling to myself as I eased my Maruti 800 in to our new home. We had shifted to a modern, more spacious apartment last year, courtesy my new job. The Indian economy was on the upswing and like millions of other Indians, I was tasting the fruit of India's economic success story. It sure tasted sweet.

I was beaming broadly as I rang the bell. I could hear laughter coming in from within, the loud, uninhibited laughter that Gaurav brought on during his infrequent visits home. I could feel the vibrancy and happiness within, hear his long strides approaching, and then Gaurav hurled open the door and hugged me in a tight father-son embrace.

"Gaurav," I half- laughed, half-sobbed at the sheer pleasure of seeing him again. I caught the newly acquired leanness around his arms and shoulders, the fine lines of decision forming around his lips, the deep confidence in the eyes, and also the strands of white – just two or three of them around the temples, which only a parent would notice. He looked good, my son.

I hugged him again, held him at arm's length to take a closer look, "You are looking good. How long are you here? I hope it is not your usual touch-and- go trip."

Gaurav laughed, slapped me across the shoulders with that teenage playfulness which had never quite left him. Ouch. He didn't know his strength now, "Oh no! This time it is for two full weeks. A long time."

A long time? Two weeks would go like this. Ever since he had been posted to Anantnag, in insurgency-ridden Kashmir, his spells of leave had been few and far in between.

Over the next two weeks, I realized that my son had matured faster than his 26 years. I also realized the reasons for the strands of pre-mature grey in his hair. It was not only the trauma of daily patrolling in Kashmir, or the nerve wracking tension of a likely ambush at virtually any corner. It was more with the conflict of emotions that he faced as they battled insurgency in Kashmir. The knowledge that they were facing a segment of their own countrymen, misguided maybe, but countrymen still the same, was not a pleasant one. The knowledge of the widows, the young dead, the deathless dead was not an easy one to live with. Fighting an insurgency is a dirty business. It can maim for life and the wounds it inflicts on the mind never really heal.

The two weeks of his leave went by fast – way too fast. Then again, it was the drive to the station, putting him on the train, waving as it pulled out, and then returning to an incomplete home. We had done it for years now, but could never really get over that feeling.

He came again, just for two days, at Divali. That would be the last Divali we celebrated together. He would never come home thereafter. Just a few months later, he would move to a place called Kargil. There on a remote and insignificant mountain top he would fall, and there we would lose him forever.

# PAKISTANI SIDE OF THE LINE OF CONTROL

### Skardu, January 1999

The staff car carrying General PervezMusharraf, the Chief of the Pakistani Army, rolled in to Shahnawaz's Brigade Headquarters at nine on the minute, the time he had said he would arrive. That was one of his better traits. He never kept subordinates waiting.

He returned Shahnawaz's salute, greeted him warmly and allowed himself to be escorted in to the Operations Room. There was no one in the room. It was just the three of them; General Musharraf, the Corps Commander and Brigadier Shahnawaz Khan, the commander of the elite Skardu Brigade. What they had to discuss was for their ears only, at least for now. Soon the whole world would hear of it.

General Musharraf took his place at the briefing table, accepted a cup of tea and lit up a cigarette. Shahnawaz had ensured that a packet of Wills Kings cigarettes – Musharraf's favoured brand – was on the table. The General smoked occasionally, and as was common knowledge, only when he was tense.

Shahnawaz unlocked the padlock on the map cabinet, unfurled a map. He had marked the map himself the last night. No one else had been involved, not his Deputy, not his Operations Officer, not a soul. No one had an inkling as to what was afoot – hopefully.

The map of the sector unfolded and the Line of Control – a jagged line in red and green – slashed its way across it. On both sides of the line were defensive positions, marked in red on the Indian side, blue in theirs. A thin, red ribbon of road meandered behind the Indian positions. For the most part, the map was barren, except for the contour lines of brownrunning over it. Those thin lines depicted mammoth heights on the ground and held the key to the plans that would unfold.

"Shahnawaz," General Musharraf exhaled blue smoke, "I served with your father, knew him well. He almost got Kashmir for us in 1947. He came very close to success in 1965. I have now appointed you to complete his work."

He walked over to the map, taking over the operations room completely. He knew each line of that map. He had served in these heights himself.

"What I want you to do," he turned to the map, pointed to a line of ridges on the Indian side of the Line of Control and traced his finger slowly along them, "Is to occupy these positions".

"These are the heights around Kargil. From there you will be able to dominate the Indian National Highway 1A." He indicated to the red ribbon of road meandering along on the Indian side, "This is the road over which their suppliesto Northern Kashmir travel. Block this road and the entire Indian positions in the sector will collapse."

"The heights you are to take are not occupied by the Indians in the winter. All your brigade has to do is occupy them and then sit tight."

"But Sir, they will not just let us sit. They will react violently."

"Shahnawaz, you have seen these heights. They are cliff tops, each over 11000 feet high. Do you think it will be easy for the Indians to reach there, if you and your men are on the crest above? You will be able to wipe them out before they even come close."

Shahnawaz knew that was true. At those altitudes, attacking a well-entrenched defender would be almost suicidal.

General Musharraf continued, "You will occupy these heights, very slowly, very gradually. Secrecy is the key here, remember that. We have surprise on our side. The Indians are not expecting this. Get hold of these peaks. When the Indians attack, you will be able to beat them back. We will say that Kashmiri freedom fighters are occupying them. It will shift world focus back on Kashmir. Once we have attained victory in Kargil, we will again press our claims for Kashmir."

"And, yes. We will take some of the Mujahedeen with us. I think we need to use those friends of yours once again." He smiled, "After all, we have paid them a small fortune over the years. Let us get back our money's worth."

Even Shahnawaz had to admit that it was a bold, simple plan – almost brilliant by its sheer audacity. But what if the Indians attacked elsewhere?

Musharraf seemed to read his thoughts, 'Don't worry. The Indians will not attack Pakistan. They will not dare. We have the nuclear bomb now."

# INDIAN SIDE OF THE LINE OF CONTROL

## Kargil Heights, May 1999

Shahnawaz shifted uncomfortably. In spite of his coat parka, his snow boots and inner thermals, it was freezing up here. There was no escape from the icy wind that penetrated each pore of his body. The wind never let up, night or day. It howled its way across these mountain tops, carrying with it a chilling, soul-numbing menace.

Suleiman came up, a metal mug of tea in hand, "*Janaab, Chai*". He had been with Shahnawaz throughout the years after Afghanistan. Shahnawaz had ensured that he remained posted with him. Over the years the bonding between the two men had grown. If anything, he was even more dependent on Suleiman now.

He took the tea gratefully. In these heights, one had to replenish fluids as often as possible. He had lost thirty of his men to high altitude illness already and he knew the importance of getting acclimatized to these heights. He finished his tea, and began his usual walk around his positions. He could see the craggy peaks all around him, bare, bleak peaks on which his brigade had been stealthily taking up positions over the past six weeks. They were now almost three-kilometres inside Indian territory and still undetected. So far, so good.

He climbed upwards towards the highest ridgeline and the recently constructed line of *sangars* – makeshift bunkers – there. His men were in their positions there with a few *mujahedeen* fighters interspersed between them. They had been got to give credence to the lie that the operation was being conducted by Kashmiri freedom fighters.

Baitullah Wazir was sitting on a rock around the nearest *sangar,* his Kalashnikov slung around his shoulder. Dressed in his usual shaggy overcoat, fur boots and felt cap, he seemed impervious to the cold. He smiled as Shahnawaz approached and rose.

*'To janaab. Ham to taiyar hai. Bus ab woh Indians ka intezar hai."* (So, we are ready. Now we are only waiting for the Indians)

"Don't worry. The Indians will come soon. For now you must remain hidden and not give away our positions. The longer we remain undetected, the more time we get to strengthen our positions".

He was not too happy at Wazir's presence here. But Musharraf had insisted that the Mujahedeen be incorporated with his brigade to project the image that the heights were indeed occupied only by Kashmiri fighters. And then this man had his uses.

His brigade was now almost in place and his men were beautifully camouflaged and hidden. Below him he could see the ribbon of road, the Indian National Highway 1D which fed its troops. There was no traffic on it now, but that would soon begin. Soon, the Indians would come in too. Soon, very soon, everything would be in place. Soon, History would be calling.

## II

Shahnawaz stood up and stretched. It was a clear day, one of the few they had received in the past month and it felt good to see the sun again. The grey fog that had enveloped them all these days had been depressing.

His men were almost ready now. They had crept forward to the positions they intended to occupy and even his supply lines were slowly coming in place. An Indian patrol had encountered them, but had been eliminated to a man, before it could relay the information back. In fact, the only other humans who had seen them were some Bakewal shepherds grazing their sheep in the lower reaches of these sparse, inhospitable heights. They were still undetected and it suited him. He needed a week or two more to completely stabilise his positions. Then he would be perfectly poised.

From the distance, he heard the sound of an approaching aircraft and instinctively ducked. There was no need for it though. From that distance the aircraft would be able to see nothing.

From its flight path, it seemed to beheading it directly towards his positions. It was a Canberra – the old fighter-bomber, the Indians used for reconnaissance. Even if it overflew their positions, the photographs would reveal little. His men were well concealed, his positions beautifully camouflaged.

The Canberra droned overhead, then banked lazily. He hoped his men had remained under cover as he had ordered. He himself could see no movement. Then a spiral of smoke rose from the adjoining ridge and raced upwards towards the slowly moving Canberra.

The Stinger missile hit the aircraft on the right wing. He saw it judder, saw it bank violently. For a while it seemed that the pilot had lost control and then miraculously, it straightened, levelled and turned back towards Indian territory.

Shahnawaz ran towards the direction where the smoke spiral had emanated. Fuck. He knew who was there. Wazir. Damn him. He had told them repeatedly to just lie doggo. Why the hell did he have to fire the missile? He had given the game away now.

It took twenty minutes of lung-bursting effort to reach Wazir's position. Wazir was there, his wild tribesmen surrounding him in a dance of celebration. He held his missile launcher high in triumph and ran towards Shahnawaz as he approached.

"Did you see that? I have shot down an Indian aircraft."

It took all of Shahnawaz's will power to control his temper. "I think I told you – all of you. There was to be no firing. You have merely given away our position."

'So what,' Wazir was unrepentant, "Let the Indians come. We are ready for them".

It was no use. The fool could never see the big picture. The missile attack would only confirm to the Indians that the heights around Kargil were indeed occupied. He had hoped for another week or so to fully consolidate, but now the Indian attacks would soon begin. But he was ready for them. Almost.

### III

Nivedita was watching the evening news when I reached home. She turned to me, her face a mask of worry.

"They have shot down an aircraft near Kargil. And they have even captured one of our patrols." Her face seemed to crumple. "Will there be war? Will Gaurav be safe?"

I held her, stroked her hair, the way I always did to calm her. "Don't worry. There won't be any war. And Gaurav is safe. He is not in the Kargil sector."

To be honest, I had no idea where Gaurav was. I knew that his unit was still based somewhere near Srinagar, but then units had been moving to Kargil ever since things began heating up there. He had not even called for over two weeks.

The call came that evening. We knew it was him. The single ring of a long distance call could only be his. Nivedita grabbed the phone.

"Gaurav, *beta* where are you? Are you okay?

Standing behind her with Vikram and Supriya crowding around, I could hear his voice, falsely cheerful. "Ma, I am fine. I am still in Kashmir. Wish we had been moving to Kargil though. The excitement is all there."

It was a short call. Less than a minute. He prattled on and then hung up abruptly. "I have to hang up now. There is only one phone here and there is a whole line behind me trying to call home. Will call again soon, bye."

The phone clicked silent. Nivedita replaced it on the cradle. "He has moved to Kargil, hasn't he?"

I didn't say anything. But I knew Gaurav's unit had indeed moved to Kargil. He would never say it on the open telephone, nor would he want us to get worried. But I knew my son. The inflexion in his voice revealed it all. He could never tell a lie in any case.

## IV

Gaurav led his patrol cautiously towards the heights of Tololing. He had intentionally selected a small patrol. It was just a reconnaissance and a small group had lesser chances of being detected. They moved slowly, pausing frequently. At these heights, movement was murder. The lungs struggled merely to suck in some oxygen from the rarefied air.

His unit had been rushed to Kargil two weeks ago and no one really seemed to know what was actually happening and what they had to do. Today was his first task – to check the Pakistani positions in the heights around Tololing.

The Pakistanis were indeed there. They were skillfully camouflaged and had remained undetected for over a month. Even as Gaurav's patrol climbed, their every movement was being observed by their adversaries hidden above. Though, he himself could see no trace of them. There was just one give-away sign – one makeshift bunker wrongly sited and not too well camouflaged. It was his only clue and he kept his eyes focused on it.

He stopped. Behind that small slit hole on the bunker he thought he had seen some movement. Yes, there it was again, he could swear on it this time. He motioned his men to get under cover, edged himself behind a rock, and waited. Waited and watched. Watched that damned bunker till his eyes ached.

There it was again. A brief glimpse of movement behind that small opening. He had to be sure. He unslung his weapon. He had got a 7.92 inch Dragunov sniper rifle just for this. With this high-precision weapon, he could hit a six inch target at 600 yards. He set the range, adjusted the sniper scope and focused the sights on that small weapons slit on the bunker. He closed his eyes for an instant, let them rest. Then he laid the aiming mark on the slit hole of the bunker, took a shallow breath, held it and fired. The round sped upwards, entered through that small slit, penetrated, and then ricocheted wildly in the closed confines of the bunker above.

He had no way of knowing if he hit anybody inside the bunker, but the shot producedjust the effect he hoped for. From the bunker a Browning machine gun opened up, its dull *thump-thump-thump* resounding across the hills. Then the bunkers adjoining it opened up as well, their fire targeting them viciously, pinning them down.

It took four hours to extricate his patrol after that, their move covered by own artillery fire. The moveback was slower and far more painful, weighed down as they were by the bodies of two of his men, who had been hit by the vicious plunging fire. But they had got the information they wanted. The enemy positions around the heights of Tololing were confirmed, their locations somewhat ascertained. Now would come the difficult part, evicting them from these heights.

## V

It had begun. In fact, Shahnawaz wondered why it took so long in coming. The shooting of the Indian Canberra had stirred a hornets' nest and the Indian patrols had increased thereafter. The air attacks had begun too. They had shot down two Indian MIGs and a helicopter and now their aircraft no longer came low, but stayed high, well above the range of their missiles. The Indian attacks too had begun. Initially these were uncoordinated, disjointed attacks which his men beat back with ease from their carefully prepared positions atop. But now the attacks were increasing. Slowly the Indians were closing in, capturing a locality here, a hillock there, a crest elsewhere. And their damned artillery never let up. The salvos just kept pouring in, harassing them, shattering bunkers, breaking morale, and taking a constant toll of casualties that just kept rising.

It was not worrying, at least not as yet. His men were well entrenched and he knew that dislodging them from their heights would be almost impossible. "Hold on," he had been repeatedly told, "Just hold on. The Indians will crack."

And hold on he did. For all of May and most of June. But those damned Indians did not crack. If anything their attacks intensified. Beat back one attack, and they would come back again. Beat that back and they would emerge from another direction. Beat that back, and they would come again, from a third. His overall defensive layout still held firm, but the strain of the continual attacks was telling.

His radio set crackled. It had been set on an Indian frequency that they had identified and intercepted. "Akbar to Bravo One. Reached Charlie Pappa Three Two."

He recognized that voice. It was call sign 'Akbar' one of the Indian officers who had been in the forefront of most of the recent attacks. He was informing his superiors of his location. Too bad it was in code or he could have ordered a mortar salvo on it.

He heard another voice. He recognized that voice too. It was Major Mohammed Akram, one of his best company commanders. His company had withstood three attacks and still stood firm.

*"Akbar. Tum phir se aa gaye. Mubarak ho. Tumhare swagat ke liye ham taiyar hai"* (Akbar, so you have come back. We are ready to welcome you)

Mohammed Akram continued. "*Kyo aa rahe ho upar. Marne ki kya zaldi hai. Bas hame Madhuri Dixit do, ham chale jayenge.*"(Why are you coming up here? What's your hurry to die? Just give us Madhuri Dixit and we will go away)

There was no answer. Even though the Indian would have been seething at being detected, he maintained enough control not to give himself away further. That was what the Pakistanis were hoping for. Another transmission and they could have homed on to his exact location.

The exchanges of insults were a daily occurrence now. And behind it lay the harsh reality. The Indians had closed in so much that they were within touching distance of the peaks. If they captured any of the major heights on the Tololing ridgeline, it would give them a base from where they could roll down and overrun their entire defences. They had beat back three frontal attacks on Tololing so far and he knew the next would not be long in coming. He just hoped that PervezMusharraf was right and that the Indians would call it quits. But quite frankly, at the moment it did not look like it.

## VI

Gaurav halted in his climb. Damn. He should not have made that radio transmission. It had alerted the fucking Pakis. His only consolation was that it was in code and they had no way of knowing where he was. But, he had managed to pass his own location to his Battalion commander so they could monitor his movement. Now, if he could finish that climb by first light, he would be able to reach the heights of Point 5140, the highest point on the Tololing ridgeline. Then if he could just capture the line of bunkers on that height, the same bunkers that had opened fire on him during his first patrol, it would provide the base from where the rest of the battalion could roll downwards to the main line of the Pakistani defences.

He paused. The Pakis had not seen him as yet and they had just a hundred meters more to go. Only it was hundred meters of almost vertical climb and in the darkness it seemed never ending. The cliff side which they were climbing seemed impassable, the climb almost suicidal, but it was the only way to get behind the Pakistani positions undetected.

They resumed their climb again, crawling upwards inch by slow inch. It was so silent and inky black, this night. Each sound his men made, each clink of rifle barrel on rock, each crunch of boot on gravel, each crack of a falling rock seemed to be amplified. But at least the darkness concealed him, and the continual crump of artillery shelling helped muffle their sounds. Just a little more to go now, just another forty meters or so.

They reached the top by four, still cloaked in inky darkness. God, it was a miracle that they had reached undetected. The Pakis obviously did not imagine that anyone could come up from that impassable cliff-side. That side was unguarded.

Even in his exhaustion, Gaurav smiled. He had done it. He was behind the Pakistani positions. Just 400 meters ahead of them was the line of bunkers on Point 5140, six of them – the same ones he had identified on his reconnaissance. In the half-light of the coming dawn, he could see the enemy positions; see the sentries shuffling against the cold, the soldiers asleep in their sleeping bags. Perfect. No one was expecting them now.

Gaurav's platoon formed up in the semi-darkness and then moved downwards, slowly and silently. He wanted to get as close to the bunkers as possible without opening fire, and maintain surprise before the final charge. They had closed in to within 80 meters from the bunkers when the sentry spotted them, shouted and fired a long burst in their direction. Then Gaurav and his men let loose their own answering bursts and raced downwards, screaming like demons, in an adrenal charged fury that carried them on to the Pakistani bunkers below.

Gaurav burst into the first bunker, fired unseeingly in the haze within. Saw a brown uniformed body stumble towards him, fired again, saw him fall. He changed his magazine and raced towards the second bunker, slowed down and lobbed a grenade within. Even before its shock wave subsided, he had rushed in, fired again and again and again. He fired at everything that moved within and continued fired long after they were still.

It took just twenty minutes to clear that line of bunkers. It was always that way. Either the surprise and ferocity of a charge got it immediate victory, or the attack would linger on interminably. He went round bunker to bunker, clearing the remnants, organizing his men to face the Pakistani counter-attack that was bound to follow, and then radioed his success signal.

The Indian flag came up on Point 5140 that morning, but Gaurav had not yet finished. Below him was the next line of bunkers. In that adrenal charged moment, those bunkers, just a few hundred meters away seemed too enticing. He saw the Pakistanis below rushing to their positions, still confused at what was happening. If he could get even one of those bunkers now, it would unhinge them completely.

He charged downhill like a man possessed, just him and his buddy. His men were still holding the bunkers on the heights that they had captured, as he had ordered them to. He raced towards the bunkers, firing continuously; he saw the line of Pakistanis scatter and fall. He saw a huge bear like man, dressed in Afghan felt cap and *firhan*, try to rally his men – they seemed to be in civilian clothing and looked like *mujahidin*, not Pakistani soldiers. He fired towards them, saw three of them fall, he saw the twinkle of gun flashes returning his fire. He saw it all through a red haze, and then felt a thump in his chest, felt himself collapse, saw his buddy fall next to him, and then felt and saw nothing. Nothing at all.

## VII

Shahnawaz raced towards Tololing heights. He had heard of the Indian capture of Point 5140, and understood its implications. That was the highest point of his defences and held the key to his entire defensive layout. The Indians now had the upper hand. Literally. Damn, it was serious.

Major Akram was there, re-organizing his men, trying to get some order back in his defences. He looked fatigued, like all of them. Shahnawaz wondered how long he and his men would be able to take it all. Wazir was there next to him, shuffling uncertainly. He seemed to have lost much of his cocky self-confidence.

"What happened?"

Akram pointed towards Point 5140, the tricolor flying over it. In the bunkers there – bunkers occupied by his own men till this morning – he could see Indian soldiers establishing themselves. Other Indian soldiers were clambering up on ropes over the cliff side, scrambling up, gradually strengthening their positions.

"Those bastards attacked from the cliff side. Nobody expected it. It was impassable. I don't know how they did it."

Shahnawaz exploded. "What the hell do you mean nobody expected it? Were you sleeping? Why haven't you counter-attacked and retaken it as yet?"

"We counter-attacked. Twice. We lost eleven men. They are above us now."

Shahnawaz knew what he meant. The Indians were on the highest point of his defences. Counter-attacking them from below, especially in daylight would be suicidal.

His experienced eyes took in the Indian atop, siting their machine guns and mortars. Already their fire was raking his own positions below. They were building up now.

He knew what would follow. They would build up there, attack from above and just roll down on them. He had no option now. He would have to withdraw his men from the Tololing Heights, move to another position behind and then hold there.

"Okay. It will take the Indians all day, maybe more, to build up in sufficient strength for another attack. They will not attack by day. Withdraw your men from hereand move to the alternate position on the next ridgeline."

Akram nodded, saluted and went on to pass the orders to his men.

Then Wazir spoke, "And what about him?" He pointed to a figure lying supine besides a bunker next to them. It was an Indian officer, badly wounded, barely alive.

"He led the attack that captured Point 5140. He charged us single-handedly and got three of my men before I got him. What do I do with him?"

Shahnawaz looked at the officer, turned him over. He was badly wounded. A burst of fire had got him in the chest and abdomen. He was alive, but just.

Even as he looked, the Indian moved his hands feebly. He was still reaching for his weapon. He tried to turn over, moaned with the agony of the movement.

"What of him?" Wazir asked again.

Shahnawaz looked at him again. For some reason, the memory of an

Indian NCO at a Prisoner of War camp in Barrackpore came back to him. An Indian NCO showing him the photograph of his son, beaming with pleasure.

"What do I do with him, before I withdraw?"

Shahnawaz could have said anything. He could have said, 'Take him along, have him treated in the Medical room.' He could have said, 'Just leave him behind, let the Indians take care of their own.' Or he could have said, 'Finish him.'

He said nothing.

He merely nodded. It was a nod which could have meant anything or nothing at all. A nod, which could have saved or finished Gaurav. A nod which could have been interpreted in any way – and deep down, he knew the way Wazir would choose to interpret it.

Wazir nodded too and moved away. Shahnawaz turned away and as he walked, he heard a staccato of gunfire – a three round burst from an AK 47 rifle. He walked faster, away from the decision he had not made, away from the death his unspoken words had condoned and heard another shot – a single shot this time. Then he heard no more. He just saw Suleiman rushing towards him, saw him hurl himself at him, felt himself pinned down beneath him and heard a huge crump of artillery fire just thirty yards away from him. Something warm and sticky flowed over his face, then the waves of concussion hit him and he passed out.

## VIII

My son died today. He died atop a mountain so remote and insignificant that it did not even have a name. It just had a number. They called it Point 5140.

I saw it on television on the eight o' clock morning news. Saw the pretty announcer – the one who dressed in army camouflage jackets and reported the news live from Kargil, and became a national celebrity for it – announce in her measured tones, with just the right hint of drama in her voice, "The Indian Army achieved its first major success of the war with the capture of Point 5140…." I don't know why, but for some reason my heart turned cold. My eyes followed the pixels on the TV screen, saw images of soldiers, the shots of Bofors guns firing, the tricolor flying atop a craggy mountain peak; saw the photo of Gaurav – his identity card photo taken when he was just out of the Indian Military Academy – and then didn't hear or see any more. I didn't see Nivedita keel over, didn't hear her wordless animal scream; didn't see Supriya collapse with a low moan, didn't see Gaurav's photo fade from the screen, didn't hear the announcer say, "was killed in the capture of Point 5140" ; didn't see Vikram rush in to the room to hold up his mother, didn't see the room swirl. I didn't see or hear anything. Just the flicking pixels dancing on the TV screen like stars before my eyes, saying, "He is gone. My son is gone. My son is dead."

## IX

It was nightfall when Shahnawaz recovered. He was lucky, far luckier than he ever imagined. The Indian artillery salvo had landed just 30 yards away from him. Had Suleiman not hurled himself at him he would have been gone.

Suleiman had taken the brunt of the blast. He had a back full of shrapnel, but he would survive. He had been evacuated to the Base Hospital at Skardu and was now on the operating table as the overworked doctors removed piece after piece of shrapnel from his lacerated back.

But then the rest of his Brigade were not so lucky. From their positions at Point 5140, the Indians just swept downwards, as Shahnawaz knew they would, capturing locality after locality. Major Akram's company was gone, overrun in the first assault itself. The shattered remnants of the battalion had withdrawn to the next ridge line. There Shahnawaz intended to hold on with the rest of his brigade.

But could they hold? Yes. Shahnawaz was sure of it. He had prepared for this contingency and their new positions were already prepared and ready. By the next morning, his men would be poised to take on any attack. Of course, they could hold.

So when the next order came, it shocked him. It came directly from the Corps Commander himself, "Shahnawaz," his voice was grave, "You are to pull out from all the positions you are occupying inside Indian territory."

Pull out? What on earth for. Yes, there had been casualties, they had lost a few key positions, there had been setbacks. But these things always happened in war, his brigade could still hold.

"There are no discussions. Our Prime Minister is in Washington. We have received direct orders from him. You will commence pulling out immediately and move back to your original positions on our side of the Line of Control."

The line clicked silent. There was nothing more to say or discuss. Once again Shahnawaz remembered the radio transmission he had received in December 1971, ordering him to surrender. Once again that pang of disappointment of having been let down by the senior leadership hit him.

Yet, he was a soldier and he did what he had been ordered to do. He slowly extricated his Brigade back across the Line of Control in to Pakistan. It was not an easy withdrawal. The Indians were attacking almost continually now, and along each step of their way back, they were pounded by artillery fire. Slowly, the scale of the disaster was unfolding. Entire battalions had been wiped out; vast quantities of equipment had been simply abandoned in the snow. His hospitals were full of the wounded, the armless, the legless, the frostbitten, the shell-shocked, the almost-dead. So many of their dead had been simply abandoned on those heights when they withdrew. An army always carries its dead – it is a point of honour. What hurt most was leaving their dead behind, exposed, unmarked, unhonoured.

And the roll of the dead was long. The list ran into dozens of pages, the names ran into hundreds. Shahnawaz pored over the names late every night, wrote personally to each one of their families. He remembered the faces of some of them and the look in their eyes kept him awake at nights. It was a look of betrayal, and he saw the same look in the eyes of those who survived.

Yes, his Brigade, like he himself, did feel betrayed. They felt betrayed by both their squabbling political and military superiors who could not see eye to eye even on a matter of such national importance. They felt betrayed at having been pulled out prematurely. But then what ever be the reason for the debacle, the blame, if any, lay squarely on Shahnawaz. He was the Commander, after all.

He carried his letter of resignation in his pocket, when he went to meet General Musharraf and give him personal briefing of the operation. But, he never even got a chance to put up that letter. In fact, the entire discussion took him completely by surprise.

Musharraf greeted him warmly enough, "Shahnawaz, the nation is proud of you. Your men have won a great victory."

A great victory? What kind of victory was that? He could not resist the response, "But Sir, if it was a victory, why did you order us to withdraw?"

Musharraf steepled his finger, smiled, "There were political reasons for that. The Prime Minister got cold feet. But for the army, it is a victory."

It seemed a hollow victory, but Shahnawaz didn't press the issue. He had half-expected to be relieved of his command and be sacked in disgrace.

That did not happen. Quite the contrary. Yes, he did hand over the brigade in due course. But then almost immediately he was ordered to take over command of another brigade – a prestigious brigade whose command was invariably given only to the very best. The 111 Infantry Brigade located at Islamabad.

# The Ghosts of Kargil

## New Delhi, July to October 1999

The dead don't die. They merely become wraiths and remain behind. They sit at their place on the dinner table every meal, they walk in to the kitchen, they ring the doorbell in their own distinctive manner; sometimes they even participate in family conversations. You hear the statements that they would have made, or the answers they could have provided. At times you smell them too, the tantalizing aroma of a much–loved body. Sometimes you hear their voice so sharply that you turn – and then realize, once again, that they are not there at all, there are only the ghosts in your own mind.

Gaurav remained in our home for years thereafter. His wraith weakened with time, but he remained in some form or the other. We received him at the airport, when he came in a coffin with a tricolor wrapped around it – we later heard that money was made on the coffins, but that was different. His remains – God, am I actually calling him that – never came home. We just said our final goodbyes at the Punjabi Bagh crematorium and watched him disappear in a wisp of smoke.

They came to say their goodbyes. The Army Chief, the representatives from his unit, his friends, his comrades, complete strangers. There were hundreds of them. The letters poured in too. We cherished those visits and the words. It was a small balm we could apply on our grief.

And the vultures came in too. On the thirteenth day ceremony – Bharat Haladi, MLA, the same instigator of the anti-Sikh riots, and one of the rising stars of Indian politics came to our home. Hewas a MLA now and walked in with his oily, ingratiating smile with a massive wreath with "Presented by Bharat Haladi, MLA" emblazoned on it, followed by an entourage of hangers-on and a battery of photographers.

He strode in to the drawing room where the thirteenth day prayers for Gaurav were being held. We had wanted it to be a quiet, solemn evening with just our immediate family, but the house filled up with visitors who poured into the adjoining rooms and the space outside. He walked in to the gathering with his hands folded, came towards me, embraced me and burst in to tears.

*"Yeh hamara beta tha. Yeh hamara beta tha. Hamare desh ka beta. Hum sab ka beta. Aaj maine apna beta khoya hai"* (He was my son, he was my son, he was my son. I have lost my son)

I stiffened at his touch. Benumbed with grief, I did not want to say anything, but the hypocrisy of his words jarred.

He continued, turning now to face the gathering, *"Par ham unko nahin chhod denge. Hum iska badla lenge. Yeh mera vaada hai.Hum apne bête ka badla lenge."* (But we will not let them go. We will take revenge. That is my promise. That is my party's promise),

Nivedita stood up, her eyes welled with fresh tears as she stumbled towards her room, Supriya following her.

That bastard still didn't stop. He placed the wreath, the one he had been holding up so the TV cameras could get a good look at it – placed it by Gaurav's photograph. Oh, my son! How handsome he looked in his uniform.

He stood up, "*Yeh mera vaada hai, yeh meri party ka vaada hai...*"

Vikram interrupted, "*Abaap jayeye. Ab hamare parivar ko akela rahene dijiye*" (I think you should go now. Leave our family to ourselves)

Haladi's face did not lose expression. He smiled even more ingratiatingly, bowed in a low *Namaste,* turned around, waved to the gathering of mourners and swept out of the room, the TV cameras dutifully following his passage.

His arrival, the sheer hypocrisy and opportunism of that man – a man for whom I had no regard, in any case – tarnished the solemnity of the occasion. That swine was making political capital on the death of my son. In the outpouring of support we received, his actions and that of other politicians like him, reopened wounds that we were trying so hard to staunch.

We tried to salvage our crumpled lives. Tried to let the routine of the day fill the huge emptiness in our lives and simply tried to go on. Vikram went back to his Management course, Supriya immersed herself in her dance. I went back to work at office in Accent InfoSolutions.

We couldn't really get our lives back on the rails again, but we could slip in to a numbing routine, which helped. And then, three months later, again came Bharat Haladi.

He got a box of sweets this time; a large, expensive one.

"*Pranam*," he folded his hands, bent low, "I was here. I just came to see how you are and if I could be of help in your hour of grief."

I wanted to say, "You could be of help if you just leave" but chose not to. I responded listlessly to his '*Namaste,*' and motioned him to sit in the chair adjoining.

He tried to hand over the box of sweets. I ignored it. He placed it on the side-table instead.

We sat in silence for a while. Then when the silence got uncomfortable, I asked him if he'd like some tea. More out of habit than any desire for his company.

The tea came. We sipped in silence. At least I was in silence. He prattled on about "our *shaheed*," our Gaurav, how he would never be forgotten, etc.

Then he said, "You know, I have already taken up a case to have this road named after your son. I have even raised the proposal with the local corporator."

It meant nothing to me. Gaurav would have never wanted all that nonsense, in any case.

"And the government is giving a petrol pump to the families of the *shaheed*. I have started that scheme. You will be allotted a petrol pump in this same area. Just at the corner of this road. We will name it after your son and put a statue of him there."

That meant even less. I was not interested in a petrol pump. All I wanted was for him to leave.

He seemed impervious to my feelings or emotions. He patted my knee and continued. "Don't worry. I will push it for you. I am just here to serve my constituency. I will take personal interest."

He came back six weeks later. I was alone at home. I mean, it was just Nivedita and me, two ageing, grieving, unthinking parents. Vikram and Supriya were out.

He got a box of dry fruits this time. And a huge sheaf of papers.

*"Pranam,"* he bowed low in his usual '*Namaste*'. I realized later that he bowed so low only when he wanted something.

"Good news," he waved the sheaf of papers. I have got the petrol pump sanctioned for you in the name of your son. All you have to do is fill up a few formalities."

*"Mantriji*. I am not interested in this. I want no petrol pump. I want nothing."

"But you don't understand. It is your '*Haq*' your due, your right. You have to do nothing. Pay nothing. See. I have all the papers ready. All you have to do is sign these papers saying you are indeed the legitimate parents, he was killed in Kargil – mere formalities. *Aap in cheezon me pareshan bhi mat ho jayeye. Main sab sambhaal loonga"* (You don't worry about all this, I will handle it for you)

He put the papers before me. There must have been about 40 or 50 of them, full of legalese and jargon.

He pointed. Handed me a pen. I signed.

He turned the page. I initialed on the left bottom corner.

Next page. Signed the right corner again.

Again.

And again.

I signed mechanically, not seeing, not even bothering to read. Till it finally finished.

He gathered the papers with a satisfied smile. Stood up, bowed. Not so low this time. *"Ab aap phikre mat kijiye. Main sab sambhaal loonga."* (Now you don't worry. I will handle everything)

I actually forgot all about the visit and the promised petrol pump after a while. It did not matter to me. In any case, the only thing the pump would have done was bring back memories of Gaurav every single day.

But the pump did get allotted. A year or so later, a new pump came up in the very spot indicated by Haladi. It was supposed to have been allotted to the family of a Kargil martyr. But the large, sparkling-new "Jai Bharat" petrol pump was not allotted to me or any of the families of those martyred. Oh no. It was instead allotted to a certain Bharat Haladi, MLA, the representative of the constituency. Then I realised why he had kept referring to Gaurav as "*Mera beta* – my son". He had usurped the petrol pump that was to be allotted to his father. How that came about, I never did know. Nor did I try to find out. I just never brought petrol from that pump. Ever.

# Musharraf's Coup

## October 1999

*The Kargil war ended ignominiously for Pakistan. Forced to withdraw with heavy casualties, it lost not only its military prestige but also its standing in the world. The scale of its defeat was becoming apparent to the nation, even though the army tried hard to mask it.*

*The actions also brought a virtual breakdown in relations between the Prime Minister Nawaz Sharif and the Army Chief General PervezMusharraf. Both blamed the other for the debacle. In fact, Nawaz Sharif said that he was not even informed about the operation. .*

*With rising tensions between the two most powerful men in Pakistan, things had to come to a passé – and it did. In October 99, just three months after Kargil, Nawaz Sharif dismissed Musharraf as Chief. In fact, when he was dismissed, Musharraf was on a flight, returning from a visit to Sri Lanka. Instructions were passed that his aircraft – a Pakistan International Airways flight – was not to be allowed to land in any Pakistani airport but to be diverted to a neighbouring country. It would have been ludicrous had it not involved the fate of a nation.*

*The Prime Minister's instructions to prevent Musharraf from landing were intercepted by the army. In a swift counter move, troops from the elite 111 Infantry Brigade, stationed at Islamabad, swung into action, seized control of Islamabad airport and enabled Musharraf to land. On arrival, Musharraf ordered Nawaz Sharif to be placed under arrest and took over as President.*

*It was Pakistan's third military coup. Musharraf would continue for another eight years as President. These would be very eventful years. Democracy in Pakistan was once again interrupted and the army was back in power.*

## II

Shahnawaz moved to Islamabad in September 1999, to take over command of the elite 111 Infantry Brigade at Islamabad. His farewell was a quiet, solemn affair. There were no parties, no ceremonies – nothing. It was not the time for it.

Islamabad cantonment with its pleasant autumn and wide tree-fringed avenues was a far cry from the icy heights he had come from. He did feel a pang of guilt at being here, but he settled in to his new role quite fast. It was not too bad, if only he could forget the sights and sounds of Kargil.

But being with Shazia, Salim, Mehtab and Aftab would help. And commanding a brigade in the peaceful capital of their country would not be too daunting – or so he thought. There would be no bullets flying, or artillery shells dropping down. The brigade's role was more to ensure the security and administration of the Army Chief. They called it "The Chief's Brigade" and very soon he would know why.

## III

His mobile rang just as he was cooling off after his weekly round of squash with Salim. Salim had beaten him soundly, as always. Youth always trumped over experience.

He recognized the number – it was his Corps Commander – Damn. This had to be serious. He moved to a side where he could not be overheard.

"Sir?"

"Shahnawaz, have you heard? Have you been watching the TV news?"

'TV news? No Sir, I am out at the moment. I'll just check it."

"Nawaz Sharif has sacked General Musharraf as Army Chief. But General Musharraf is not even aware of it. He is out of the country and now on a flight from Colombo to Islamabad. What makes it worse is that Nawaz Sharif has passed orders that the flight is to be barred from landing anywhere in the country. It is to be diverted to another country."

"What!" It came out involuntarily. Sacking a Chief was one thing; the Prime Minister was entitled to do that. Preventing his aircraft from landing was another.

"You go to Islamabad Airport. Take over the Air Traffic Control Tower and make sure the aircraft lands. And keep your brigade on high alert."

The news stunned Shahnawaz. Musharraf's aircraft would be approaching Islamabad and if it was prevented from landing, it could run out of fuel and crash. He had to move fast.

He raced to Islamabad Airport with a small convoy of fully armed men behind him. He reached the airport, directed his men to take positions around the airfield and raced up towards the tower of the Air Traffic Control – the hub which controlled all aircraft traffic coming to and from Islamabad.

There were five people inside the ATC. Three were scared looking traffic controllers peering over the radar consoles. Two others, senior police officials stood over them, pistols in hand. They were obviously Nawaz Sharif's men, sent to ensure that Musharraf's plane did not land.

Shahnawaz removed his pistol. Four of his officers had gathered behind him; they unhitched their weapons too, surrounded the police officials, took their weapons and shepherded them downstairs.

He turned to the traffic controllers, "Are you in contact with the PIA flight from Colombo to Islamabad? Where is it located now?"

The Controller nodded, flicked on a switch. "It reached Islamabad 40 minutes ago. We were ordered to deny it permission to land. It is circling over us now."

He looked at the runway. There was no traffic – unusual. This was peak air activity time. The landing and guidance lights had been switched off and on the runway were two fire trucks, parked smack in the centre.

"Switch on the landing lights. And get the trucks out of the runway. And connect me, to the aircraft. Quick."

"ATC Islamabad to PK 805. Do you receive?"

The pilot came on almost instantly. "Yes. I need permission to land. I am fast running out of fuel."

Shahnawaz grabbed the mike, "This is Brigadier Shahnawaz Khan, Commander 111 Brigade. I want to speak to the Chief. He is on the flight."

There was a pause. The crackle of a headset being exchanged.

Musharraf came on the line. His voice was calm. He was not a commando for nothing. "This is General Musharraf. Why am I being denied permission to land?"

"Sir, this is Brigadier Shahnawaz. I have things under control and have taken over the airfield. Your aircraft will be able to land. Our men are here."

Musharraf paused, "What is the name of your father? What decorations did he receive?" That wily commando was checking to see if he was not being drawn in to a trap.

Shahnawaz answered, "My father was the late Major General Shahryar Khan, recipient of the *Sitare Imtiaz* and *Hilal-e-Jurat*." The darkened runway suddenly became awash with light as the landing lights came on. Through its glow, he saw his men removing the two fire trucks, clearing the runway. "You can land, Sir. It is safe now."

The large PIA Airbus with the Pakistani Chief and 197 other passengers on board touched down heavily, slowed and taxied to a halt. Shahnawaz raced to the aircraft, now surrounded by Pakistani soldiers in a protective ring.

The door opened. Musharraf emerged. Shahnawaz saluted. Though he was in civvies, Musharraf saluted back with that cocky commando salute he always preferred.

"Thank you, Shahnawaz. You and your men have done well." He was cool as a cucumber, that man. "But I think I need a cigarette now. It has been a long flight."

IV

*The Pakistani Army took over by 8.30 pm that same day. Nawaz Sharif was arrested and Musharraf came on National television, clad in a borrowed flak jacket, to announce the sacking of the Sharif government and the takeover by the army. And with this began the next era in Pakistan's tumulus history.*

V

This is why the Triple One Brigade is called "The Chief's Brigade". Traditionally the Islamabad based brigade has been used by different Chiefs for their personal protection, for administration, and of course, to stage a coup when felt necessary.

And traditionally, those who help their Chief take over power go places. Shahnawaz was no different. He continued commanding that brigade for the next two years as Musharraf consolidated his hold on the nation and the army.

When Shahnawaz's promotion to the rank of Major General came about – well, who could have doubted it – he continued at Islamabad at Musharraf's behest. Only this time he was placed in a far more delicate appointment. He went back to the ISI and took over as its Additional Director General, responsible for InternalSecurity and the affairs of India and Afghanistan. He was now President Musharraf's right hand man and one of the most powerful men in Pakistan. Life was good again.

# PAKISTAN'S WAR WITHIN

## 2001 Onwards

*11 September 2001was a day that changed the world. That morning at 8.46 am, a group of 19 terrorists, hijacked four aircraft in the USA. Two crashed in to the twin towers of the World Trade Centre at New York, one on the Pentagon building at Washington DC, the fourth crashed in an open field at Pennsylvania.*

*The attack, the largest single terrorist strike ever, brought a vengeful USA in towar with Al Qaeda and the Taliban, the groups behind the attack, based in Afghanistan. As a furious USA readied for war with these groups, it gave Pakistan an ultimatum, "Either you are with us or against us."*

*PervezMusharraf capitulated. He had no choice. The USA invaded Afghanistan and launched a massive crackdown on the groups. Faced with annihilation, many of the terrorists, slipped back into Pakistan where they took sanctuary in the rugged terrain of the border areas. After all the terrorists had friends, relatives and bases on both sides of the Pak-Afghan border.*

*The Pakistani government initially refused to act on the terrorists that had now moved into its soil. That was a fatal mistake. The groups felt betrayed with Pakistan's siding of the USA and now began turning against it. They established themselves in the border areasand unleashed the same reign of terror and Islamic fundamentalism that they had let loose in Afghanistan. Slowly their tentacles spread across Pakistan. Pakistan would soon be at war with them – the same groups that they themselves had created and sponsored – and that war would tear the nation from within.*

# THE FALLING TOWERS

## Islamabad, 11 September, 2001

Major General Shahnawaz Khan looked at himself in the mirror. He liked what he saw. He was not too bad for a 50 year old - well, okay - 53 actually. His body was still lean and fit, barring that little heaviness around his waist. His eyes and skin were clear and unwrinkled, and the salt and pepper in his hair gave him just the right touch of dignity. He preened in front of the mirror, sucked in his stomach some more, dried himself and stepped out.

He dressed carefully. Today was a big day and he knew Shazia would want everything to be just perfect. She had already left for the Jinnah Auditorium where her concert was to start at seven. She liked to stand on the empty stage before a big performance just to get the feel of it. This would be her biggest concert ever.

Suleiman was at the door waiting for him. He held the car door open, smiled and said, *"Memsaab ko hamare taraf se bhi Mubarak de jiye. Allah Mian ke dua se unke show bahut shandaar rahenga"* (Please give my best wishes to madam for her show. By the grace of Allah, her show will be a great one)

Shahnawaz smiled back, *"Unhe bata doonga. Ab aap jayeye. Rest karo"* (I'll convey it to her. Now you try and get some rest)

The car drove off, Suleiman limped away. A piece of shrapnel from the Indian artillery shell he had taken on Shahnawaz's behalf was still lodged in his back, too close to the spinal column for surgery. He was in agony most nights, but continued uncomplainingly, looking after the house and the Shahnawaz family. Shahnawaz had ensured that he remained there with him. It was the least he could do. He owed him his life after all.

They reached the auditorium well in time, and went past the posters screaming out "Shazia Khan – The Nightingale of Pakistan, Live in concert' and moved in to their seats in the front row. He made that call to Shazia, that call he always made just before her recordings or her concerts began.

"All the best, my love. I know it will be a hit, as always."

"God, I hope so." Shazia's voice seemed keyed-up, "I am as nervous as never before. What if they don't like my show? What if they boo me off the stage?"

Shahnawaz smiled. "It will be a grand hit. Like each one of your shows. And even you know it". It was always the same. Shazia had to work herself in to a state of tension before each show. The tension would evaporate the moment she walked on to the stage and then the music would take over.

The lights dimmed and the spot light followed Shazia from the wings to the centre of the stage. It hovered over her as she stood almost nervously, eyes running over the darkened auditorium. She looked so beautiful, even now – a beauty that matched her voice, now one of the most well-known in Pakistan. She bowed slightly, and then launched in to her repertoire; celebrating lost and found love, probing in to the meaning of life, taking you to mustard fields and misty meadows, carrying you to homes and families, childhood memories and ancient enmities. Her songs encompassed each aspect of life, and as always, Shahnawaz felt the hair on his forearms rise just by the sheer beauty of her music.

She was in her final number – one of her most popular hits – about a divided love on two sides of a river that ran between two nations. And as her voice broke with the yearning the two lovers felt across the divide, Shahnawaz's mobile rang.

The "Please switch off your mobile phones" sign had come on at the start of the show, but the Additional Director ISI could never have his phone off. It was on silent mode and vibrated insistently in his pocket.

Shahnawaz ignored it. Damn. It rang again. Then the SMS warning buzz sounded. There was a brief SMS in his inbox. It just said, "Please watch the TV."

Shahnawaz frowned. 'Watch TV'? What kind of message was that? But it was from one of his senior directors. He would not have sent it unless it was important.

He waited till the show ended. Shazia would never forgive him if he walked out in between. But even as she was still on stage, bowing to the standing ovation of the audience, he raced to the lobby where he knew would be a television set.

It was already on and he saw the world's most famous skyline appear on the screen. He saw the camera pan the skyline and then zoom in to the twin towers of the World Trade Centre. The right tower was in flames, smoldering in black, oily smoke. Even as he watched a second plane emerged from the left corner, raced across the TV screen and then exploded in a massive fireball on the second tower of the US World Trade Centre. The commentator's voice, already shaken, rose to a scream, "Oh, My God; Oh, My God," as the ticker tape ran "Terrorist crash hijacked plane on the World Trade Centre. USA attacked."

The attacks would change the course of the world and send the USA in a furious vengeful war to claim retribution for those responsible. And this war would come right to Pakistan's doorstep.

## II

Shahnawaz was summoned to General Musharraf's office first thing in the morning. President Musharraf's office actually – he was Pakistan's President since his coup of 1999.

Shahnawaz had spent all night in front of the television, poring over the news, analysing its import. The events taking place in USA would have serious consequences, and like it or not, Pakistan would be sorely affected. The course of his own nation was about to change.

It seemed that President Musharraf had not slept a wink all night either. He looked harassed and distraught and his ashtray was overflowing. Shahnawaz had never seen him so tense. "President George Bush called at midnight. They have traced those who carried out this attack. It is Al Qaeda and the attacks were coordinated from Afghanistan. He wanted to know if Pakistan was linked in any way to the attacks. Of course, we were not."

Shahnawaz itched for a cigarette himself, but he could not smoke in front of his President.

Musharraf continued, "I have never seen President Bush so furious before. He said that if we are involved in any way, the USA will bomb Pakistan back in to the Stone Age. How dare he? Does he think we are a banana republic that can be pushed around?"

He paused, let his anger ebb and then composed himself, "They will be attacking Afghanistan to get the terrorist groups responsible. He wanted to know it we were with them in their War against Terror or against them."

"And what did you say?"

"What could I say? I know that the Al Qaeda and Taliban are our allies. But we have no choice. We will have to renounce these groups and support the USA in their war against them."

Shahnawaz was half expecting this and he understood the implications. The terrorist groups including Baitullah Wazir's, who were operating from Afghanistan had been their allies for over a decade. If Musharraf had agreed to side with the USA they would have to combat these same groups. That could well turn them against Pakistan in the future.

Shahnawaz interjected, "But, Sir, there are over fifty different groups. Many of them we have trained, indoctrinated and cultivated ourselves. Some of them have even fought for us in Kashmir. How can we renounce them just like that?"

Musharraf gave a thin smile, "That is the balancing act we have to play. We will have to act so that we don't antagonize the USA, but at the same time just enough so that we continue our relations with them. It will be a delicate act, and we will have to play the game very skillfully and very discreetly".

Shahnawaz knew what that meant. In effect, they would be playing a double game. It was a game that could just go out of control very rapidly.

"Sir, even if we act only selectively, eventually we may turn them all against us. I only hope that this action does not rebound on us."

"Yes, but that is a chance we must take. For now we have no option, but to side with the USA in their War against Terror, even if it means acting against these groups"

Shahnawaz's apprehensions would come true. The USA invaded Afghanistan in December 2001, and from there, many of the terrorist groups, slipped across to Pakistan. The hydra that they had helped create was now on their soil. The terrorist groups would soon turn against Pakistan itself. Pakistan would be at war with them, and what was worse, it would be at war with itself.

# NEITHER FRIEND NOR ENEMY

**Pakistan, June 2002**

Shahnawaz received the call on a Sunday morning. He normally avoided taking calls from unknown numbers, but this was on his unlisted number – the one he gave only to a select handful.

Though they had not spoken in years, he recognised the voice immediately. It was Baitullah Wazir, *"Janaab, kaise ho. Lagta hai ki aapke purane dosto ko aap bhul gaye ho." (*How are you? It seems you have forgotten your old friends.)

"*Kaise ho, Wazir Saab. Khairiat me. Kaha ho aap abhi?* (How are you Wazir? Where are you now?)

*"Ham to abhi aap ke karib aa gaye hai. Kya ham mil sakte hai.* "(I am close to you. Can we meet?)

Shahnawaz hesitated. He did not want to meet Wazir, at least not now. But then he did not want to cut off all ties either. In fact, it would be best if they could have a face-to-face.

*"Theekh hai. Kahan?"* (Okay, Where)

*"Peshawar mein. Aap agle Shukhrawar yahaan aa jaye. Mere aadmi aap ko mere paas pahucha denge. Akele aaye." (*At Peshawar. On Saturday. From there my men will guide you to me, come alone.)

The call cut off. Shahnawaz stared at the silent phone for a long time. He knew that Wazir and his group had slipped in to Pakistan after the US attacked Afghanistan and were now holed up in one of the remote villages along the Pak-Afghan border. He would meet Wazir, it would be for the best.

He reached Peshawar that Saturday, incognito as always. He had been to that small town on the Pak-Afghan border very often. But now, the town had changed.

He did not feel that he was in Pakistan at all. The Afghans were everywhere. *Burqa* clad women walked the streets like wraiths; bearded Afghan youth, Kalashnikovs slung casually by their sides, distinctive black turbans on their heads, walked the streets with impunity. The Pakistani police and security forces were non-existent. Dammit, they seemed to have taken over the town.

Three of these black-turbaned, Kalashnikov toting youth escorted him to Wazir's location. They did not blind-fold him – nobody dare do that to the Additional Director General, ISI- but took him in a battered pick-up truck through the same rugged, potholed roads, over dusty tracks, non-existent paths to a village similar to the one where he had first met Wazir. Only this village was not in Afghanistan, it was in Pakistan.

But then, national boundaries meant nothing to the Afghans. Wazir and the hundreds of Afghan militants had homes and relatives on both sides of the Durand Line – the line between Pakistan and Afghanistan. They crossed that line with impunity, had wives and family on both sides, attended weddings and funerals, travelled and stayed in whichever location took their fancy. When the US attacked Afghanistan, most of the militants just slipped across the border in to Pakistan. There they were safe.

Wazir sat on a chair, a shawl loosely wrapped around him. His beard had turned white and he wore a black patch over his left eye. His body had lost the taut leanness of his youth. His skin sagged in folds, as though he had put on a lot of weight and then lost it all in a hurry.

He had not met Wazir in four years, but he knew that he had prospered. His group had emerged as one of the most powerful in Afghanistan and when the Taliban came in to power he had become the Minister of Culture and Islamic Affairs in the government. He had ordered the destruction of the famed Bamiyan statues; those sixth century Buddha statues of priceless heritage. He had also imposed Shariat – Islamic Law – engineered the massacre of Shias, banned music, kite-flying, television, dancing, or any form of entertainment. He also made a fortune along the way, with his dealings in heroin. Oh, he prospered all right, till the US pushed him out of Afghanistan.

There was little warmth when he greeted Shahnawaz, there were no embraces, no cup of tea came, "So, you have joined hands with the infidels."

Shahnawaz said nothing. Actually, there was nothing to say to this.

"We have been friends for fifteen years. We fought the Soviets together. We helped Pakistani interests in Afghanistan; we even fought for you in Kashmir. I have lost twelve of my tribe in the jihad there – WHY? For you.And now when USA, that Great Satan attacks your Afghan brethren, what does Pakistan do? You renounce us and side up with them. Them?"

Shahnawaz interrupted the harangue, "You and I remain friends. What has happened between the countries is a political decision. I had no hand in it."

Wazir continued, "No hand? You are Muslims, like us. You should be here to help us in our *jihad* against the USA. Instead, what do you do? For a few dollars, you even give them your bases from where they can attack us."

He lifted his eye patch. Shahnawaz winced. The left eye was an empty socket with a black scar running diagonally across it. "Do you know what the USA has done in Afghanistan? They have wiped out entire families, entire villages in their attacks. I lost thirty of my tribe, my wife, my two children, my nephews...," he pointed to his mutilated eye, "my own eye; my entire village in just one bombing attack. I barely managed to cross the border and reached safety here, in the village of my second wife. And what did you do when the infidels were attacking an Islamic country? You supported them. You are not Pakistan- you are *Jhootistan*"

He tried to stand, fell backwards in his chair with the force of his exertions. Apparently, his wounds were more serious than it seemed.

Shahnawaz used the pause in his harangue, "Wazir, I know we have been allies for many years. But you must understand that Pakistan had no choice. But I am glad, that at least you are safe. I cannot change my government's decision. But you can stay here inside Pakistan, till you recover fully. You will be safe from US attacks. We can provide sanctuary, but that is all I can do."

Wazir grunted. He was shrewd enough to know that this was the only concession he could extract at the moment. "Very well, but the *jihad* will continue. We will fight America and we will defeat it," he paused ominously, than added, "And if need be, we will even fight you."

# COPING WITH THE VOID

## New Delhi, 2002

We took our seats in the front row of the darkened auditorium. All four of us – Nivedita, Me, Vikram and Gaurav. Gaurav was always present for each significant event of our lives. I could imagine him there, perhaps dressed in a pair of jeans and a crisp white shirt, going through the leaflets; scanning the stage and the audience. He was not present, but as always, he was there.

Vikram guided us to our seats, helped Nivedita into hers. I liked the way my younger boy was shaping up. He was tall, taller than Gaurav, but perhaps not quite as handsome. He had the same grave demeanor; the same quiet smile seemed to flicker around his eyes. He was the brains in the family, my younger son. He had finished his management course at the top of his class, and been lapped up by a Multi-National Corporation at a starting salary that made my jaw drop. Now as he rose up the corporate ladder, he was like most of the new generation of India – bold, confident, ambitious, and well, a little cocky.

He held Nivedita gently by the hand as he helped her in her seat. It had been a long time since I had seen her bedecked, but today she was in one of her best saris – I recognized it, it was the one Gaurav had got her with his first pay. The grief had taken its deadliest toll on her. She was a whisper of the person she had once been and today seeing her resplendent after so long, my heart smiled.

He guided me to my seat as well, Me with my slow, stooping gait of a fifty-five something, my pot-belly, my white hair and the lines on my face that had become even more pronounced after Gaurav's death. I shuffled in my seat, picked up the brochure – the brochure with Supriya on the cover, frozen in a classical Odissi pose. I let my eyes linger for a long time over the photo, smiled to myself and waited for her dance recital to begin.

The lights dimmed and from the wings of the darkened stage the first dancers floated in – nymphs in a garden, where Krishna, the mischievous god hid and watched. He watched them in their games and frolic as he waited for Radha, the one he truly desired, the one whom he had angered with his faithlessness and who now sulked and pined elsewhere. Then she came – Supriya, No Radha – she was immersed in that role completely. She wafted to the centre of the stage with the wistful longing of a hurt lover, let herself be surrounded by her gossiping friends, allowed herself to be coaxed in to telling them how that lascivious Krishna had come to her every day, how he stole her clothes and then her heart, how he mesmerized her with his flute, how he drove her from mad longing to despair, how his frivolous ways hurt her, how she never, ever wanted to see him again, but Yes, Yes, Yes…, she did long for him and – she hid her face in her arms – she was too shy to ever admit it, to her friends, to him, even to herself.

Radha, no Supriya, said none of this. There were no words, it was just the accompaniment of the *pakhawaj*, harmonium and *manjira* to the beat of her body, but each cock of an eyebrow, each gesture, the flow of her hands and feet said it all. She told us the story through the steps of her dance; she took us to anger, anguish and longing. She carried us deep into *Geet Govinda* – the song of Krishna. Then we were not in the darkened auditorium at all. We were transported to Vrindavan, the garden of love and from there the first notes of the flute wafted in.

Radha startled as the melody of Krishna's flute floated across the stage. She peered over the edge of the garden, fled to the centre of the stage when he came in jauntily, first ignored him, then allowed herself to be coaxed, then cajoled, then smiled, forgave and gave in. Her feet glided in the ecstasy of re-found love, her hands were running water, her body sheer poetry in motion. When the spotlight finally dimmed with the pair transfixed in a timeless pose, it was a moment of complete abandon and surrender. The music died, the lights dimmed and the hypnotic spell around the audience broke as auditorium erupted in thunderous applause.

I had been holding Nivedita's hand unconsciously throughout the show and now as we both stood and applauded, I turned to look at her. She was shining with radiance, with a mother's absolute joy at her child's triumph. We watched Supriya bow low towards all corners of the auditorium, heard the *ghungroos* on her feet providing one final rhythm as she walked off-stage; and then as the lights came on, I saw the shadow cross Nivedita's face. I felt the shadow cross my own mind too. We both had the same thought together – if only Gaurav had been here.

We pushed that thought away, like we had learnt to do. But Gaurav remained. I think I saw him there in the audience, applauding louder and harder than the rest, clapping long after the others had stopped. And I think Nivedita, Supriya and Vikram saw him too.

II

We waited in the lobby for Supriya to arrive. I could still see her on stage, beaming brightly, accepting bouquet after bouquet, saw her smile at the flashing cameras, speak in to the microphones placed before her, saw her touch the feet of her *guru* and then she went backstage.

She reappeared half an hour later, dressed in a simple sari, her face scrubbed clean of make-up, her costume and jewelry in the small suitcase she always carried for her performances. She rushed to us waiting in the lobby.

"How was I?"

She knew she had been great. Each performer instinctively knows that, but she wanted the confirmation from us.

Nivedita held her face with both hands, kissed her on her forehead, "You were great. I have never seen a better recital."

"Yeah, and you didn't even trip once – you were great, sis." Vikram hugged her playfully, avoided the light punch she gave him.

*"Beti, bahut sundar. Mujhe to jyada samjh me nehi aata, par itna sundar dance maine aaj tak nahi dekha."* (It was very beautiful. I did not understand much about the meaning, but have never seen a more beautiful dance)

This recital was just one of many. She was slowly gaining a stature as one of the rising stars in the new generation of Indian dancers. All those years of training, her single-minded dedication were now finding culmination.

She chattered excitedly about the show, about the reviews she received, the mistakes she thought she had made, and I heard Nivedita's laughter ring out from the back seat as well. I smiled to myself as I drove my small family home and again came the thought. If only....

# In the New Millennium

## India-Pakistan, 2002-2005

*The first half decade of the New Millennium were good ones for India. The Kargil War was behind it, the economy was on a roll, jobs were being created, and foreign investments were pouring in. Under Prime Minister Vajpayee, the country seemed to be coming into its own.*

*In the elections of 2004, the BJP led National Democratic Alliance lost its majority and the Congress led United Progressive Alliance came into power. Prime Minister Manmohan Singh took over as Prime Minister. This quiet, unassuming man was the Finance Minister who had ushered in India's economic reforms, and was one of the architects of its success story. Much was expected from him, but these expectations would be sorely belied.*

*Pakistan was going through far greater upheaval. By around 2002-04 the terrorist groups inside Pakistan had consolidated along the Afghan-Pakistan border and came together under the umbrella of the Tehrik-e-Taliban, a rabidly fundamentalist organisation. They aimed to establish strict Islamic Law – Shariat – across all of Pakistan, just as they had in Afghanistan. Slowly they established their writ in the areas they controlled. Public floggings, killing of minorities, bombings and executions became a norm. Yet, for a long while, the Pakistani government refused to act against them and allowed them to spread their influence deeper in to the country,virtually up to Islamabad.*

*It was only in 2004, when the situation had already gone out of control, that President Musharraf ordered army action against them. By then, perhaps, it was already too late. The militants were too well-entrenched, their influence too wide-spread to be countered. Pakistan would soon be at war with them, and in this war the nation would be dangerously divided.*

# THE CANCER TAKES ROOT

**Pakistan, 2004**

Shahnawaz looked at the report he had just typed. He had been working on Pakistan's Internal Security Review for over a week now and wanted it to be as clear and concise as possible. After all, it would be going all the way to the President himself.

The report did not make pleasant reading, but then the Internal Situation in Pakistan was not a pleasant one. In the years during which the different militant groups had been allowed to stay inside Pakistan, they had come together under his old friend and nemesis, Baitullah Wazir, to form an organisation called Tehrik-e-Taliban. Under him, they expanded beyond the border areas and deeper into Pakistan. Their demand was simple. Impose *Shariat*, strict Islamic Law on the nation – a harsh, cruel law which they enforced ruthlessly in the areas they controlled. Purdah was enforced, women education was banned, all forms of entertainment banned. Public floggings and executions had become a norm. Why, in just the past two years they had killed over 2000, conducted 40 suicide attacks, and launched over a hundred bombings across the nation. And this was just the beginning.

He removed his spectacles and rubbed his eyes. The mechanical, impersonal words he had typed did not convey the gravity of the situation. Baitullah Wazir and his *Tehrik-e-Taliban* were now a greater threat than any had imagined. And yet, most simply refused to see the threat. They just felt that it was a local problem that would go away if they ignored it long enough.

He would go through the report one more time before putting it up to President Musharraf. But even as he switched off his lap-top, Shazia came in to his study, her face shaken.

"What happened," After almost thirty years of marriage he understood each nuance of hers. Something had affected her greatly.

She sat next to him, let him put his arms around her. Her voice was unsteady as she spoke. "Just have a look at this. A friend sent it to me on Facebook. Just see what these barbarians are doing."

She turned on her mobile and grainy images appeared on the screen. It was a badly filmed video, obviously taken hurriedly on a hidden mobile camera by an amateur, but it conveyed the message of what was happening in Pakistan more chillingly than anything else he had seen.

It showed a seventeen year old girl – more girl than woman – dressed in a white and yellow *salwar kameez*, pinned down by two black-turbaned men. Even as they held her supine, a third – it seemed to be a *burqa* clad woman – raised a whip and brought it down sharply on her back, jack-knifing her backwards with a shrill cry of pain and terror.

"What have I done? What have I done?" she screamed, only for the voice to be cut in mid-sentence as the whip came down again – again that animal scream of pain.

Thirty seven times the whip rose and fell. Twenty times she screamed. Then she just lay unconscious or dead as the whip lashed down, lacerating her back and buttocks, turning her white and yellow *salwar* in to a red, sodden rag.

The two Taliban men released their grip as the whip came down the last time. The *burqa* clad woman folded her whip. The camera panned jerkily around the crowd of silent, shocked men, watching dazedly from the sides. None had moved a step to stop this outrage.

"*'Allah-ho-Akbar,'* God is great. Let this be a lesson to you all who choose to deviate from the true path of Islam. Let this be a warning to the whores and adulterers. We have spared her life. Next time we may not be so merciful."

The video stopped. Shazia was still watching the blank screen, her hand raised to her mouth, her face shocked. "Did you see what those animals did to that poor girl? And do you know why? They caught her talking to her fiancé on the road. They said it was un-Islamic for an unmarried girl to be seen with a man who was not her father or brother. Those brutes, those animals."

Shahnawaz held her in his arms. The video had shaken him too. He knew that Wazir's Tehrik-e-Taliban had taken over the border areas and imposed their brand of Islam there. He received reports of their attacks on girls' schools, public floggings and executions every day. But this video captured even more vividly, the threat that was facing the nation. It was a threat to their concept of Pakistan. It was a threat to their religion, to their very way of life. Perhaps it was a threat to the very existence of Pakistan as they knew it.

## II

Shahnawaz submitted his report to President Musharraf the next day along with the video clipping of the Chand Bibi – that was the name of the young girl – flogging.

Musharraf read the report carefully, watched the video impassively. Then in the green ink which he preferred, he wrote at the bottom of Shahnawaz's report.

*"I direct that military action be initiated against the Tehrik-e-Taliban and the other militant groups operating within the country."*

Signed

General PervezMusharraf

President and Chief Executive

## III

*The initiation of military action against the militants proved far more difficult than was envisaged. The militants were now organized, well-armed and equipped and it was almost impossible to dislodge them from their strongholds. Instead, it was the army that took on heavy casualties. Entire battalions were captured and taken prisoner; military bases were targeted by suicide bombers and attacks. Senior army officers were assassinated; their Headquarters attacked.*

*Emboldened, the militants now began expanding throughout Pakistan. Their agenda of fundamentalist Islam had actually drawn many of the impoverished, illiterate and unemployed Pakistanis in to their fold. They pushed forth their demand that all action against them be stopped, and more ominously, that strict Islamic law be imposed on the entire nation.*

*In spite of the battle raging within, many still failed to see the threat. For them, India remained the real enemy. And they embarked on an audacious plan – a spectacular terrorist attack on Mumbai which would draw the attention of the world and bring India's commercial capital to a halt.*

# THE THIRD MOST POWERFUL MAN IN PAKISTAN

**Office of the Director General ISI,**

**Islamabad, January 2008**

Lieutenant General Shahnawaz Khan walked through the unimposing front façade of the ISI Headquarters. He crossed the lawns and fountains within, entered the bougainvillea covered inner buildings and strode up the balustrade into the office of the Director General, Inter Services Intelligence – the office of the third most powerful man in Pakistan, second only to the President and Army Chief.

He entered his plush office and soaked in the feeling of power that seemed to hang in there. Jinnah's photograph stared down at him, austere and demanding as always. The Pakistani flag hanging over his table seemed equally demanding, if not more so. On the board above were the names of past Director Generals, each one an illustrious luminary, who had helped carve the destiny of their nation in some way. And now, here he was occupying the same chair, shouldering the same responsibilities. It was a heady feeling, and an intoxicating one.

He had been promoted to the rank of Lieutenant General just the month before and had simply been elevated upstairs from the office of the Additional Deputy Director General to that of the Director General. He had been hand-picked for the job by the Chief himself. In these troubled times, he wanted the best man for this delicate appointment.

And these were troubled times all right. The actions against the militants had been continuing for three years now, but had not proved as effective as he had hoped. If anything, Taliban attacks had only intensified across the nation. They had even targeted the Army Headquarters, attacked a naval base and even took over a mosque just three kilometres from his own Headquarters. What was worse was that they seemed to be winning over supporters in droves. The poor flocked to their warped version of Islam and embraced it readily. Even within the Army and the security forces there was a wave of sympathy for them.

He lit up another cigarette. He had been virtually chain-smoking these days – you don't become the third most powerful man in Pakistan without the tensions to go with it. His doctors had been warning him to cut down, but what the hell. Maybe, after all these problems were over.

What was needed was something to divert the attention of the people. If he could engineer one major triumph against a common enemy, perhaps it would help bring all Pakistanis together again. Maybe, even some of the militant groups they were fighting would come back to their side then.

And what was the common enemy. What was the threat that all Pakistanis – militant, soldier or civilian – identified with. Simple, it was India. What was needed was one strike against it – one spectacular strike.

It would have to be a big action. And it would have to be done without it being traced back to Pakistan. He would have to rely on one of the local terrorist groups like the *Lashkar-e-Toiba* which they had sponsored for years and was still allied to Pakistan. A grand, successful strike using this group could deflect attention from Pakistan's internal woes, and if India threatened to attack, so much the better. At one stroke it would unify the nation against their common enemy.

And what would be the target. It had to be one that would really hurt their arch-enemy and draw the attention of the world to it. And what target would be vulnerable, yet prominent enough for a strike of this nature. He swiveled in his chair, gazed at the huge map of India that occupied half a wall in his office, and then placed a finger on the target he had selected.

It was Mumbai.

# 'IT IS NOT A CRICKET MATCH, IT IS WAR'

## Indo-Pak T20 World Cup Final

Joginder Sharma, the raw, unknown medium pacer from Haryana trundled in for the last over of the match. The tension showed on his face, as it did on everyone – everyone except for Misbah-ul-Haq, the Pakistani batsman on strike and M S Dhoni, the Indian Captain, cool and collected as always behind the stumps.

What a humdinger of a match this inaugural T20 World Cup final had been. Like all India-Pak matches it see-sawed madly and now hung on a razor's edge – one over to go; India 157, Pakistan 145 for 9; 13 runs needed by Pakistan, one wicket more for India. On which side would the match fall?

Joginder ran in, bowled the first ball wide – the tension was showing. One more run to Pakistan. Misbah missed the second – a dot ball. Joginder came in again-not a bad ball actually, but Misbah launched in to it, his bat arced like a sword and the ball soared over the long-on boundary in to the stands.

"It's a six," Ravi Shashtri, the commentator shouted out, "Pakistan six runs away from a sensational victory..., what will Misbah do now?"

Joginder came in again, bowled at his usual military medium pace just outside off-stump. Misbah got beneath the ball, scooped it upwards with a delicate flick and sent it soaring upwards, over the wicket keeper, up, up and above, toward the fine leg boundary....

On the sub-continent, a billion hearts stopped on both sides of the border as the ball rose high, swirled, looped downwards – and landed straight in the hands of Sreesanth fielding at the fine leg boundary.

Ravi Shashtri screamed out, "Misbah scoops, in the air, Sreesanth takes it – INDIA WIN" His voice rose to a scream, a scream drowned out by the wild roar that reverberated across the stadium and all of India.

Misbah was down on his knees in abject despair. Around him, Indian players whooped with joy, hugging each other, running around the ground in manic celebration. In the stands, Indian flags waved like banners. The commentator continued, his voice hoarse with emotion, "Wild scenes of celebration at the Wanderers Oval, Johannesburg as India win the T-20 World Cup, beating arch-rivals Pakistan in a nail-biting finish. What a game this has been; what a glorious, glorious game of cricket...."

**II**

Nine thousand kilometres away, Shahnawaz switched off his TV in disgust, as did thousands others across Pakistan. Damn. They were so close. If only Misbah's ball had cleared the fielder and reached the boundary, the roles would have been reversed now. It would have been the Pakistani team cheering, it would have been Pakistan reverberating with joy.

Damn. What the hell was the matter with the Pakistani team – why could they never win against India in the World Cup? Where were they; the Saaed Anwars, the Inzamams, Imran Khan, Wasim and Waqar – the old gladiators who reserved their best for a battle against India? Where was Javed Miandad – that Miandad whose last ball six to clinch victory from certain defeat struck a psychological blow that Indian cricket took a decade to recover. Where were those warriors now? Why had the roles been reversed?

Aftab and Mehtab groaned, Aftab with his hand on his head, "Fuck, Fuck, Fuck," he muttered. Shahnawaz chose to ignore his son's profanity. "Damn," Adnan slapped his forehead, "I don't mind if we lose, but not to India. Shit."

Suleiman was there, standing in one corner, prayer beads in hand, his face a cloud. He looked like he wanted to hurl something at the TV screen. Perhaps had he been in his own room and not his master's study he would have.

Shahnawaz went out, poured himself a large, stiff drink and lit another cigarette. He drew the curtains and looked outside. The entire city seemed silent and gloomy. But then, it would be in mourning. A loss to India was always a national calamity.

### III

Joginder Sharma pitched the ball short and Misbah stepped out and lofted him cleanly over long-on for a six.

"Oh no" The groans rang out across the room. Vikram and Supriya had got their friends over to watch the match at home and they now lay sprawled on the rugs and sofas of our drawing room, cheering and moaning alternatively, as the match headed for its nail biting finish.

Joginder trundled in again, Misbah bent low, scooped the ball over the wicket keeper's head – the room groaned again, it seemed the ball was headed for the boundary; it swirled interminably in the air and then landed safely in the hands of Sreesanth at the fine-leg boundary. The commentator screamed, "Misbah scoops, in the air, Sreesanth takes it, INDIA WIN – India win by five runs."

I jumped up and down the sofa like an excited child. By my side, Vikram, Supriya and their friends hugged and high-fived each other and the room erupted in wild, raucous cheers.

Nivedita came in, a plate of *pakoras* in hand. Vikram ran up to her, took the plate from her hand, twirled her in a small pirouette and laughed out, *"Maa. Jeet jaye. Hum jeet gaye"* (*Mom, we have won; we have won*)

*"Oh ho. Yeh to aakhir cricket match hi hai,"* (It is only a cricket match after all)Nivedita could never really get the cricketing fever that caught us all.

*"Match hi nahi hai Maa. Yeh Jung hai."* (It's not just a match, Mom. Its war) He pirouetted her again.

Outside, I could hear crowds cheering, car horns blowing in celebration, fireworks lighting up the night sky. It was not just India winning the World Cup. It was India beating Pakistan and that made the victory even sweeter.

Dhoni was striding across the screen now and the room erupted in cheers again as he lifted up the trophy, his teammates crowding behind. How different they were, this young team of ours. This generation of players that swaggered out in to the field as if they owned it. I had grown up with that generation that took the field to avoid losing matches, not to win them; those who looked upon a draw as a victory. Not this one. They went after victory like it was a birth right and more often than not claimed it.

*"Aaj to drink ban hi jaata hai,"* (This calls for a drink). I rushed to my small bar, pulled out my best whiskey, passed it to Vikram, who poured it in glasses, paper cups, whatever was available and passed it around to his friends. I raised my glass with them in a toast of celebration. This was India's generation, these confident young people crowding around our drawing room. This was India's new generation, full of fire, talent and self-belief, demanding victory in the same way that Dhoni's young team claimed theirs. All they wanted was a level playing field where they could attain it.

Vikram, Supriya and their friends trooped out to continue their flag-waving celebrations outside. Nivedita and I sat down on the sofa together, the house suddenly silent, except for the post-match replays on television. We both liked this. We liked the feeling of our house being full of people, of hearing the sounds of laughter within our home. I poured myself another drink, pulled her close to me in a sudden wave of tenderness. The television screen still flickered, but now I was no longer watching. It just felt good to be just sitting there with her like that.

# 'AMAN KI ASHA' – THE HOPE FOR PEACE

**Mumbai, August 2008**

I wanted to stroke Nivedita's hair one last time – stroke it the way she always liked me to do. She lay so still now, her face calm and unlined, her white hair combed neatly back, the *sindoor,* blood red in its parting. She looked serene, so very serene. I wonder what thought had passed her mind in the last instant of her life. It must have been of Gaurav.

She was restless all night, tossed and turned repeatedly. Then when I woke her up at her usual seven, she merely said, "I'm tired. I think I'll sleep some more." Then she just continued sleeping.

We placed her flower bedecked bier on the platform of the electric crematorium. The platform tilted, slid her body through the small circular door and carried her in to the furnace within. In the brief opening of the door, I felt the waves of heat emanating from within. Then the door clanged shut and I was left with nothing but cold loneliness.

They say that when a parent dies you lose your past; when a spouse goes, you lose the present; with a child you lose the future. I had lost my parents – both sets; I had lost my dearest son, and now my life's companion. What was left was just a vague and empty future staring emptily back at me.

But there were at least Vikram and Supriya to fill my empty thoughts. But they too would soon leave to follow their own lives. Vikram had already left. He was at Mumbai now, with an MNC, flying in often, calling every day, but living his own life – just as it should be. Supriya was here with me, flitting in and out from rehearsals, dance performances and TV shows, slowly making her mark as one of the rising dancers of this generation. She too would leave to follow her own destiny. And then, I truly would be alone.

So I did what I could. Pushed aside these negative thoughts, immersed myself in the solace of my job, which I had been performing for seven years now. I had seen the company grow from a start-up by two whiz kids from small-town India to one of India's most innovative software solutions companies. The company had grown with India's economic boom and I had grown too. From looking after a small office space with 30 employees, I was now in charge of the entire building and the growing staff of 150 odd employees. My job as head of Admin and Security in Accent InfoSolutions was my support system and that small cubicle of an office, my sanctuary. There, with the small army of drivers, security staff, lift operators, peons and sweepers under me, I filled my days.

It was on one of those days when I returned from work, that Supriya greeted me at the door her hands waving a small white envelope.

"Dad, guess what. Guess what I received."

She didn't wait for a reply, "I have been invited to perform at the Indo-Pak 'Festival of Friendship.' Some of the best artists from both nations will be performing – Rehat Ali Fateh, Shazia Khan, A R Rehman, Shankar Mahadevan – and Me. Can you imagine it, Me? She kissed the envelop, "I can't believe it"

I hugged her, "Well, I can. I knew that one day you would be there. When is the show?'

"This August, at the Taj Hotel in Mumbai. God, that gives me just four months to choreograph and rehearse.... And you are coming with me. We will stay in the best place in Mumbai, we'll meet the best artists of both countries. You'll love it."

"More than that, I'll get to see you on stage again," I hugged her indulgently, "And I know that you will be the best of them all."

## II

Shahnawaz reached home at ten that night, a little later than usual. But then his plan was in its final stages and he wanted to fine-tune each aspect of it.

Shazia was waiting for him as she usually did. Even at this late hour she was perfectly dressed as always, and in her hand she held a small white envelope.

"You know," she held up the envelope, "We are going to India."

"India? What on earth for?"

"I have been invited to sing at the 'Festival of Friendship.' It's a gathering of artists from India and Pakistan to bring our nations closer – at least culturally. After all, we have so much in common. You know, my records have sold better in India than in Pakistan."

"Well, if they have invited you, I know you will want to go. When is the show?"

"This August, in Mumbai. And it is not 'I' going; it is 'We'. You are coming with me. I don't want you making any excuses this time."

Mumbai. What a bloody coincidence. That was the target he had selected for his strike. Yes, of course, Shahnawaz would go. He would see the show, see Mumbai, see the Taj Hotel – it would give him a first-hand glimpse of the target he had in mind.

## III

My jaw dropped as I entered the lobby of the Taj. I had never seen anything like this before. That marbled floor, those exquisite carpets, the crystal and chandeliers, the onyx reception table – and that rich, luxurious smell of money and class.

I felt out of place in these surroundings. This was a place for the elite, the very rich, the ones who had really made it. I was glad Supriya was here with me – checking us in, smiling to the staff, allowing us to be guided to our room – and then my jaw dropped again.

What a room. The large bay windows opened out to the Gateway of India and the vast Arabian Sea beyond. On the horizon a line of ships waited, closer to the shore hundreds of small boats bobbed up and down in the inky waters. Beneath me, on the road below, an Audi roared past a horse-carriage – I didn't know they still had them here, but they did, for the tourists. I took in the sights of Mumbai; Mumbai, the city of dreams, the city where you could make your fortune, or break your heart, the city that never slept, acity which never had the time to.

I turned to Supriya, "*Beti*, how much will this room cost?"

She laughed gaily, "Don't worry about that. The organizers are paying for it. Let's just enjoy it for the three days we are here"

She traipsed out of the room. Her show was tomorrow, and though she had practiced a million times, I knew she would want one last look, one final rehearsal, before the big night tomorrow.

## IV

Shazia smiled graciously as she accepted the large bouquet – tulips – her favourite flowers. Obviously, they had researched her likes and dislikes well.

Shahnawaz shifted uncomfortably as they placed the garland on him, put a 'tikka' on his forehead. Yes, they had gone out of their way to make them feel welcome in India, but he was never one for ceremony. Also he was here for things far more important than a cultural meet.

The tall Sikh doorman opened the door and ushered them in to the lobby. Shahnawaz had seen some of the best in the world during his travels, and he had to admit, the Taj was right up there.

He took in the throng of guests – the rich, the well-heeled, the foreigners; he took in the mural of MF Hussein at the Reception Table, the grand piano in the corner. His eye registered the Harbour Bar in one corner, the Shamiana Coffee Shop in the other; it followed the corridors from the lobby leading to the rooms above. He took it all in, though not with the eyes of a connoisseur, but of a hunter surveying its prey.

He liked the view from his room too. The view of the Gateway of India and the wide Arabian Sea. Hundreds of fishing boats dotted the harbour, one more could come in virtually unnoticed. Thanks to the invitation Shazia had received, he had a God-sent opportunity for a confirmatory reconnaissance of the target he had in mind. The plan was clear now. It would be Mumbai, it would be the Taj Hotel, and the attackers would come in from the Arabian Sea.

## V

I slid in to the outdoors auditorium, trying to make myself as inconspicuous as I could. Vikram guided us to our seats – one of the first row ones. That was the advantage of being the father of a performing artist. We always got the best seats.

I felt out of place in this audience. The who's who of the city, and of Pakistan, seemed tobe here. I recognized some film stars, saw the vice-captain of the Indian cricket team, beer barons (you know the one with his starlets, and jet-setting lifestyle – the one who had not paid his staff in months) the usual politicians, writers and artists from both nations. This was a must-do on the social scene.

Yes, that was hope for peace, there was a reaching of hearts. If our two nations could not meet politically, at least we could meet as people sharing a cultural bond;meet as individuals undivided by borders, untarnished by hate.

And this shared hope for peace played all of the evening. It came through Abida Parveen with her soulful sufi mysticism, it was there in the magical voice of Shazia Khan, in the driving beat of Junoon's eclectic mix of rock, sufi and classical music. It found echo in Shankar Mahadevan's soaring voice, in A R Rehman, in Indian Ocean as they sang of peace, of hope and togetherness and their sentiments seeped in to me – slowly, perhaps even reluctantly, but it did.

And then came Supriya for '*Aman ki Asha*' – the hope for peace – the final recital of the evening. The dancers wafted on to a darkened stage illuminated by flashes, with a jagged line of barbed wire, sand bags and bunkers separating a field of green. On both sides of the wire, the dancers in the colours of their nations, danced to their own rhythm in steps that seemed almost antagonistic. Then the music rose. I recognized the voice; it was Shazia Khan, 'The Nightingale of Pakistan.' Her voice seemed to strike at the wire and bunkers on stage and slowly the dancers followed her rhythm, their steps became as one. In their dance they moved closer, reached across the wire, touched hands, withdrew, and reached out again. Then their hands rose in unison, cut the wire in deft flicks, removed the sand bags, and dismantled the bunkers brick by brick. The wire fence broke and was winched away by a miracle of back-stage technology. Then it was only a field of green – an open undivided field across which the dancers moved uninhibitedly, their greens and whites and saffron blurring and joining, their hands linking, their steps becoming one, as Shazia Khan's voice rose in a heartfelt plea for peace.

Shazia's voice faded, the stage darkened, the curtain fell. Her voice and the dance had gripped us completely in its spell. I had built sand-bagged bunkers myself, laid miles and miles of barbed wire, reinforced them with mines; and I knew that once laid, they remained. The bunkers and wire fences were far more difficult to remove than to install. But in that moment, I too felt that the wire would collapse; that the sandbagged bunkers would be dismantled as they had on stage. I too felt that the balloons that rose in the colours of the two nations would rise together in harmony; that the doves that had been released would wing their way to each other's hearts. And I too believed that the sounds of firecrackers erupting in the background, would be just that – firecrackers – and not the cracks of gunshots.

## VI

It took Supriya two hours to emerge after the show. By now we knew the signs – the better the performance, the longer was the wait.

Vikram and Iwere waiting outside the Taj when Supriya joined us, a huge bouquet of flowers in hand. And there, I bumped in to my past.

I recognized the lady who was coming up to us, who could not. She was Shazia Khan, the Nightingale of Pakistan, who had sung the final number for Supriya's recital. What a voice. And how beautiful she was. She was immaculately dressed in a white *shalwar kameez*, with a green *dupatta*. Her jewelry – though not much – were all in pearls and emeralds, white on green. She had obviously coordinated each aspect of her attire.

Supriya started with pleased surprise as Shazia approached her, then bent down instinctively and touched her feet. "Shaziaji, I could never imagine that one day, I would dance to your voice. I will always cherish this moment."

Shazia held her face in both hands and kissed her lightly on the forehead. That maternal gesture reminded me achingly of Nivedita. God, how I missed her.

"Such talent. And that too in one so young. What a beautiful dance."

Supriya turned to introduce us, "My father, my brother, Vikram".

I bowed in Namaste to her, turned towards her husband. I had seen him before, but where. His face, his body structure seemed so familiar. I knew him.

He shook hands, a firm strong grip, and in that moment of contact I felt a strange connect pass through us.

He was a little taller than me, definitely far more fit. His hairline, like mine was receding and formed a deep 'U' shaped indentation above his right eyebrow, so akin to the contours of my own hairline. He looked at me with strong, grave eyes and introduced himself.

"Shahnawaz." It was a simple introduction made with the brevity of a man who does not want to divulge too much. Of a man who half expects everyone to know who he is.

And then I remembered who he was. Captain Shahnawaz Khan, that Pakistani officer in the Prisoner of War camp at Barrackpore.

I thought I detected a flicker of recognition in his eyes. Then the brown eyes behind the spectacles retained its old impassive look and he smiled, "You have a very talented daughter."

Perhaps I could have reminded him of our past. Of that year spent together in 1972. But I did not have to. His eyes told me that he remembered. His voice said he did not want to acknowledge it.

We stood uncomfortably as Supriya and Shazia prattled on about the show. Then more to break the silence than anything else, I asked, "And what are you doing, now."

That 'now' just slipped out. It should have not been there.

"I am a businessman," again the taciturn reply of one who broaches no questions.

Vikram chimed in, more to keep the conversation ball rolling than anything else, "Great show. I hope we really do have peace between our two countries."

"I hope so too. Perhaps when the Kashmir issue is resolved, we can have permanent peace."

Vikram stiffened. We had lost Gaurav in Kashmir. His voice had a hard edge when he replied, "Or when you stop sponsoring terrorist acts inside our country"

Shazia turned, "I don't think this is the time to be discussing these things. There will be peace between our people. Didn't you see it in today evening's show? Both our people want it." She said it with conviction, she obviously believed in it.

"But, we had better be going now," and then she slowly unclasped the pearls and emerald bracelet from her hand.

"Here," she pressed it in Supriya's hand, "Just a small token from me to you."

She waved aside Supriya's protests, "Or, you could take it as a small token from a Pakistani to an Indian," she smiled, kissed her gently on the forehead.

I saw Shahnawaz touch his wife lightly on her elbow. He obviously wanted to leave soon. I turned to him, "It was a pleasure meeting you again", Ouch. Why did that 'again' have to come out?

He nodded impassively. We stood awkwardly, half reaching out towards each other, for a farewell handshake. Then the heavens split. A flash of lightning lit the night sky, and the clouds of the retreating monsoon that had been gathering overhead, broke. Then the first drops splashed down – strong and heavy.

Mumbai rains erupt suddenly and this one came in faster and harder than usual. The first sheets of rain cascaded down. We moved back, our extended hands retracting, not touching, not making contact. Then he nodded again, put his arms around his wife and hurried her to the shelter of the Taj lobby.

They never did complete the handshake. But then, Mumbai's retreating monsoon did not want it; the heavy air did not desire it, the rain cascading in waves now, did not permit it. The elements themselves did not want that contact. The hands would remain extended and would retract, without touch, as they had so often before. And as before, the songs of "*Aman ki Asha*" would be drowned by the sound of approaching thunder.

# OPERATION MUMBAI

## Mumbai, 26 November 2008

*At 8.20 in the evening of 26 November 2008, a group of young men landed from a small rubber dinghy at Badhwar Peth, a small fisherman's colony in uptown Mumbai. These men, young, illiterate and impoverished had been recruited by the Lashkar-e-Toiba, to carry out a deadly attack on the unsuspecting city.*

*In groups of two they reached their targets. One hit the Leopold Café, a popular watering hole in uptown Colaba, another went to the Chatrapati Shivaji Terminal, one of the busiest and most crowded railway stations in the world. A third hit Chabad House, frequented by Jews, a fourth went to the Trident Oberoi and the fifth (later to be joined by the group from Leopold Café) struck the Taj Mahal Palace – one of the city's most prominent landmarks.*

*The wanton trail of destruction left 166 killed with over 300 injured. At the Taj Hotel itself thirty three perished as four terrorists stormed their way in to the lobby, across the restaurants, and then in to the rooms, killing and maiming indiscriminately. For almost 96 hours they held it in a state of siege – their actions covered by world media, their activities coordinated by handlers in Pakistan.*

*Virtually till the last moment the attackers were in touch via cell phone with their handlers in Pakistan. Yet in spite of the emphasis in ensuring that the operation could not be traced back to Pakistan, the planners failed. One of the attackers, an illiterate, 21 year old named Ajmal Kasab, was captured alive and gave out the details of the planners in Pakistan and the involvement of its security agencies. The finger now pointed directly at Pakistan.*

*With this attack the prospects of peace between the nations receded. 'Aman ki Asha,' proved to be just a hope. As had happened so often before, it was a hope that would not be realised.*

## II

Shahnawaz received the news that the party had landed at 8.20 pm on 26 November. Operation Mumbai was underway.

There were just three other officers from the ISI who were involved in it. For the most part, the Lashkar-e-Toiba had been doing the dirty work. It was better that way. Nothing could be traced back to them, and even if it was, state involvement could be easily denied.

9.30 pm. It would soon be starting now. He switched on his television. He would get all the news on the progress of the operation on TV now. Operation Mumbai would be covered live on TV.

## III

The ten young men who landed at the fisherman's colony near Colaba embraced each other before departing, promising to meet again in *jannat* – heaven. They had been together for over a year now and were closer than brothers, why they had even made a pact to die together.

They didn't speak much. Each knew what had to be done, they had rehearsed it repeatedly. The first pair entered the Leopold café; another reached the Taj Hotel, a third went to Chatrapati Shivaji Terminus, a fourth to the Oberoi Trident and another to the Chabad House. There they opened their rucksacks with their deadly cargo of one AK 47 rifle, twenty magazines, 10 Chinese made grenades, packets of raisins and almonds and bottles of energy drink inside.

And then the mayhem began.

## IV

Supriya picked up the phone. It was Vikram.

"Hey Sis, I know I had promised that I would fly down for the weekend, but I am stuck in Mumbai. Our Vice President is here from the USA and I have to brief her over dinner on our India activities."

"Brief *her,* eh? And over dinner, is it. That sounds interesting. And who is the *her* – a tall, blue-eyed, blonde American that you seem to be fond of?"

I heard Vikram laugh, "Right, Tall, blonde, blue-eyed – all of the three. Plus she is 65 and a grand-mother. She would be better suited for Dad than me. Ask him if he is interested."

Ouch. I could never get used to the cheeky, irreverent humour of this generation. We had far more respect for our elders in our days.

Supriya laughed, "Well, enjoy your dinner date. Where are you taking her by the way? At the Taj, is it? That's a great place if you are on company account. – See you, bro, have a good time."

She clicked off. "Vikram says he's going for dinner to the Taj this evening. Lucky guy."

V

Vikram entered the plush lobby of the Taj. He had dressed carefully, his briefcase with all the papers he needed were by his side. Christine Marion, his company's Vice President, was an important person and he wanted to make an impact.

She came down to the lobby a few minutes after he arrived – a tall elegant lady with a sense of quiet power. "Vikraaam, how good to see you. We have spoken so often over the phone and must have exchanged over a million emails by now. Good to finally meet in person."

Vikram shook hands, "Good to meet you too, Maam."

She waved her hand, "Call me Christine, everyone does." Her voice became very business-like, "I have been through your report and recommendations and have a few observations. Let's move in for a quick bite, and over dinner you can give me quick run-down."

Even as Christine and Vikram moved towards the Harbour Bar restaurant, two men, one in a red T-Shirt and baseball cap worn backwards, another in a Yellow T-Shirt and dark trousers, entered the lobby. For a while they seemed a little overwhelmed by the glittering chandeliers, the carpets, the frosted glass and onyx – the sheer opulence of the place. They looked like schoolboys in a forbidden playground. Then the elder – the one in a red T-shirt, nodded imperceptibly. In a smooth, well-rehearsed motion, the two unslung their rucksacks, removed the AK-47s within, clipped in the magazines taped together in pairs for rapid loading and began firing.

The tall Sikh doorman, the one who had sniffed disparagingly when they entered, was the first to fall. He collapsed on the marble floor, his starched white uniform slowly turning crimson. The next burst sprayed across the reception, shattering the onyx counter, ripping through the floor Manager. The two pretty receptionists fell with him. A guest having vermillion applied on his forehead in the traditional Taj welcome collapsed on the carpet – and then the screams began.

Vikram started as he heard the sounds of the first shots. Christine laughed, "Must be firecrackers. There is always a wedding here at the Taj." Then he saw the two men at the mouth of the lobby – AK-47s in hands – dived at Christine and pulled her to the floor.

That instinctive act saved their lives – at least for a while. The next burst went over them, smashing the plaster on the walls, ripping across the priceless mural by M F Hussein, shattering the chandelier above them, spraying them with glass.

Vikram remained lying there with Christine, their bodies partially concealed by a large sofa. The two gunmen fired indiscriminately and then headed for the Harbour Bar restaurant and its uncomprehending guests within.

Even now Vikram could not understand what was happening. Then from the back-entrance two more entered, both with rucksacks, both with AK-47s in hand.

"Run," he held Christine's hand, pulled her towards the narrow corridor leading to the rooms on the upper floors, dragged her up the stairs as a fresh burst of gunfire tore through the lobby beneath.

"Your room. Let's go in there. Run."

They raced up the three storeys to room 424, Christine's suite, rushed inside, and bolted it from within. Christine was crying.

Vikram sat next to her, "Maam – it is Okay. We are safe in here. There are about a thousand rooms in the hotel. The terrorists won't be able to search each one of them. And the police will soon be here. We'll just stay here till they arrive."

They switched off the lights, placed a mattress by the door for additional support and then opened the large bay windows overlooking Mumbai Harbour. It was too high to jump.

Below he could see the police jeeps arrive, hear the blare of their sirens. He could see people thronging the famed promenade – see the barricade being set up there by woefully ill-equipped, *lathi* wielding policemen. Beneath, the sounds of firing continued; there was a *whoomp*, then another – grenades; and then his mobile rang.

The sound coming from the closed, darkened room made him start. He grabbed at it.

"*Bhaiyya,*" Supriya screamed, "Are you Okay? Are you there in the Taj? What's happening there?"

"How do you know," the words came out incredulously.

"The news are full of it. *Bhaiyya*, are you Okay?"

"Supu, calm down. I am at the Taj. We are holed up in a room here. But we are fine. We will be out of here soon."

*Bhaiyya,* stay inside there. Don't come out. Just look after yourself, *Bhaiyya,* we are coming there."

Vikram switched off his phone. At least they knew where he was. All they had to do now was to stay calm and remain hidden till help arrived. And help would come soon, hopefully.

## VI

I wanted to speak to Vikram too, but Supriya had cut the call. God, I hoped he was fine. I had lost one son already. Oh God, look after my younger one.

Supriya took charge of the situation; called the police, told them of Vikram being trapped in the Taj. Then we rushed to Delhi Airport and caught the midnight flight to Mumbai.

The one hour forty minute flight to Mumbai was the longest I ever had. It was bad enough at Delhi airport with every television set flashing the news – MUMBAI UNDER ATTACK. The toll was over a hundred dead now, another 300 wounded – they had captured a terrorist – that bastard, I hope they skin him alive. Again and again the cameras zoomed on to the Taj Hotel, – the hotel where terrorists still roamed and where my son remained trapped inside.

I fell in to a brief fitful sleep during the flight – that half-awake, half-asleep kind of sleep. And after many years, that old nightmare of childhood came back to me. Only this time it was different. I dreamt that I was standing at Palam Airport, waiting for Gaurav's coffin to arrive from Kargil. Then suddenly the airfield became a vast refugee camp full of faceless figures in blue saris peering over a tricolor wrapped coffin, which Nivedita and me tried to open. I told her, "The politicians have even made money on these coffins – that's why they don't open."

Then the coffin opened and I peered inside. And it was not Gaurav in there. It was Vikram.

I awoke with a start. Supriya was over me, patting my hand, "it's okay, Dad, it's okay" Then the plane banked, the lights of Mumbai came in view – incongruously bright – and we landed to a city under siege.

We reached the Taj Hotel around dawn, crossing around fifty check points, on the way. They had caught one of the terrorists alive, eliminated the others. But four still remained in the Taj, prowling its plush interiors, searching the rooms, pulling out terrified guests and shooting them in cold-blooded slaughter. And my son was still in there. Oh, God, look after him.

## VII

Shahnawaz had not left his office all night. The operation was still on and going beyond his wildest expectations.

His television was tuned on to the Indian news channels and he flicked channels repeatedly, gradually forming a picture from the jig-saw puzzle of information that emanated from the screen. Virtually every channel in the world was focused on what was happening in Mumbai.

From the speaker phone by his side, he could hear the handlers calling the terrorists holed up inside the Taj. The calls were made from a stolen SIM card and were routed via internet, to prevent them from being traced back to Pakistan.

He heard the phone ring- it would be ringing inside the Taj now.

'*Salaam Aliekum.*" He recognized the voice. It was Major Iqbal – one of the ISI officers assigned for the operation.

"*Aliekum Salaam*" – this from the terrorist inside the Taj. The tongue rolled over the 'L' and 'S' in the rustic peasant accent of Pakistani Punjab.

"*Bhai*, you have done well. Your team has killed over 200 infidels. Just hold on. Hold on for as long as you can, the eyes of the world are on you."

"Abu is wounded in the leg. But we are fine. We have just executed ten hostages. What do we do now?" The voice sounded slurred, disoriented, as if on narcotics.

That was very likely. Most suicide attackers were pumped with drugs, especially as the end come close.

"The television says there are guests trapped in the rooms. Set fire to the hotel. That will get them outside. Go round each room. If anyone answers shoot them. Go now, kill as many as you can before they get you. Today is *Jumma* – Friday, a good day to die. Remember, Paradise awaits you."

The handler disconnected. Shahnawaz switched channels on the TV screen. It focused on the Taj, and from the sixth floor came an explosion.

Then tongues of flame leaped out from the windows, fanned by the sea breeze.

He flicked channels again, saw the now familiar image of the Taj, and from below, the ticker tape emerged, 'Mumbai under attack. Terrorist captured alive. Siege of Taj continues."

One of them captured alive. It was the one thing that he had been dreading. That could trace the whole operation back to Pakistan now. Damn. That was the problem with these local home-grown terrorists. They couldn't even become martyrs properly, like they were meant to.

## VIII

The smoke wafted in their room late at night. Christine screamed, "The hotel's on fire."

Vikram looked out of the window. The upper storey of the Taj was in flames, fire licking at the sixth and fifth floors. It was a matter of time before the fire crept up to them.

He opened the window; let the cool night air come in. They could not afford to be asphyxiated inhere. Images of the 9/11 bombing of the World Trade Center at New York came back to him, of people jumping from the burning building. Would he and Christine go the same way?

The phone rang again. It was Supriya. "*Bhaiyya,*" she whispered. There was no need to whisper. Had a terrorist been prowling nearby, he would have heard the phone ring in any case.

"We are here in Mumbai. We are beneath the hotel now. Don't worry, just stay where you are. The army will soon clear the place. You will be safe."

"When the fuck are they coming," after being trapped inside that room all night, Vikram's nerves were frayed.

And then there was a knock on the door.

Vikram put down the phone, one part of his mind screaming with relief at the thought that help had arrived, the other telling his mouth to be shut till they could verify who was outside. He raised his hands to his lips to Christine, gesticulating, 'Be silent, don't answer'.

It was too late. Her own nerves at breaking point, Christine responded to the knock almost instinctively. She stood up, moved towards the door, "Who's it?"

It was the last words she spoke. The heavy AK -47 bullets pierced the door, ripped through the flimsy mattress placed across it and tore through Christine, hurling her on to the carpeted floor.

Another salvo of bullets poured in through the still bolted door. They were firing blindly, unseeingly, but in the confined space it was still lethal. And this salvo headed straight towards Vikram.

## IX

They cleared the hotel completely only on the third morning- when the National Security Guard commandos went in and cleared the surviving terrorists – shot them down like the dogs they were.

I stood with Supriya near the driveway of the Taj. No one was still allowed close, but tearful relatives were permitted to go near to see and identify a mangled body, wail over a lost one, sob with relief as a loved one appeared, shaken but whole. How would my own son be?

They came out on stretchers, one by one – A blonde American lady shot through the head. Her papers identified her as C Marion. Wasn't that the name of the same lady, whom Vikram had come to meet? I could feel my knees beginning to give way as the next stretcher came in view.

It was Vikram. Lying ashen faced there. It was Vikram. Supriya and Me pushed our way through the security cordon, saw him lying there on the stretcher, saw the blood through a roughly bandaged shoulder – I noticed that it was a Taj monogrammed napkin. His eyes flickered, they registered Supriya and me – and then he smiled.

If someone asks me of my most treasured memory of Vikram, it was this. This wan smile. That smile through blood-caked lips was barely a smile. But it told us all that we wanted to hear. A smile that said that he was alive and that he was still there with us.

X

But in my relief at seeing my son alive, came an incident that tarnished the sanctity of the moment. As my son was being carried out in to the ambulance, with the other injured, even as the bodies were being identified and slowly carried out, in came a face that I loathed. It came in with a huge entourage of white Ambassador cars, beacons flashing. It came in with two car loads of special commandoes for protection, it came in the Taj lobby with cameras and journalists in tow. It came in with that sneering swagger that one associated with it.

It was Bharat Haladi – now the Minister for Internal Security – the man responsible for keeping us safe – the man who had been on a foreign jaunt when all this was happening. With him was his son, an aspiring Bollywood actor and another dark, oily man bedecked in gold chains and rings. We found later that he was one of the wealthiest film producers of Bollywood.

They strode through the burnt-out lobby, laughing and joking. They seemed to be discussing a movie that they would make on it, with his son in the leading role. They went around the hotel, Black Cat commandoes surrounding him, turned to the TV cameras, and then waved and left.

That bastard. Here, in the deadliest attack on the country, the man responsible for keeping us safe was concerned about making money through a film on the event – a film that would launch his son. The smugness of that swine. I had the urge to yank a weapon from the NSG commando next to him and empty its magazine in his plump oily face. I pushed that thought away. Fuck that scumbag. My son had survived and in that moment, that was all that mattered.

## XI

Yes, Vikram survived. He stayed in hospital for three months, but he lived. He did not leave. And when the Taj reopened a year later, we were there. All three of us. We were there in the solemn crowd of diners, those who had been there on the night of 26/11 and had survived. We stood in a minute of silence for those who did not. And we had a drink for the first time after that evening. We drank to the memory of Christine Marion and the hundreds like her, we drank to the courage of the security men who died saving countless others, we drank to the Taj; we drank to the spirit of Mumbai – a city that responded to the nation's deadliest terrorist attack in the only way it knew. By getting on its feet and back to work the very next day. It was the city's way of telling its attackers, "FUCK YOU."

# Deeper into the Abyss

## Pakistan 2009

Shahnawaz walked out of the Prime Minister's office and mopped his brow. It had been another grueling session. Ever since that idiot Ajmal Kasab had allowed himself to be captured alive, virtually every eye had been turned accusingly at the ISI. He had denied all involvement, of course, that was standard operating procedure. In any case, nothing could be traced directly back to them.

These had been tense days. The world had pointed its finger accusingly at Pakistan and an angry, wounded India called for vengeance. Then gradually, the rhetoric eased off and the fears of war receded. But, in all this there had been little let up in their own internal war. Militant activity did not abate. Acts of sabotage, assassination, bomb blasts and sectarian killings continued across the nation. Military actions against them too intensified. Then came the call.

It was from an unknown number, but he recognized the voice instantly.

*"Salaam Aliekum Janaab! Aap ne Mumbai ko bahut bada jhatka diya hai. Mubarak ho! Aakhir who kaafir hi hamere sahi dushman hai."* (You have struck a big blow at Mumbai. Congratulations. After all those infidels are our true enemies)

Shahnawaz did not reply. There had to be more. Baitullah couldn't be calling just to offer his congratulations.

*Mere pass 35,000 Mujahidin hai aur 400 suicide bomber jo shahadat ke liye taiyar hai. Agar tum kaho to main unhe kal India bhej sakta hoon"*

(I have 35,000 Mujahidin and 400 suicide bombers with me. At your command I can send them in to India)

Was this guy offering some kind of truce, "*Aur tumhe kya chahiye?*" *(*And what is it that you want in return)

*"Bas, aap ke military operations band kar do. Tumhara bhi faida hoga, hamara bhi" (*Simple. Just stop your military operations against us. It will be better for both of us).

Shahnawaz knew the implications of this. Over the past few months military operations against the militants had intensified. If he called off military operations against the militants, it would free a lot of troops. And if Baitullah agreed to call off his activities inside Pakistan – why his nation would have a reprieve from the violence that had engulfed it all these years. But there had to be something more to it.

"*Theek hai, aur kya"* (And what else)

*"Janaab, hameri ek aur maang hai. Pakistan me Shariat aa jaye ga. Pakistan ek Islamic state banega*" (And our main demand. Bring in *Shariat* in Pakistan. Make it an Islamic state)

"Impossible. I am willing to call off operations against you, if you agree to a cease-fire. But your second condition is unacceptable. Pakistan is governed by its own laws and constitution. Islamic laws cannot be imposed upon it."

"Oh, no, my friend. We will impose Islamic law here. Just as we imposed it in Afghanistan. That is what we want. That is what the people want. And you are a Muslim. That is what you should want too."

"Baitullah, Pakistan is not Afghanistan. It is a liberal nation. I have seen what your brand of Islam did to Afghanistan. I will not allow you to impose it on us."

Baitullah's voice hardened, "*Shariat* is the law of Allah. And we will impose it. Even if we have to eliminate every man who opposes it. We will make Pakistan the Islamic Emirate of Pakistan. And from here we will teach the world what Islam is."

The call disconnected. Shahnawaz looked at the silent phone. Baitullah and his Tehrik-e-Taliban had been demanding the imposition of *Shariat* for years now. But he knew what it would do to his nation. It would put Pakistan back to the medieval ages. The Pakistan the Taliban wanted to create was a radical Pakistan with public floggings, beheadings and executions, with a ban on entertainment and anything joyous. It was not the vision of Pakistan that Jinnah and its founders had envisaged. And this was not the Pakistan he would allow Baitullah and his creed to create. Oh no, he wouldn't. Not now, not in his lifetime, never.

**II**

The next call came two months later. It was a different number, but the voice at the other end was the same, "*Salaam Aliekum, Janaab.*"

As always, Shahnawaz said nothing. He knew what was coming.

"*Janaab*, you have not stopped your military operations against us. And I hear that you have ordered two more divisions to be sent against us. We are true Islamists, your brethren. You should be with us, not combating us."

That was true. Shahnawaz had ordered an intensification of military operations against the Taliban. He had taken charge personally of these operations and had put in everything the army had against them- tanks, attack helicopters, artillery- everything. After months, the operations were achieving some measure of success.

Though how did he know about the two additional divisions. He had ordered that just yesterday and they had not even begun moving. But then, his own Headquarters, like every other institution in Pakistan had been infiltrated by the militants and their sympathizers.

Yet, his spy-master's antennae had caught on to the inflexion in Wazir's voice. Its usual contemptuous arrogance was missing. He seemed a little defensive now. Good. That meant the operations were hurting him.

"What do you want?" He kept his voice cold, deliberately so. He was not willing to make any concessions now.

"Call of your operations. We will order a truce. We can discuss a solution then."

It was an old trick. Each time, army operations began succeeding; the militants would propose a truce- and then promptly break it once they had recovered their strength.

"A truce? Yes, we will have a truce. But you and your men must lay down your arms first. Then we will discuss."

Baitullah's voice hardened, "We have never laid down our arms. You think we will do it for you. Remember. If the military operations you have started against us do not stop, it will be you, and you alone, that will be responsible for the consequences. Let this be my last warning."

The call disconnected. Baitullah never spoke for more than 30 seconds or so to avoid his calls being traced. If he could get him to talk longer, his signal agencies would be able to home on to him.

Forty eight hours after the call came another message. It was delivered to his residence in a large brown envelope, along with his official *dak*, sealed with the insignia of Army General Headquarters.

He opened it – it seemed to be just routine official mail, though the envelope was larger than usual and there seemed to be something soft inside. He tore open the seal, ripped the brown, coarse envelope – and the contents poured out.

There was no official correspondence inside it. It just contained just a simple white sheet, a thread, a needle, and 1000 Rupees in crisp 100 Rupee notes.

He stared at it a long time. It was Wazir's signature warning. He had asked him to prepare his own burial shroud, and sent him one thousand Rupees as funeral expenses. One thousand Rupees, that's all. One thousand Rupees, the cost of a funeral; One thousand Rupees, the cost of a life in Pakistan.

### III

The first attack came just two days later when a suicide bomber rammed his truck into the gates of the ISI Headquarters, around five fifteen in the evening, the blast shattering the quiet unobtrusive gates, the truck, the bomber and thirty five operatives and clerks who were leaving for the day.

That attack was just a warning. The real attack came a week later.

He was returning to Islamabad late one evening after a meeting with his commanders engaged in operations against the Taliban. He did not know how they found out about his route, or the time he would be there. But then the Taliban had infiltrated deep – far deeper than anyone imagined.

His cavalcade raced towards Islamabad. It passed the fields that lined the National Highway on both sides, approached the bridge on the Rohi Nala – the British era flood drain that carried sludge and waste away from the city. There was little traffic, but nowadays people rarely travelled late. The only person in view was a peasant lolling around the bridge, nonchalantly chewing a blade of grass. He couldn't have been more than 16, that bare-footed boy in his ragged *dishdasha,* skull cap and sparse beard. But why did he have that shawl around him, and that too in this heat. Shahnawaz felt a faint premonition of danger; something was wrong. He leaned ahead to tell the driver to slow down – and then the boy exploded.

They were still around forty meters from the bridge, but the force of the explosion hurled the heavy, armour plated car off the road. The driver struggled to get the car back under control and braked to a halt. Ahead of him, the leading pilot vehicle had careened of the road in flames, the driver and crew killed almost instantly by the force of the blast. There was no trace of the boy. Just a small blackened crater by the side of the bridge where he once stood, chewing a blade of grass.

They discovered shards of him much later – shards, that's all, not even enough for an identification. He had detonated himself pre-maturely and that had saved Shahnawaz. Even as his security men closed in and formed a protective ring around him, from the mosque in a nearby by village came the muezzin's call for the evening prayers. Shahnawaz turned to that sound and involuntarily bent his head in prayer. But it was not a prayer of thanksgiving for his survival – it was more a plea for the survival of his nation.

## IV

That close shave did not affect Shahnawaz's resolve. He continued his operations against the Taliban, if anything, he further intensified it. But the next warning worked.

It came in the same coarse, brown envelop with the emblem of Pakistan Army GHQ stamped on it, delivered the same way as before. And it was not directed at him. It was at Shazia.

It contained just two lines in crude, ill-spelt Urdu, "Your wife's actions of singing and being seen by men is improper and un-Islamic. She is warned to mend her ways and spend time in prayer instead." There was no signature, just two crossed scimitars – the insignia of the Tehrik-e-Taliban – at the bottom.

He did not tell Shazia about it, but discreetly increased her security. She was busy recording her latest album, "The Nightingale Sings Again" and he knew that the note – whether sent by a crank, or by Wazir himself- would definitely affect her.

She had been working on a collection of 12 songs, a fusion of ghazals, sufi, classical music and modern rock for over a year and was halfway through the recording. He did not want anything to disturb her now.

Her call came when he was in the middle of a conference. He knew it was her instantly. The ring tone for her number had been set to "Aar ya Paar" his favourite composition of hers.

She would never ring unless it was an emergency. Damn. He excused himself, went outside the conference hall and took the call.

But it wasn't Shazia on the other end. It was someone else. Someone spluttering in confusion and fright, "Sir – myself Ibrahim Ilahi – Manager Mehboob Studios – Sir – Madam".

Shahnawaz's heart turned cold. It had been just two weeks that the warning letter had arrived. "What happened, man? Get a grip on yourself. Where is my wife? Get her on the phone."

It was no use. The studio manager was too flustered to say anything coherently.

Allah. Let her be safe. Shahnawaz rushed to his staff car and raced towards Mehboob Studios – the studio where Shazia was recording- and was there in seventeen minutes flat.

Suleiman was there at the gate, looking shaken and sheepish. He had assigned him for her personal security and insisted that he accompany her whenever she left the home. At least, him, he could trust.

"Sir," Suleiman blurted, "*Madam andar hai. Woh theekh hai.*" (Madam is inside. She is Okay)

That was all he wanted to hear. He rushed past and sprinted inside the studio. Shazia was there – thank God – sitting on a sofa in the Manager's office, crying softly to herself. For the first time in all these years, she looked her age.

He held her close, let her cry in his arms, let her feel safe again, let the sobs subside.

He placed her gently on the sofa, turned to the trembling manager, "What happened?"

"Madam received this parcel. Then she fainted."

He handed over a small white cardboard box, beautifully wrapped and decorated – the kind of box in which her fans often sent small offerings.

There was an offering inside, but it had not come from an ardent fan.

There on a pristine white bed of cotton, stained by just a few small beads of red lay a nightingale. A beautiful white and brown nightingale, small enough to be nestled in the palm of a child's hand. It lay stiff and silent in its coffin of white cotton, the white of the feathers around its neck darkened by a bright red ring of blood around it.

Its throat had been slit.

## V

Shazia never did finish her album. She never went back to the recording studio either. She went up to her rehearsal room at times, but she rarely, if ever sang, not even in the privacy of her room.

Shahnawaz tried to coax her out of it. But there was little he could do. The small brown and white nightingale with a ring of blood around its throat was too stark a symbol for Shazia to put behind her.

Shahnawaz could not forget that symbol either. It was a symbol of all the silenced voices of Pakistan. It was a symbol of all the beauty and joy that the Islamic fundamentalists wanted to destroy. It was a symbol of their reach. If they could silence the voice of the wife of the Director General ISI, they could silence every voice that dared speak out against their puritanical values. And they were succeeding too. Slowly, the dissenting voices and saner minds were falling silent as their own shrill shrieks resounded all over Pakistan.

## VI

Baitullah's call came three months later. This time from another number later traced to Okara.

'*Mubarak Ho! Suna hai, Bhabhiji ne gaana-waana band kar diya hai. Woh ab sahi raaste par aa rahi hai. Abhi aap bhi samajh jayiye*" (Congratulations. I heard your wife has stopped her singing. Good. She is coming on the right lines. Now you must understand as well)

Shahnawaz controlled himself, "*Kya chahiye tumhe*?" (What do you want?)

*"Bas, Apke military operations band ki jiye. Band karo yeh operations. Aakhir, aadha Pakistan to hamare saath hai.* (Stop your military operations against us. After all, half of Pakistan is on our side)

Shahnawaz knew that was true. The military operations he had ordered were taking a heavy toll of lives, both of the enemy and his own soldiers. But surprisingly, in spite of the atrocities of the militants many of the people still looked upon them as the soldiers of Islam and their model of radical Islam as the panacea for their nation. The fools.

And the politicians were no better. They would go rushing to appease the same militants who were destroying their country if they felt it would give them some kind of political mileage. There was this cricketer turned politician who now espoused their cause quite openly. And as far as their Prime Minister was concerned. That so-called "Mr 10 Percent" couldn't care what was happening to his country as long as he got his commission on every deal being made there.

Even the few voices that dared stand up to the Taliban were being silenced. Salman Taseer, the liberal Governor of Punjab, who spoke out against the radicals, and stood up for the minorities of his state, was killed by his own body-guard, who was then applauded and garlanded as he went to jail. No *maulvi* was willing to read Taseer's funeral prayers, but 500 lawyers pledged to defend his fanatic killer. The nation was sinking deeper in to the abyss of fundamentalism.

"I will not halt military actions, till you agree to drop your arms and abide by Pakistani law. This is Pakistan, not Afghanistan."

"We will never drop our arms. Nor will we give up our demand for *Shariat* in Pakistan. And we will achieve it. We have defeated the Russians, we are defeating the Americans. You think we can't beat the Pakistani Army?"

"No you can't, you bastard."

The call dropped. The thirty second rule. But it was encouraging. Baitullah asking so often for a truce meant that the army operations were succeeding. If he could increase the pressure and perhaps he could still break the Taliban and prevent Pakistan's slow descent into chaos.

He called all his Divisional Commanders to his office the next morning. "Gentlemen, we are intensifying operations. We will get Wazir and we will finish the Taliban. Remember, our country's future depends on it."

# 'THE JIHAD WILL GO ON'

## Pakistan 2010 Onwards

Shahnawaz gazed through his binoculars across the rolling mountains of the war-ravaged Swat Valley. What a beautiful place it had been at one time, full of holiday goers who came there to trek, take in the cool air, ski, eat the famed river trout, maybe even go hunting for antelope in the hills. He and Shazia had honeymooned there themselves; not that they had done any skiing or trekking – they were far too pre-occupied in other even more pleasurable activities. And now Shahnawaz was not admiring the beauty of the place. He was viewing it with the eyes of a tactician, taking in each peak, each likely defensive position, escape route and ambush site. The operations he had launched against the Taliban here were now in its final and most difficult phase.

Shahnawaz had intensified his operations against the Tehrik-e-Taliban and were now slowly closing in on their stronghold in the Swat Valley. Shahnawaz had taken charge of the campaign personally. He had unleashed attack helicopters and artillery, probed, closedin, taken control of the area village by village, ridgeline by ridgeline. His own men had taken heavy casualties, but he pushed them hard and slowly they had cleared the area of the Taliban. They were poised at the outskirts of Mingora, the capital of the Province and the stronghold of the Taliban.

Wazir was reported to be holed in there and he was the one Shahnawaz wanted. If he could get Wazir, it would give cripple the Taliban. And now his battle with Wazir was personal.

It took Shahnawaz three days before they finally cleared the last pockets of resistance and entered Mingora. He was amongst the first to enter the town, now shattered and ravaged by the fighting. And in there he realised what the Taliban had done to it.

He passed the town square, where the Taliban had hung their opponents from lamp posts and then let their putrefying bodies rot, with none daring to bring them down.

He passed the burnt out schools – the girls' school torched by the Taliban, where ten teachers had been executed before their shocked students for daring to defy their diktat.

He passed the closed video parlours and movie halls.

Crossed the mosque with 'Al Jihad, al-Qital' – Holy War, Bloody Battle – emblazoned on its walls.

Passed the abandoned *Mohallas*, whose inhabitants, mainly Shias, Hindus and Christians had fled after the initial massacres.

Passed the wailing women whose children had been abducted to become suicide bombers.

Passed the shattered buildings, the abandoned orchards, the broken homes and destroyed lives.

Saw a black-turbaned body on the street – a dead Taliban fighter – and resisted an urge to kick the inert body. You swines. What have you done to my country?

But there were only a few of the Taliban dead around. The dead were mainly the rank and file, the foot-soldiers. None of the big fish had been captured or killed. Wazir and his senior commanders were nowhere to be found.

But then Shahnawaz knew that the Taliban leaders would slip away and avoid a pitched battle. And he had prepared for it. All along the trails, on the escape routes, on the peaks, he had established Commando teams – his best. They had set up skillful ambushes, cutting down the fleeing Taliban as they tried to escape.

It was from one of these teams that he got the call, the long-awaited call, "Sir, we got him. We got Wazir."

## II

Wazir. Wazir himself. Shahnawaz could not believe it. He knew that Wazir and his key aides had been holed up in the valley, but his intelligence said that they had slipped out before the attack went in. Could it be possible? He had to go there and see for himself.

One of his Commando teams had engaged a large group of fleeing Taliban fighters the previous night. The encounter went on all night and by morning most of the Taliban – all 18 of them – had been eliminated. When the Pakistani Commandos closed in the next morning, all were dead – except one.

He reached the site of the encounter when the sun was just coming up. Major Shahid the young team leader of the Commando party was there waiting for him. He knew Shahid well. A fine upright officer, untouched by the fundamentalism that affected some of the others. He saluted as Shahnawaz approached.

Even in his exhaustion, the excitement showed, "Sir, we got Wazir."

He led him to the valley, in the bed of a dried up stream, where a dozen black-clad bodies lay. And there surrounded by three heavily armed commandos sat a figure that Shahnawaz remembered from his youth.

He was in his mid-twenties, lean, pale sun-burnt skin, sparse beard, narrow brown eyes rimmed with *kohl*. The Taliban fighters were fond of decorating their eyes with *kohl* before a battle. They felt it would make them appear even more attractive to the 72 virgins that awaited them when they attained martyrdom.

It was the Baitullah Wazir of thirty years back. A replica of the Baitullah, Shahnawaz had met for the first time in the terrace of his hut in a remote Afghan village. The same glaring eyes, the same cruel, upturned lips, the same arrogance and scorn. But it was not Baitullah, of course. It was his son Rahimtullah – his first-born, his heir, his successor, his military commander. The man who conducted the executions that his father had ordered. The man whom Baitullah loved above all else.

He glared as Shahnawaz approached. The kohl –lined eyes did not flicker. They stared with hatred and then he turned and spat; a thick glob of bloodied phlegm.

He was wounded. Not very badly – but was wounded all right. The wounds had prevented him from escaping and had left him helpless till the Commando party closed in. They could take him to the Military Hospital, treat him and interrogate him. But that bastard would reveal nothing. And in all probability, the Taliban would connive with the politicians and have him released just a few months later.

Major Shahid came up next to him, his weapon cradled beneath his armpit. He looked at Rahimtullah, turned to Shahnawaz and asked,

"Sir, what do I do with him?"

For a fleeting moment, the memory of a wounded Indian officer on the Kargil heights came back to him. Then it had been Baitullah who had asked the question. He had not replied then. He had not taken a decision, though he knew how it would be interpreted. The man whose life lay in balance on his reply then was a soldier, an Indian soldier, no doubt, but one fighting for his nation, dying for what he believed was right. This man was vermin. And this time there was no confusion in his mind. He made his decision instantly.

"Shoot the bastard."

He did not turn and walk away from his decision as he had done that day. He stood by and watched it all. He watched as Shahid cocked his weapon, stared at Rahimtullah as he glared back at him. He watched as Shahid got his weapon in line with Rahimtullah's face. Even then those eyes did not lose their contempt, He watched as Major Shahid thumbed down the safety catch, saw his finger begin a gentle squeeze on the trigger – saw the kohl-rimmed eyes flicker with fear for the first time – and then the burst smashed through his face, shutting the eyes forever, ripped the black, coiled turban from his head and hurtled him face down on the damp earth.

Shahnawaz watched the dark red blood seep out of the fractured skull in to the ground – that venomous blood would corrode the soil of his country. Then he patted Shahid lightly on his shoulder and said,

"Get me my Communications Officer."

### III

The call came the next evening as he knew it would.

*"Haraam Zaade. Madher chod.* I'll kill you. I'll kill each one of your family. That whore of your wife, I'll get myself. Then I'll have your sons brought to me alive. You bastard. I'll kill them slowly and every night you will hear their screams. And then, I'll get you."

Shahnawaz let the harangue continue for a minute or so. And when he paused he said, "If I were you, I would be more worried about saving my skin, Baitullah. Because I am coming after you next."

"You mother fucker. You think you can get me. The Russians could not. The Americans cannot. You think you will get me. You? A whore's son like you?"

"Yes, Baitullah. You have seven sons, no. Three have already died. One I killed yesterday. Start saying your funeral prayers for the other three as well."

"I'll kill you, you bastard. I'll kill you with my own hands. I'll wipe out each trace of your family..."

Shahnawaz liked the way the conversation was going. He had to make it continue, "Buy a funeral shroud, Baitullah. Buy four of them. One for you, one for each of your sons. Don't worry about the funeral expenses. I'll pay for that myself."

*"Madher chod.* I don't have just one son. I have thousands. How long do you think you can escape? I'll get you, every one of your family".

The harangue stopped abruptly. The phone switched silent. Shahnawaz looked at his watch. One minutes twenty eight seconds. Not bad.

He turned to his Communications Officer next to him He was hunched over a delicate looking instrument, adjusting its dials. The Communications Officer removed his earphones, looked up at Shahnawaz and smiled, "Sir, I have got his fix down to twenty meters."

## IV

The attack went in within the next twenty minutes. In any case, his commando teams were ready and waiting.

Baitullah's call was traced to a village just around thirty kilometres from where they were. The Huey Cobras Attack helicopters came in first with their rockets and cannons blazing, homing on to the exact hut from where the call had come.

The commando teams that came in the second wave, twelve minutes after the Huey Cobra had completed their third and final run, had to extricate what was left of Baitullah from the rubble. There was little – in fact only the DNA tests confirmed that it was indeed him. The final confirmation, if at all it was required came through an announcement by the Tehrik-e-Taliban the next day.

"Baitullah Wazir, the valiant warrior of Islam has attained martyrdom. His son has been appointed as the Emir of the *Tehrik-e-Taliban* and vowed to avenge the death of his father. The *jihad* will go on."

# INDIA – THE FALLING DREAM

## 2009-2012

*By around 2009 or so, the India success story was slipping. It was not the result of terrorist attacks on Indian soil, or any external factor. The seeds for its decline came from within. A nation that was all-set to give its teeming millions a better future, now paused, slipped and started falling. The India story seemed to be over.*

*And the fall broke the dreams of millions – the millions of young, talented, hard-working youth who had waited, degrees in hand, for a better tomorrow. It halted jobs, it reduced the rate of growth from a whopping 9.5 % to less than 5; it devalued the rupee; it dried foreign investments and projects; it stalled development and growth. Mere statistics don't tell the story. They don't reveal the extent of the tragedy that had befallen so many Indians, orphaned and betrayed by the policies of those who had created this situation.*

*The reason for India's decline was not hard to find. It had more to do with bad policies, it was more to do with corruption that raged unchecked in every walk of life. The corruption that allowed politicians and bureaucrats to amass millions without accountability, the corruption that made it impossible for any work, or business to fructify. The cancer of corruption ate in to each aspect of governance and everyday life, corroding its entrails.*

*The list of scams that emerged in the period were endless. In each case, the guilty, usually the well-connected politicians got away shamelessly and blatantly. A few, very few, spent small terms in jail, got out on bail and continued their shameless loot of the nation. Their actions was destroying not only the image and the progress of India. It was destroying the hopes of an entire generation and the anger of the failed generation was rising fast.*

## II

Vikram remained in hospital for three months before he returned home, and then took another two to recover sufficiently enough to start going back to work. In that time the support we received from all quarters surprised me. Vikram was treated as though he had returned from a war – though in a way he had.

We did not know it then, but the battles were just beginning. It would be battles that Vikram and millions of Indians would fight. The attack on Mumbai and the spate of terrorist attacks on India's soil could not diminish its spirit. What could was the vicious assault being inflicted upon it from within.

India's meteoric economic rise that had seen it climb steadily upwards since 1993, and had lifted millions out of poverty, was now coming to a close. And it had little to do with outside attacks. It was floundering because of the actions of its leaders.

For years now, the nation had been systematically looted. The corruption was rampant. It began at the top and seeped all the way below. And as the corruption corroded the nation, India's economy slipped and fell. It was going back to the era of slow growth and unemployment. In this environment, the companies that had established themselves with so much enthusiasm were closing down, putting hundreds without jobs.

Vikram had re-joined his job with his MNC with his usual enthusiasm. It was an exciting, highly- paid job, the kind that thousands of young, talented Indians had been occupying in the New India. Only, as he would often confide to me, things were changing.

The orders for his company were just not coming. The licences and permits required remained unsigned for months in different departments, any plan for expansion or forward movement was ruthlessly stymied. As his own company stagnated, it impacted the lives of Vikram and all who worked there.

The lay-off began. Sometime in mid 2011, Vikram and 250 like him found themselves without a job. Armed with degrees, skills and qualifications. But no opportunities.

In the time in which Vikram spent aimlessly at home, looking for another job, I realised what he had lost. I saw the frustrations rise, saw him drink far more heavily than ever before, heard the hard edge in his voice. It took four months to find another job, one not so paying, not so exciting, but a job nonetheless. Thousands of others were not so lucky.

That is what our so called leaders were doing to our country. They were not only emptying its coffers. They were destroying the hopes of an entire generation. They were orphaning a nation.

## III

Then it was my turn. I had been with Accent InfoSolutions for over ten years now and that little cubicle of mine had virtually become a second home. I enjoyed walking in there every morning, seeing the rows upon rows of work-stations, with T–shirt and jeans-clad software programmers hunched over them. I liked the hum of talk and activity and the sense of energy within its walls. Here, I belonged.

I had been part of the slow growth of the company, had seen it rise from a start-up to a premier software solutions firm. I had shared their plans, the excitement of clinching a new order or finalising another product and had seen a stream of young, talented men and women come and go through its walls. It had been a heady journey and I enjoyed being a part of it.

There were changes now. Over the past year or so there was the slow, imperceptible sense of decline. Expansion plans were put on hold, recruitment had halted, few new products rolled out. The bonuses and pay rises which had been doled out so generously before, became a trickle. I guess you couldn't really blame them. Business had been slow and there had been no new orders for a while now.

One had seen it before. After all, a cycle of ups and downs are part of a company's growth. But this time, the trough seemed longer and steeper. The rot in the environment outside had become far more endemic. Accent InfoSolutions had prided itself on its ethics and culture and its strict adherence of never offering any bribe or gift, whatever the circumstance. But now in the environment of corruption that steeped the nation, its very ethic seemed to be a drawback.

We did not receive any Divali bonus that year. And three months later, Sanjeev, my boss, called me to his office.

He began without preamble, "It's not been a very good year for us. You know it. We have lost those three major government contracts – those bastards wanted us to pay a whopper just to renew them. And when we refused to pay, they slapped us with about a million in retrograde taxes. That has wiped out what little we made."

"Fuck," he pounded his fist on the table, "I am sick of doing business in the country. You can't get the simplest thing done, till you grease every outstretched palm along the way, and then if you do get an order, they slam a dozen restrictions on you to make sure you still can't do it. It is getting impossible to do anything here."

I said nothing. I knew it was true.

"But anyway, we got to tighten our belts and hope things improve. But we're going to have to cut corners, if we want to survive. You will have to cut your staff by around twenty percent. Draw out a list of the people in your department we can let go. We'll wean them out slowly."

That was the beginning. Accent Software, like so many companies across the country, had downsized. Sorry, 'right-sized'. That was the term the HR guys used.

I went to my cubicle – made a small list of the administrative staff under me. There were nineteen of them. Four would have to go. Who?

Susheel – my assistant, who had been with me for five years now. He had just taken a company loan to put his daughter in college.

Javed – the Mr Dependable, who smiled his way through each job, scrounged each paisa, just to save enough to send home every month.

Mangal – the 19 year-old canteen boy, who studied late each night after his day's work, hoping to carve out a better future for himself.

Manmohan – reasonably efficient, wife, two young daughters. He had landed this job just two years ago.

The list continued. It said none of these things. It only contained an impersonal bio-data of each of my staff. But I knew them as people. I knew the impact that losing their jobs would have on them and their families. It would be a death sentence for their future hopes.

I identified four, convinced Sanjeev to reduce it by one, and watched the three on whom the axe had fallen, leave with despairing eyes and hunched shoulders at the end of the following month. And well, life went on.

But the effect of these changes were visible in the office. I saw the tensions creep in, saw the young executives hunch silently over their computers trying hard to prove that they were worth their salaries. They were all part of the young, bright generation of India. Many had worked themselves to their roles at immense cost and personal sacrifice. Like most of the young, they took their futures for granted, but now their very futures seemed to be in jeopardy.

And then the axe fell on me. Sanjeev called me to his office, "I'm afraid we are going to have to let you go."

"You know with the economy failing, we have been getting no new orders. We have lost each government contract. Even are foreign clients are keeping away. It is the state of the country. The politicians have fucked-up everything. They have put in rules that suit no-one but themselves. They are making the money, while the rest of us get screwed. We just have to cut costs now, if we want to survive"

He tried to soften the blow, "But don't worry. It's temporary. As soon as we get back on the rails, you'll be back in."

But all the sweet talk did not hide the basic fact – I had been fired. And on the 31st of that month, I closed my table, put my few personal belongings inside my briefcase and walked out of my home at Accent InfoSolutions without saying goodbye to a soul. No one said goodbye to me either. They all had their eyes averted in any case.

## IV

I drove past the Gurgaon-Delhi highway one last time. How I hated the peak-hour traffic jams I encountered there every day on my way to work and back. How I would miss them now.

I drove past the incomplete flyover that had been under construction for over a year and a half.

Went past the banners wishing Happy Birthday to a rising political leader – our beloved Bharat Haladi himself.

Crossed the traffic light where a seemingly educated man, reasonably well-dressed, tried to sell me a set of CDs.

Past the labourers family at work on a construction site. Their six year old daughter was playing with an infant in her arms, hurling him in the air, catching him again – both gurgling and laughing at each other. I don't know why the sight bought a lump in my throat.

Went past the 'Jai Bharat' petrol pump, now expanded to thrice its original size, with a huge poster of Bharat Haladi dominating one side. The same petrol pump, Haladi had usurped in my son's name.

Turned in to the lane and bumped in to the water tanker lurching in the narrow road leading in to our colony.

It had been a good monsoon that year but for some reason the supply of drinking water to the housing colonies had been drastically reduced. Water tankers were doing roaring business ferrying water to different colonies at exorbitant rates. This one had 'Jai Bharat Water Suppliers' emblazoned in red on its sides.

"*Behen Chod, Madher Chod*" the driver left his tanker cab and advanced menacingly towards me in my small car.

It was that bastard's fault in any case, but even before I got out of the car, he was on me. "*Buddhe. Dikh ta nahin hai kya?*

"What the...," even before I could complete my sentence, he slapped me viciously across the face, sending my spectacles flying, splitting my lip.

He turned, climbed in to the cab of his truck and drove away. Nobody tried to intervene, one stopped to help. The water-tanker cartel was part of a well-organised mafia, and this one was headed by the most powerful of them all – Bharat Haladi's cohorts themselves.

I turned to my house, clicked open the main door and slumped in to the empty chair in the drawing room. The house seemed very, very silent. And the silence seemed to be closing in on me.

# The Enemy Within

## Islamabad, 2012 Onwards

Shahnawaz was a little surprised at the mixed reactions to Baitullah's death. Although the television channels and the enlightened press hailed the death of the brutal warlord as a victory, most of the vernacular press condemned it, and even mourned the death of 'a true soldier of Islam.'

Prayer meetings were held in mosques on his behalf. And of course, the politicians jumped on the band-wagon, many of them now demanding an end to army operations, and calling for a truce with the Taliban. Even as the nation burned, they were still willing to join hands with the enemy to make political capital.

There came the usual wave of retaliation attacks. Bombs ripped through the GHQ building in Islamabad, a suicide bomber blew himself up in the dining hall of the troops that had participated in the operation; a wave of bombings hit Pakistan, the most deadly being at a mosque in the garrison town of Rawalpindi which killed 35 soldiers during their Friday morning prayers.

Shahnawaz did not let it deter him. The operations he had begun against the Taliban continued. They were the enemy now; they were the threat to his nation, not that bogie of India which they had been fighting all these years. He had identified the enemy now and it had to be kept at bay.

Attacks on his life continued as well. A suicide bomber slammed his explosive laden motorcycle on his vehicle – only the detonators did not work; the bombs did not explode. He survived yet again. Allah was looking after him. Perhaps he had entrusted him with the task of saving his country.

## II

Major Shahid walked into Shahnawaz's study. Shahnawaz had appointed him as his Personal Staff Officer. He needed someone like the tough, die-hard Commando with him. Someone he could trust.

"Sir, we have been receiving reports. There is likely to be another attack on your life. His voice dropped to a whisper. "The militants are trying to infiltrate into your personal staff. I am going to intensify the security here."

Shahnawaz waved it aside. Shahid was paranoid about security. "What more do we need. You have already got a full company here. My wife and I can't walk the lawns without one of your men appearing behind the bushes. Forget it. It's okay."

"No, Sir. It's not okay. I have vetted your entire personal staff. I have changed some of the security men who I felt had militant leanings and replaced them with some of my own men. We cannot be too careful, Sir."

Shahnawaz shrugged it aside. He did not like all this security around him, but knew that it was essential. He went back to his table as Shahid left.

He liked being here in his study. He liked sitting on his large, ornate teak table with its open view of the lawns. The table was his father's, a family heirloom. How often had he seen his father sit behind it in his study? He himself had sat there almost every day now for the past ten years or so.

Suleiman hobbled in to the room, placed a cup of tea by his side. It would be perfectly made, as always, at just the right temperature. He knew Shahnawaz's every requirement.

He had been at the Shahnawaz household ever since his injuries at Kargil. Shahnawaz kept him when he retired from service, gave him a comfortable retainer fee, gave him a place to stay within his bungalow and let him remain. It was the least he could do.

The Indian shrapnel he had taken on Shahnawaz's behalf was still lodged in his spine. He was in pain much of the time, his nights spent awake in spasms of agony. But he would emerge every morning, attend to Shahnawaz, hobble around the house to oversee its functioning, and generally make a nuisance of himself with the other staff.

He stood uneasily around the table. Shahnawaz recognised the body language and knew what was coming.

"*Saab,* I want leave for the rest of the day.

"Leave? You just went on leave a week ago. What do you want it for now?"

"Saab, I want to go to the Mosque and pray. The pain I get is because I have not been a true Muslim. I need to pray more."

Shahnawaz shrugged. "Okay, Go." He had got used to Suleiman's frequent leave requests by now. But he always granted him that. After all he was more than a retainer, why he was almost family.

**III**

Suleiman limped in to his study next morning. It was five thirty, but Shahnawaz was at his table as always, noting down the points for the day.

He was limping more than usual and his eyes were racked with pain. He would have spent another sleepless, pain-racked night, reading his Quran, letting its words take his mind of the pain.

He shuffled towards Shahnawaz's table, a cup of tea in his hand, and then the door burst in.

Major Shahid was there, gun in hand. Behind him was the new Guard Commander that Shahid had just got in. His carbine was levelled as well, its muzzle pointed towards Shahnawaz's table.

In that split-second, Shahnawaz understood. The assassin in his home which Shahid had spoken about yesterday was Shahid himself. Hehad even replaced the guard with his own men. Even as the thought crossed his mind, Shahid pointed his gun in his direction.

Suleiman dropped the tea cup, lurched towards him, coming in the line of fire. Both guns were trained on him now. Oh God, Shahnawaz thought, he is taking the bullet for me.

He heard the crack of Shahid's pistol, the staccato burst of the Guard Commander's carbine and saw Suleiman fall. Even as Shahnawaz ducked instinctively behind his desk, the room exploded.

The blast smashed through Suleiman, Shahid and the Guard Commander, hurling them like puppets. Shahnawaz felt waves of scorching heat hit him. Then the heavy teak table hurled down on him. He could smell burning hair and then the table splintered above him and he felt nothing more.

## IV

He remained in a coma for nine days. Nine days in which the doctors had almost given up hope. Nine days in which he lay poised between life and death.

Images floated through his mind as hovered in his dream-like state. His mother was there and she seemed to be calling him. *Abbajan* was there too, in his uniform, smiling down at him. He was in *Abbajan's* study – he was telling him, "So close, we were so close to Srinagar then". He was in the heights of Kargil, Wazir pointing a gun at a wounded Indian officer at his feet, saying "What do I do with him?" Suleiman came in to his office, limping into the line of fire in his office. Wazir was there again, just a disembodied voice threatening to eliminate his entire family. They all seemed to be calling him. And there was Shazia. She was singing, calling out to him. It was a soft call, but it was stronger than the other voices that filled his mind.

He opened his eyes to the call. Shazia was there above him. Was that Salim, Aftab and Mehtab behind her? Why wasn't Salim in his university at Berkeley? He closed his eyes again.

He opened them again the next day. They registered Shazia. Opened them again in the evening. Smiled. The next day Shazia fed him a few sips of juice. He drank and slept again.

It took a month before he was finally declared out of danger. His iron constitution had withstood the effects of the blast and concussion. The heavy teak table which had crashed into his ribs had taken the brunt of the shock. He survived, but just.

He found out the truth much later, when he asked about Suleiman. "He's dead," his Deputy Director told him.

"And Shahid? And that Guard Commander?"

"They are dead too. No one could have survived the blast."

His heart reached out for Suleiman. Crippled, pain-wracked Suleiman who had taken the bullets fired towards him. Oh God. Give him relief from his pain now.

And then the thought struck him. "That blast. What caused it? Did Shahid throw a grenade at me?"

His Deputy Director bending over him stiffened. He seemed to struggle for words.

"Sir, it was not Shahid. He was not trying to kill you. He saved your life."

"What do you mean? That bastard had his gun pointed at me. Had Suleiman not come in the way, I would have been dead."

"Sir, he was not aiming at you. He was aiming at Suleiman. Suleiman was the assassin that had come for you."

Shahnawaz felt his heart turn cold, "What do you mean?"

"Sir, Suleiman had been indoctrinated by the Islamic fundamentalists. They convinced him that you were an enemy of Islam and had to be eliminated. Shahid suspected it all along. A few of your guards had also been indoctrinated. That's why he changed them. Suleiman had an explosive vest around him that morning. Shahid found the casing of a detonator in Suleiman's room that morning and realized what he was going to do. That's why he rushed into your office. To stop Suleiman. To save you."

"What." Shahnawaz slumped back into his bed. Suleiman, an assassin. It was impossible. He had been with him for twenty years. Become a family member. It couldn't be Suleiman. Not him. .

But it was true. Suleiman, like so many others had been indoctrinated by Islamist militants. His loyalties had shifted to a warped version of jihad. And that was why the war inside Pakistan was so difficult to win. The enemy was within their own home.

V

The Taliban never succeed in getting Shahnawaz, but another cancer did. A cancer as insidious and deadly as the one eating his nation.

It had been growing within for years now. He had fed it with a rich diet of thirty cigarettes a day, he had ignored the warning signs – ignored the racking cough that had persisted for months. He hid from Shazia the fact that his sputum was ringed with blood every morning, suppressed the nausea and weakness that hit him with increased frequency. It was nothing, he said. It will go away if I ignore it. His country had said the same to its own cancer.

The doctors detected it when he was in hospital. By then it was already too late. Its tentacles had infected his lungs and were now reaching for his heart. Slowly the rapidly multiplying cells were infecting every organ.

Yet, he did fight it. Fought it for a year more – when the doctors had no hope of him lasting out more than three months. Fought it for six months more, and then seemed to recover. And then it struck again, more malevolently than before and took him away on the night of 13 August 2014.

## VI

But the Taliban had to have their revenge didn't they? They had to stamp their imprint. And they did.

They hit him next morning around midday, when his white-shrouded body had just been interred into his grave. When the aged *maulvi* who had recited prayers at the death of his parents and the birth of his sons, was intoning the funeral prayers. When the crowd of mourners – over a thousand of them who had come to say farewell to a much respected Pakistani – were standing by, their faces downward, when his sons Salim, Aftab and Mehtab were saying the final prayers for the dead. The blast hit them all.

It was triggered just around fifteen yards away. It could not touch his body, it had already been interred. But it claimed Salim and thirteen others. It wounded Aftab and the aged *maulvi*. It hit the psyche of all those who were there – like it was meant to. It demonstrated that Pakistan's war with itself was not over. It had merely transcended generations.

## VII

*Pakistan's war within threatens to tear the nation apart. It is a hydra that has been created on its soil. Lop off one head, another appears, kill a leader, another comes in his place, eliminate one, ten more arise.*

*Yet Pakistan has given birth to that hydra themselves. Spawned it, nurtured it and let it rise to its present form when it began consuming Pakistan itself. It has paid a heavy price for its ill-directed policies. Over 67,000 have perished in its internal war; over 2 million have been displaced. It has lost more security personnel battling the militants than in all its battles against India. The cancer that has been implanted now feeds on its soul.*

*Perhaps the realisation has come that their enemy lies within. It was not the India bogie that had been fighting. The sixty years of turmoil with India were wasted years – both for India and Pakistan. The wars achieved nothing. If anything, it only weakened Pakistan and brought it to the present state. The wars drained India too, diverted resources from both nations that could have been better used for their people.*

*As the militant cells multiply there are fears for the very existence of Pakistan. But Pakistan will survive. The inherent strength which saw it come through four wars with India, helped it withstand a cruel dismemberment, sustain itself through military takeovers and inept politicians, could help it withstand even this threat. Its strength could help it win the war within. And win it, it must. There is more at stake in this battle than was in all the wars with India. This battle is more than just for the continued existence of Pakistan. It is for its very soul.*

# A GUNSHOT IN ANGER

## New Delhi, 15 August 2014 and Onwards

Have you ever spent months with nothing to do? Just sitting at home, doing nothing, looking forward to nothing. I hope you never have to go through it.

It is one of the most sickening, deadening feelings that one can go through. The days are so meaningless, the thoughts so empty. I would awake early, more out of habit than anything else, go through the newspapers one by one, try to clean up the house a little bit, watch TV, have lunch, sleep, take a walk, watch TV, sleep. Each empty day like that eroded a small part of me and my self-esteem.

I was alone then. Vikram was with his new company and Supriya too had more or less shifted permanently to Mumbai – the scene of all cultural activity. I was alone here, with just my thoughts and dark negativism to keep me company.

Like Masterji, I turned to the newspapers to fill my empty thoughts. I read it from page to page. From the first page, where the headlines screamed out about the latest scam, the growing unemployment, the falling economy, to the sports page, where Dhoni's young team was fortunately still winning. I read about collapsing businesses, rising prices, the rapes and murders in the capital. I read about farmers' suicides, about students and housewives being water-cannoned as they protested against rising prices. And most of all, I read about the corruption.

My God, that story seemed unending. There was the 2G scam, the 3G scam, the Food grains scam, the Cattle fodder scam, the International games scam, the Army War Widows housing scam, the recruitment scam, the Railways scam, the Highways scam, the mining scam.... You name it. It seemed that everything was up for grabs. It seemed to have become an organised racket where whatever could be taken was plundered. And behind most of it was the smiling figure of Bharat Haladi.

He had now risen to amongst the top five political figures of the country. A shady, malevolent figure, close to the family in power, whom no one could touch. He had remained as Minister for Internal Security even after the Mumbai attacks; continued with his foreign jaunts and junkets. It made no difference when his involvement in any of the scams came up. He was merely shifted to another ministry, given another portfolio and then was back in business once again. His latest responsibility – if you could call it that – was organizing the International Games in Delhi – an extravaganza the country could ill-afford, a spectacle that seemed designed only to enable all involved to siphon out what they could of the debacle.

Bharat Haladi made hundreds of crores out of that. He purchased buses that broke down, made stadiums that collapsed and were never used again, purchased expensive sports equipment that did not work, brought toilet paper at $ 80 a roll, mirrors at $220 and soap dispensers at $60. And when the news broke out in the press he simply denied it, smiling shamelessly all the time.

But then it was not just him. Everywhere across the country were politicians like him, making thousands of crores and looting the exchequer dry. Few, if any were ever convicted, and if the long, convoluted process of the law caught up with them after decades, they simply went to jail for a while, came out on bail in a few months, if not weeks, and then the loot went on.

But the clamour was getting louder. I think the people were getting fed up with the systematic loot of the nation. When the media finally exposed Haladi's antics, the outrage rose loud enough to provoke a full-fledged investigation. Finally, after a long and lengthy trial, Haladi and a few of his minions were sentenced to jail. Justice had been done, or so it appeared.

Haladi remained in jail for less than a month – just three weeks in fact. He came out on bail from Tihar jail with hundreds of his supporters – those goons of his party – greeting him outside. He emerged garlanded, carried on their shoulders. He emerged hands upraised like a victorious boxer, with that oily ingratiating smile still on his face. But then he was a winner all right. He had beaten the system hadn't he?

**II**

I saw it all with the same sick sense of frustration and impotent anger, which millions of other Indians felt. Oh, I did my little bit. I took part in the midnight vigil with candles. I took part in the student rallies at *Jantar Mantar* protesting corruption and price rise. I was there when Anna Hazare – an old soldier like me – sat on a hunger fast demanding a legislation to curb out corruption – I saw the police break up the rally with their *lathis.* And all the time the politicians continued, impervious, shameless, smiling down at us from election banners, their hands folded, their Gandhi caps firmly in place.

The banners were coming up all over the city now. Elections were due, that five yearly ritual, when we used the only weapon we had – our vote. I had never voted so far. My weapon was rusted and unused.

And in the fray were people like Bharat Haladi – standing on the dais, promising people water, jobs, electricity – everything they had taken away from them. They promised quotas and reservations – so what if it divided society thereafter – they promised to hang rapists, and then condoned them, depending on which audience they were addressing. They promised rice, laptops, saris and subsidies – anything – just give me your goddamned vote.

And amazingly, in spite of Haladi's criminal background and all that he had done, his own political stock was on the rise. He still had 17 criminal cases pending against him – ranging from kidnapping to murder. But in spite of that he still remained one of the most influential politicians of the nation. His own party was very likely to emerge as one of the largest – and then, who knows. In the dangerously fractured mandate which most analysts had predicted, he could well go on to become the next Prime Minister – the signs were all there.

And he was everywhere now. He was there being photographed with his other political allies, most of them in the same mould as him – holding hands, feeding each other *laddoos* and raising two fingers up in a 'V'. He was there in the rallies, where his supporters had got crowds by the truckloads, he was on the streets, walking heavily garlanded from house to house, he was being photographed having a meal in the house of the poorest of the poor. He was there flouting his name 'Bharat'. He used his name to evoke Indian nationalism, though I don't think that swine even knew what nationalism or national character meant.

He came to my house sometime during the campaign, "*Namaste,*" he folded his hands, bent low ingratiatingly, *"Mera naam Bharat Haladi. Bharat mera naam. Bharat mera Dharm. Aur me bandhe haath se apke vote mangne aya hoon"*(My name is Bharat Haladi. Bharat is my name. India is my religion. I have come to ask you for your vote)

I don't think he even remembered that twelve years ago he had come my house after my son's death, and had cheated me out of a petrol pump allotted to his name. Why, I was just one of the hundreds he would have swindled. He was swindling the nation wasn't he? A nameless individual was of no consequence.

And seeing him, the anger and revulsion rose again. This was the man who had led and instigated a anti-Sikh mob at my doorstep thirty years ago. This was the man who made political capital of my son's death and then stole his petrol pump. This was the man I had seen laughing and joking in the lobby of the Taj Mahal Hotel where my younger son was lying wounded, concerned only with making a movie of the incident. This was the man with 17 criminal cases pending against him, who wanted to become the Prime Minister of our country. Was this the man who would rule our nation?

I said and did nothing at that time. I just saw him, hands folded, neck garlanded, the well-orchestrated cries of "*Bharat Haladi ki Jai; Bharat*

*Mata ki Jai*" rising in the background and the thought came to my mind for the first time. It came to me with the clarity of a vision. I knew what I would do. I would not cast my vote. I would use another weapon.

That vision increased in clarity as I brooded inside my empty house. That vision of Bharat Haladi standing with his arms folded in '*Namaste.*' In my mind he became the symbol of all that was corrupt and venal in our country. He was the one who had stolen our nation dry; he was the one who had robbed our youth of their future. He was the one who had plundered our nation out of its destiny. He was the one – he and politicians like him.

And then my plan formulated. I took my weapon out from my cupboard. That old .38 Revolver that had been lying unused there for over 15 years, ever since I had carried it with me from the army. It had never been used, had never once been fired in anger. It just remained resting in its case, lying there cleaned and well-oiled, awaiting its moment.

Its moment was coming. And so was mine.

### III

I began following Haladi after that. I was there for each rally, I ran along his car, I waved out to him in the crowds, tried to come close to him, tried to touch him.

I needed one moment of contact, and it would come. Haladi prided himself on being 'The Man of the Masses' – Oh, he loved being seen as the man who would reach out to the common man – his vote banks. He prided himself on seemingly shunning security and moving into crowds to touch the common man. I was waiting for his moment of contact with me.

The criminal cases pending against him had also mysteriously evaporated. Three witnesses died suddenly, one in a car accident, one who drowned swimming in a canal, another found with his throat slit – a victim of a gang-fight they said. Others turned hostile, refused to testify. His road to absolute power seemed clear.

I followed him throughout the campaign. I attended each election rally, reaching very early to be there in the front rows, I was outside his party headquarters, I was on the route his SUV would take. I was there each time, always with a huge garland of marigolds in my hand. I think after a while even his cronies and bodyguards around him, saw me as just another die-hard supporter. God knows he had thousands like that, why, I never could tell.

I just needed that one moment when I could get close enough to him. And my moment was coming soon. That Independence Day – 15 August 2014, Bharat Haladi was to address a huge rally at the Ram Lila *maidan.* This was to be his culminating rally, his final demonstration of strength, before the count down to the elections began.

That bastard had chosen Independence Day for that rally. One of our most sacred days, whose import people like him never understood and whose significance they besmirched repeatedly. It would be one of the largest rallies ever held, and more importantly, my last chance to get close to him.

I studied old footages of his previous rallies, went through them repeatedly trying to understand a pattern. And a pattern did emerge. After each rally, Bharat Haladi would leave the stage, go down to meet his throng of supporters. Invariably he descended from the right and then mingled with the audience, his hands folded in Namaste, the trademark smile fixed on his face.

That would be my moment. I had to get close to him after he descended from the steps and moved into the audience. I had to position myself in the front rows, on the side where he would descend from the stage and then get close. I began going to the site of the rally a week before it was due, watched the scaffolding come up, saw the rows upon rows of banners festoon the area. Saw the dais, where he would be seated, the steps leading to it, and the chairs and tarpaulins for the audience. I went to the site daily, assessing distance and time and rehearsing my actions over and over again in my mind. I practiced my actions in front of a mirror at home. Went through the motions over and over again. I would have less than ten seconds to do what I had to. What would happen after that, would be of no consequence. I never really gave it a thought.

I positioned myself in the front row of the audience a good 24 hours before the rally was to commence, standing there with a plastic bottle of tepid water and a huge garland of marigolds, done up in the colours of Haladi's party, and interwoven with his photographs and five hundred rupee notes. I hated touching his photo and placing it on the garland, but I had to appeal to his vanity to get close. And the five hundred rupee notes – over a hundred of them woven in to the garland – well, their appeal to Haladi would be obvious.

I was elbowed from the first to the third row of the audience, but managed to hold my place in the corner as the audience built up. They came in truckloads, herded in by Haladi's party workers, most of them probably with just a promise of a sari, a sack of rice, or a bottle of cheap booze. And by nine, the time Haladi was to arrive, the ground was packed to capacity.

Haladi came late, almost an hour late, but that was true to form. Yet he arrived to thunderous cheers, and began climbing slowly up the stage, dressed in his trademark pajamas and *kurta* – man of the masses after all. He came up, turned and waved to the audience, and almost on cue, his supporters took up the war cry.

"*Bharat Mata ki Jai; Bharat Haladi ki jai.*"

Oh, what a lovely slogan it was. But then it was all he and his ilk provided; slogans, nothing but slogans. I took up the cry too, but stopped at "*Bharat Mata ki Jai,*" I could not get myself to complete the next half.

And then he launched in to his litany of promises. He was a speaker all right. His voice had a right rustic touch to it; his speech had all the right symbols. And he promised the moon. He promised more quotas, and reservations, and the removal of foreign influence, and more sub-quotas – everything, but what we truly needed, development, opportunity, honesty and a chance to truly grow. But the audience lapped it up. And

I must say as the last cries of *"Bharat Haladi ki Jai, Bharat Mata ki Jai'* went up once again, I half believed in what he was promising.

Then he raised his hands in another 'Namaste.' The audience were cheering now and in a perfectly timed gesture, he waved at the crowd, seemed to shrug of the cordon of security that surrounded him, and moved ponderously, down the stage and into the audience.

That was my moment. I edged closer to him, watched him being engulfed by his supporters. I pushed my way closer, and even as the crowd jostled around me, I got within touching distance,. Less than a yard separated us now and I reached out towards him with my huge garland of marigolds and 500 Rupee notes. I felt my palms begin to perspire as my hand closed around the butt of the .38 Revolver concealed within the garland. It was cocked already, had been so ever since the rally began. Haladi leaned forward, slightly, to receive the garland, I almost lost my footing as the crowd jostled around me, but recovered, placed the garland over Haladiand then fired.

I fired when the garland was around his neck, and the concealed gun was just six inches from his heart. In the cheering, raucous crowd, I don't think anybody even heard the first shot. I saw his face start, his body begin to move backwards, and then fired again, closer to the heart now and his body jerked violently backwards. .

I pulled the trigger again as he started falling, but the ancient pistol failed me then. It jammed, the hammer clicked harmlessly on the firing pin. I pressed the trigger again. This time the trigger mechanism itself did not work – and then a vicious hand slammed across the side of my head and I felt myself being hurled sideways, the pistol wrenched from my hand. Then another hand came down and I collapsed on the floor.

Even as the blows rained down on me, I could hear the roars of the crowd – cries of bewilderment, of anger, dismay – and I think from some corner, or was that my imagination – of cheers.

I don't know how I survived the onslaught from Haladi's goons. They would have killed me had the police not arrived. In my haze, I heard the wail of sirens; saw an ambulance rush by, saw Haladi being carried on a stretcher inside, and then the police whisked me in to the waiting van alongside before his mob of supporters could beat me to death.

We love to crib about the police, but they are quite efficient actually. They whisked me to the Police Station, then to a cell, then photographed and fingerprinted me. They took my watch, wallet, chain, shoe-laces and hanky and made me sign a receipt for each one of them. They got a doctor to treat my wounds – the three broken ribs, the fractured left hand (broken at almost the same place as Masterji's hand), the split forehead that required sixteen stitches and God knows how many bruises and cuts. I heard them talk about getting in a psychiatrist as well. After all, I was grinning like a loon through it all.

## IV

I stayed in that cell for days, then weeks and months. I saw the headlines on the papers. Hey, I was on the front pages – my photo dwarfed by the photos of Haladi's funeral procession – but on the front pages all right. It was my moment of glory, and this time I had earned it.

I saw it all on TV. Saw the repeated footage of a small, nondescript man – how much like Masterji, I looked – edge close to Haladi in the jostling crowd, place the garland of marigold flowers and 500 Rupee notes around him, saw Haladi jerk backwards and fall; saw his security staff swamp me, and grinned even more as I saw my actions being played over and over again on national television.

Vikram and Supriya were there, of course. There were with me all through it all, trying to raise bail for me, trying to give me support in every way they could. And never once, in public or otherwise, did they question what I had done. There was no condemnation; no recriminations. Nor did they mention about the threats that they had been receiving, or the fact that they had been allotted police protection to save them from an attack from Haladi's goons. I only got to know of it from the newspapers.

For weeks thereafter the newspapers were full of my act and frankly, I was a little surprised by the reactions that came in. Most of the newspapers condemned my act, but quite a few, actually condoned it – justifying it as a last act of futility against a system that allowed people like Bharat Haladi – a man convicted of corruption, and with 17 criminal cases still against him – to rise to a position where he could project himself as a likely Prime Minister of the nation.

And then the news leaked out about how he had usurped the petrol pump allotted to me after the Kargil War and the papers began playing up the revenge angle. But it was not that. I killed Haladi not because he stole the petrol pump allotted in my son's name. That I had even forgotten. I killed him because he was stealing the future of millions of other sons.

The letters also poured in, thousands of them; some with threats, most of them in support, and a few with a small cheque enclosed. Supriya replied to each one of them on my behalf, thanked them individually and ended with the gentle admonition, "Do not emulate what I have done."

The lawyers and activists came in too. My God, there were so many of them who offered to raise money for my defence, so many of the lawyers who agreed to take up my trial for free. Even the police began treating me with some kind of deference after all the *hulla-bolla* died down after a while. After all, amongst the 17 criminal cases pending against Haladi, two had been registered in this very police station.

They sent me in Tihar Jail after my first hearing. The same Tihar jail I am still in now. The same jail where my father spent a month during India's freedom struggle; the same Tihar jail where the swine Haladi had been incinerated for three brief weeks when he was convicted of corruption. And here I have become somewhat of a hero with the other inmates. They smile and wave at me as I walk around the courtyard. At times they offer me a banana, or a boiled egg, or *beedis* and cigarettes. Sometimes, a hardened criminal will come by, slap me on the back and say, "*Maan gaye, guru*".

Oh, it is not too bad here in jail. As I await the outcome of my trial, I keep myself quite busy with my letters and newspapers. They have permitted me to get papers in my cell, and my lawyer has even got me a dozen folders. I have followed Masterji's old habit of reading each newspaper from word to word, making cuttings of the important articles and putting them in neat folders. I have a folder for each subject now – politics, the economy, the neighbours, terrorism, Pakistan, corruption, my own trial. The folder on corruption is the largest and it grows by the day. The scams continue unabated.

I guess my act against the cancer of corruption is not enough. By killing one, I did not remove the cancer; I merely destroyed one of its cells. But then I am no surgeon. I am just an ordinary Indian, responding in futility and defiance to a scourge that I feel is destroying our nation.

But that's okay. I did what I could. But it is not something I will recommend to anyone. There are other processes of law, which take longer maybe, but which will be more effective. There are hundreds of other Indians – ordinary people like you and me – who are now standing up against corruption, protesting the loot of the nation by people like Bharat Haladi and his ilk. And there is hope. I see a new crop of leaders, and new political parties, who are emerging with the promise of development and honesty. I don't know how long it will last, but there are winds of change in the offing. And that change has not been brought about by me or my act. It has been wrought by You, and the millions of Indians who clamour for the change.

As for me, don't worry. I am quite fine here in Tihar jail. The Indian judicial system will take its own time to decide whether to send me to the gallows or to set me free, or maybe something in between. I am not too uncomfortable here. I have my visitors, I have my letters, I have my newspapers. And I have this pencil.

So let me fill my days by telling you about what I have seen. About our Nation. About Me, about Me and You. Let me tell you the story of its birth – of how I came to its soil on 15 August 1947. About Nehru and Gandhi. Of the 1962 and 1965 wars – I breached a canal and halted the Pakistani tanks then, remember. Of 1971, and my small part in the historic surrender ceremony; of the Pakistani so akin to me whom I met in the Prisoner of War camp; of Mrs Gandhi and the Emergency; of Operation Blue Star and the anti-Sikh riots. Of Kashmir; of Kargil and my son who fell there – of the Mumbai attacks; of our cricket matches and dances, of our economic success story and its decline – and of its revival which I am sure will happen again.

And so I picked up this pencil, took this scrap of paper and began my story, *"I do not know the exact year of my birth, but then I don't think anyone does. It was the year of the great flood. That would make it around 1943 or 1947 or so. It could also make it at any time in the past 2000 years when the floods hit the Indus Valley.... But then the date of my birth is not important. On paper they record it as 15 August 1947, the year I was carried numb and shocked in my father's arms in the land of our new-born country...."*